Young Dual Language Learners

A Guide for PreK–3 Leaders

Editor

Karen N. Nemeth

with 45 contributing experts

CASLON PUBLISHING

PHILADELPHIA

Caslon, Inc.
825 N. 27th St.
Philadelphia, PA 19130

caslonpublishing.com

9 8 7 6 5 4 3 2 1

Library of Congress Cataloging-in-Publication Data

Young dual language learners : a guide for PreK–3 leaders / Karen N. Nemeth, Editor, with 45 Contributing Experts.
    pages cm
    Includes bibliographical references and index.
    Summary: "Provides clear and concise expert responses to questions that early childhood and elementary education administrators and preschool directors ask about educating young children who are learning through two languages"— Provided by publisher.
    ISBN 978-1-934000-14-4
    1. Education, Bilingual. 2. Language arts (Preschool) 3. Language arts (Elementary) 4. Children of immigrants—Education (Preschool) 5. Children of immigrants—Education (Elementary). 6. Children of minorities—Education (Preschool) 7. Children of minorities—Education (Elementary) 8. English language—Study and teaching (Preschool) 9. English language—Study and teaching (Elementary) I. Nemeth, Karen N., editor of compilation.

LC3723.Y68 2014
370.117'5—dc23   2014001321

Printed in the United States of America.

Contributing Experts

Iliana Alanís
Associate Professor of Early Childhood
  Education
University of Texas at San Antonio
San Antonio, Texas

Erin Arango-Escalante
Assistant Director, Academic Language
  and Literacy Initiatives
World-Class Instructional Design
  and Assessment (WIDA)
University of Wisconsin–Madison
Madison, Wisconsin

Laura Ascenzi-Moreno
Assistant Professor
Childhood, Bilingual, and Special Education
  Department
School of Education
Brooklyn College
Brooklyn, New York

Sandra Barrueco
Associate Professor of Psychology
Fellow of the Institute for Policy Research
  and Catholic Studies
Catholic University of America
Washington, D.C.

Douglas D. Bell, Jr.
Kennesaw State University
Kennesaw, Georgia

Laura Bornfreund
Senior Policy Analyst
New America Foundation
Washington, D.C.

Pamela Brillante
Assistant Professor of Special Education
  and Counseling
William Paterson University
Wayne, New Jersey

Margarita Calderón
Professor Emerita
School of Education
Johns Hopkins University
Baltimore, Maryland

Luz Marina Cardona
Cabrillo College
Aptos, California

Jennifer Chen
Associate Professor of Early Childhood
  and Family Studies
Kean University
Union, New Jersey

Nancy Cloud
Director, MEd in TESL Program
Rhode Island College
Providence, Rhode Island

Linda M. Espinosa
Professor of Early Childhood (Ret.)
University of Missouri
Columbia, Missouri

Diane Staehr Fenner
President
DSF Consulting, LLC
Fairfax, Virginia

B. J. Franks
Language and Literacy Associates for
    Multilingual and Multicultural Education
Bradley Beach, New Jersey

Cristina Gillanders
Scientist
Frank Porter Graham Child Development
    Institute
University of North Carolina–Chapel Hill
Chapel Hill, North Carolina

Claude Goldenberg
Professor
Graduate School of Education
Stanford University
Stanford, California

Janet Gonzalez-Mena
Professor Emerita
Napa Valley College
Napa, California

Margo Gottlieb
World-Class Instructional Design and
    Assessment (WIDA)
Madison, Wisconsin;
Illinois Resource Center
Arlington Heights, Illinois

Vera Gutiérrez-Clellen
Professor
School of Speech, Language, and Hearing
    Sciences
San Diego State University
San Diego, California

Ellen Hall
Executive Director
Boulder Journey School
Boulder, Colorado

Judie Haynes
everythingESL
Wyckoff, New Jersey

Judy Hicks
Doctoral Candidate
Curriculum and Teacher Education Instructor
Teacher Education Program
Stanford University
Stanford, California

Kathleen Leos
President/CEO
Global Institute for Language and Literacy
    Development (GILD)
Washington, D.C.

Lisa M. López
Associate Professor of Educational Psychology
College of Education
University of South Florida
Tampa, Florida

Alison Maher
Education Director
Boulder Journey School
Boulder, Colorado

Kate Mahoney
Associate Professor
State University of New York
    (SUNY)–Fredonia
Fredonia, New York

Jennifer Mata
Assistant Professor of Early Childhood
    Education
DePaul University
Chicago, Illinois

Sandee McHugh-McBride
Adjunct Professor
Graduate School of Education
Rutgers University
Camden;
Rowan University
Glassboro;
ESL Instructor
Brookdale Community College
Lincroft, New Jersey

Laura C. Morana
Superintendent
Red Bank Borough Schools
Red Bank, New Jersey

Karen N. Nemeth
Consultant/Author
Language Castle, LLC
Newtown, Pennsylvania

Diep Nguyen
Teacher Education Department
College of Education
Northeastern Illinois University
Chicago, Illinois

Anita Pandey
Professor and Coordinator of Professional
    Development
Morgan State University
Baltimore, Maryland

Elizabeth D. Peña
Professor
Department of Communication Sciences
    and Disorders
University of Texas–Austin
Austin, Texas

Ruth Reinl
Independent Consultant
Early Dual Language Learning Consulting,
    LLC
Middleton, Wisconsin

Theresa Roberts
Professor Emerita
California State University–Sacramento
Sacramento, California

Monica Schnee
ESL Coordinator/Teacher
River Edge Public Schools
River Edge, New Jersey

Leslie Sevey
Assistant Professor
Rhode Island College
Providence, Rhode Island

Sonia W. Soltero
Associate Professor and Chair
Department of Leadership, Language
    and Curriculum
DePaul University
Chicago, Illinois

Patton Tabors
Cambridge, Massachusetts

Zoila Tazi
Associate Professor and Chair
Childhood Education Department
Mercy College
Dobbs Ferry, New York

Barbara Tedesco
Language and Literacy Associates for
    Multilingual and Multicultural Education
    (LLAMAME), LLC
Colonia, New Jersey

Tracey Tokuhama-Espinosa
Universidad San Francisco de Quito
Quito, Ecuador

Maria N. Trejo
Associate
Margarita Calderón & Associates
Washington, D.C.

Wayne E. Wright
Professor
College of Education and Human
    Development
University of Texas–San Antonio
San Antonio, Texas

Debbie Zacarian
President and CEO
Debbie Zacarian, Ed.D. & Associates, LLC
Amherst, Massachusetts

Preface

Elementary school administrators and preschool directors work in schools that may look quite different from those described in their university textbooks, and these schools continue to change rapidly. Today, growing numbers of elementary schools, both public and private, provide general education, special education, and inclusion classes for 3- and 4-year-olds. Young children who are growing up in homes with languages other than English (LOTE) are the fastest-growing segment of our population. New state standards and their connection to the Common Core State Standards are changing the way administrators approach learning, accountability, and professional development. Furthermore, budget cuts and demanding new funding streams are coming and going at an alarming rate. This guide helps administrators make sense of the many factors at play as they build the best services possible for children who enter school speaking a LOTE.

Young Dual Language Learners is essential for the following people:

- Principals, directors, supervisors, and other administrators in schools or programs that serve children from age 3 to grade 3
- Administrators of programs for children who speak a LOTE at home
- General education teachers with young dual language learners (DLLs) in their classrooms, English as a second language teachers, bilingual education teachers, and special education staff working in schools serving young DLLs

This book puts the answers to all of your questions at your fingertips, giving you guidance from the leading experts in our field. You will be able to proceed with confidence as you set up rooms, hire and prepare staff, assign appropriate placements, and make sure that best practices are understood and observed.

Administrators may have to work with a variety of specialists to establish appropriate services for young children who are new to English. Many specialists have experienced rather isolated forms of professional development. Administrators therefore need to consider the following types of questions:

- Has your special education staff taken coursework on adapting instruction for DLLs?
- Has your English as a second language or bilingual education staff taken coursework about the specific learning needs of children under age 6?
- Do your general education teachers feel supported and prepared to meet the needs of children in the early grades who come with differences in language, culture, and ability?

These are issues that require the leadership of a well-informed administrator.

Regulations that affect early childhood education come from many different fronts. Elementary schools have to follow state regulations that may or may not include kindergarten. States have one separate set of special education regulations and a separate set of bilingual education regulations, but many states do not spell out what schools should do when a child is identified in both of those categories. Many public and private elementary schools offer preschool classes as well. Depending on the state, those classes may or may not be subject to the same rules as K–3. Furthermore, many schools provide preschool by partnering with local private preschool programs or Head Start programs. These programs generally follow regulations from the state office of health and human services. In addition, Head Start programs are subject to many federal rules tied to their funding. There is a lot of information for an administrator to understand and put into place to make this all work.

This array of regulations also means that administrators have to be in contact with more state, county, local, and even federal offices. When different streams of funding are involved, each stream also comes with particular rules. In this changing landscape, no book could cover or anticipate everything you would need to know. Instead, we put administrators on a path to success and alert them to changes they need to be aware of.

Our expert contributors carefully describe the ways in which young DLLs are like K–3 learners and the ways in which they are quite different. The contributors help preschool administrators understand more about the rules, regulations, and expectations faced by their elementary school counterparts, and they help district administrators understand the nuances of operating preK–3 programs. You will find answers to questions such as how to interview, select, and prepare the right teachers for the right settings, and you will find a combination of research based and real-life experience to give you the answers you need.

The role of a child's home language in the educational process and environment in the early years is subject to a great deal of misunderstanding and controversy. Our experts take on this topic from several perspectives, including how to use paraprofessionals appropriately to support home languages and how to address different home languages when assessing children and classrooms.

Features

To enhance the reader's experience using this book, we provide several learning support features. These special features allow the book to be used as an in-depth planning tool, an easy-access desktop reference for any early childhood education administrator, and a great resource for graduate courses and high-level professional development.

Key Considerations for Language Plan

Each chapter begins with a set of Key Considerations for Language Plan to show administrators how they can use what they read to create a specific language plan for their schools that represents the shared knowledge and vision of the entire school community. With so many factors to consider and so many changes and challenges to face, it is very important for early childhood educators to develop written language plans. For classroom teachers, this plan should address the overall approach to first and second language supports for students by taking into account the languages used by the staff and the context of the curriculum and resources available. Classroom teachers may also add a daily language plan to their lesson plans to spell out exactly how they will make adaptations for DLLs on any given day.

Directors, principals, and other administrators must have a building- or program-wide language plan that addresses broader issues while incorporating the elements of the individual classroom plans. The general language plan should address how the school will provide for student learning opportunities, staff support, family engagement, and teaching strategies as appropriate for the needs and requirements of that program. In its 2008 seminal report—*Dual Language Learning: What Does It Take?*—the Office of Head Start emphasizes the importance of having a comprehensive language plan: "Successfully serving children and families from various language and cultural backgrounds cannot be accomplished without a program-wide, comprehensive plan" (p. 2). As the full report clearly indicates, supporting children in the acquisition of two languages is a complex, multi-faceted task that requires intentional support at all levels of a program.

Terms and Glossary
Elementary school administrators and preschool directors may encounter a wide array of terms when attending meetings or reading guidance about working with young children who have home languages other than English. In addition to the officially sanctioned terms used in conjunction with federal funding and assessment initiatives, other terms arise from state policy, local tradition, and other factors. For example, the National Association for the Education of Young Children (NAEYC) has joined with the Office of Head Start to use the term **dual language learner** (DLL) to refer to young children who have home languages other than English, and DLL is the term we see more often in preschool. The international association Teachers of English to Speakers of Other Languages (TESOL) uses the term **English language learner** (ELL) to refer to those students who are officially designated for **English as a second language** (ESL) instruction, and ELL and **English learner** (EL) are the terms we see most often in school districts. We are also beginning to see the term **emergent bilingual** used to refer to students who have home languages other than English and who are acquiring English in preschool and in K–12 districts. Terms that are boldfaced in the text are defined in the glossary.

Resources and Questions
Each chapter concludes with tools that can immediately be used in practice:

- Self-Assessment Checklist
- Planning Guide
- Language Development Graphic
- Assets/Resources/Needs Assessment Grid
- Assessment Comparison Chart
- Resource Connections
- Advocacy Planning Tool
- Questions for Reflection

These practical tools help administrators and teachers apply their understanding of important issues in educating young DLLs within their school context.

Young Dual Language Learners has been created for you—the educational leader in early childhood education—the all-important foundation for our nation's future success.

Contents

2 Identification and Planning   36

3   How Young Children Learn in Two or More Languages   56

Key Considerations for Language Plan   56
Introduction   57

4 Developing Instructional Programs for Young Dual Language Learners 78

Key Considerations for Language Plan 78
Introduction 79

5 Policies, Accountability, and Program Effectiveness 106

Key Considerations for Language Plan 106
Introduction 107

6 Working Effectively with Families, the Community, and Volunteers 132

Key Considerations for Language Plan 132
Introduction 133

Young Dual
Language Learners

CHAPTER 1

Leadership and Professional Development

Key Considerations for Language Plan

- Our language plan will take into consideration the first and second language development and learning needs of children from grades preK–3.

- Our language plan will be created with the understanding that **dual language learners** (DLLs) in the early years need support of their **home language** and English in the context of a developmentally appropriate curriculum.

- Our language plan will clearly state the dispositions and qualifications needed by teachers and paraprofessionals who will work with our young DLL students.

- Our language plan will describe human resource policies and practices to ensure that properly prepared staff are selected, assigned, supervised, and supported appropriately.

- Our language plan will include professional development goals for administrators, as well as teachers, specialists, and paraprofessionals, to ensure that we provide a cohesive and effective program of instruction for diverse young children.

E ducational leaders are familiar with the challenges presented by diverse and changing populations. For many years, however, concerns about children who came to school speaking a language other than English focused on older elementary and secondary students. Several recent factors are elevating the complexity of these challenges, not the least of which is the booming population of children under the age of 9 years who are living in homes where a language other than English is spoken. Estimates vary, but most experts agree that right now at least 25% of young children are learning in two or more languages in the United States. Whether these children are enrolled in private childcare, Head Start programs, or publicly funded preschool, their needs are becoming increasingly apparent and program administrators are looking for answers.

Fortunately, this set of increasingly complex demands facing early childhood administrators has motivated some of the nation's top experts to join forces and provide the best information available in a user-friendly format. Some of the nation's thought leaders and respected practitioners share evidence-based strategies and resource foundations to ensure a confident planning and implementation process for early childhood administrators in any setting.

Some of the additional challenges that arise in the work of administrators of diverse programs include new state requirements for identifying young children who are DLLs and understanding whether they may also have disabilities that need services. Outcomes measures for the school may be affected by the growing number of children who are new to English, yet must be assessed in English to contribute to the school's data.

Administrators are struggling to find highly qualified bilingual teachers, but in most cases that process is aggravated by the variety of languages needed. It is great to find a qualified teacher who is English/Spanish bilingual, but that strategy falls short when the district has several other languages as well. English as a second language (ESL) teachers are in demand, but many of them completed an entire undergraduate or graduate course with little or no mention of the unique learning needs of students in early childhood education.

With funding sources scrutinizing how funds are being used to implement appropriate services for children who speak two or more languages, grants are coming with many more strings attached. Common Core State Standards are being developed and implemented for grades K–3, and some states are adding standards to guide preschool teachers as well.

The makeup of the particular student body of each school is unique, and the match of languages and cultures between the staff and the students begins with many obstacles. New initiatives supporting high-quality preschools have changed the way preschool programs are operated, evaluated, and funded. A growing number of elementary schools are offering preschool or partnering with neighboring preschool programs. This means changes for preschool directors who, though they may have plenty of experience with the under-5 set, are learning a whole new world of regulations, requirements, staffing, and curriculum leadership when partnering with school districts. Most administrators who work in elementary school environments, on the other hand, have little or no background or experience in working with children under the age of 5 years. Fitting effective supports for young children who are new to English will certainly complicate all these adjustments.

Chapter 1 helps preschool administrators and elementary administrators understand the nuances of each other's work. Topics include the basic information necessary for identifying the needs of young children new to English and how to find and prepare staff appropriately to teach them. Use the self-assessment checklist at the end of the chapter to gather information about your status as an educator in a linguistically diverse environment and about the methods, policies, and practices you currently employ to teach young DLLs. This starting point will enable you to use the information in the book to build on your strengths and directly address the areas you wish to improve.

A. What do program administrators need to know about young dual language learners?

■ *Linda M. Espinosa*

Everyone who works in a Head Start, public preK, private preschool, or community-based childcare program has experienced a shift in the demographics of the children and families they serve. During the past several decades, the proportion of young children who speak a language other than English in the home and are not fully fluent in English (**dual language learners** [DLLs]) has grown dramatically. From 1990 to 2010 ten states experienced more than 200% growth in their population of young DLLs while their overall student growth increased by only 20%. This group of young children has also been academically vulnerable, with chronic underachievement and elevated school dropout rates.

In my experience, these dire school outcomes have been the result of deep misunderstandings about the nature of second language development during the early childhood years. These commonly held misperceptions have led to well-intentioned but misguided policies and practices that have both contributed to poor school performance and failed to capitalize on the talents and cognitive potential of **emergent bilinguals** (see Espinosa, 2013, for a discussion of common myths about DLLs). Fortunately, we now have the scientific knowledge to better understand the linguistic, cognitive, social, and academic development of children who are learning through two languages during a period of rapid brain growth. We are also witnessing policy formation at the federal, state, and local levels that reflects our expanded knowledge of the processes and consequences of growing up with more than one language.

These scientific advances are truly revolutionary. When I was a program administrator in child development and primary programs in California in the 1980s and 1990s, I was often amazed and challenged by the shift in our demographics from primarily low-income, monolingual, English-speaking families to low-income, monolingual, Spanish-speaking families who had recently immigrated from rural Mexico. These children and families brought with them specific family and cultural strengths, which we frequently did not recognize, as well as great linguistic and cognitive potential, which we also did not always understand. Our policies and practices were constrained by outdated beliefs about the capacity of young children to learn multiple languages during the first years of life and the potential advantages of early **bilingualism**. We struggled over basic questions from parents such as, "Which language should I speak to my child? Since Maria needs to learn English, should I stop speaking Spanish because it might confuse her or slow down her English language development?"

Now we can answer with confidence that infants and young children have the innate capacity to learn two or more languages from birth and that if early multiple language exposure is sufficient in quantity and quality, young children can successfully become fully proficient in multiple languages. We also know that exposure to two or more languages during infancy changes the way the brain processes language and results in different patterns of linguistic and cognitive development. For example, recent research has shown that very young bilinguals develop heightened attention during speech processing (because of the need to sort out two separate linguistic systems) that leads to well-documented metalinguistic advantages. In addition, multiple studies over the past decade have shown that preschool bilinguals demonstrate more advantages in self-control and **executive function**, and they show advantages in tasks that require selectively attending to competing options and the ability to suppress interfering information. These early bilingual benefits have been found across cultural and socioeconomic groups as well as across different language combinations. However, these cognitive advantages have been tied to the extent that the child is bilingual; those who are more balanced in their bilingualism show larger advantages than children who are more strongly dominant in one language.

It has also become clear that young DLLs show different patterns of early language and literacy development. Recent studies have consistently shown that bilingual children take longer to recall words from memory. They have slower word retrieval times in picture-naming tasks and lower scores on verbal fluency tasks. Young bilingual preschoolers also tend to have smaller vocabularies in each language when compared to English-speaking monolinguals. However, a DLL's vocabulary is distributed across two languages; when both languages are included, their vocabulary size is often comparable to monolinguals. These differences are normal aspects of early bilingualism and should not be interpreted as language delays. However, when educational policies assess only English abilities, young DLLs are judged to be less competent rather than as developing important but different abilities across *two* languages.

We also know that there are consequences of losing one's **native language**. Young children who shift to English at the expense of continuing development in their native language will never experience the linguistic, cognitive, or social advantages of becoming fully proficient in two languages. They also risk becoming disconnected from their family history, culture, and identity. History is replete with examples of what happens when groups of people are "cut loose" from their cultural and linguistic roots. However, when DLLs become proficient in their **home language**, they are able "to establish a strong cultural identity, to develop and sustain strong ties with their immediate and extended families, and thrive in a global multilingual world" (Espinosa, 2006, p. 2).

The message for program administrators is that we all need to adjust our beliefs about how to best support the development and achievement of young DLLs; new scientific evidence compels us to revise our policies toward the instruction and assessment of children who are learning about the world through more than one language. The overwhelming consensus is that *DLLs need support for both languages through intentional instruction, specific language interactions, frequent assessments, and culturally sensitive engagement with families*. The specific instructional adaptations and assessment procedures are detailed elsewhere (Espinosa, 2010, 2013). Finally, it is imperative that all program administrators integrate this new scientific evidence into improved practices for young children who have tremendous unrealized potential, but who have been seriously misunderstood and inappropriately served. We now know enough to design effective curriculum and classroom practices—and it is up to all of us to understand this research, apply it to our program practices, and advocate for improved services.

B. What are the nationally accepted terms used to describe young children who speak different languages?

■ *Kathleen Leos*

Appropriately identifying a child whose language background is not English can be perilous at times and prone to unintentional errors. Understanding the basic definitions and terms used to identify the students, why they are used, and what to do with them should help administrators clarify any misconceptions that have been in operation for decades in early childhood programs and schools.

Early childhood education in the United States relies on two legal definitions and a variety of terms to describe children ages 3 to 8 who speak a language other than English at home or are considered "language minority children," according to the 1974 Supreme Court case *Lau v. Nichols.* An **English language learner** (ELL) or **limited English proficient** (LEP) student—as defined by Title IX of the Elementary and Secondary Education Act (ESEA), which governs children in preK–12 public education— is a student between the ages of 3 and 21 who has difficulty "speaking, reading, writing, or understanding the English language" sufficient to deny the individual the "opportunity to participate fully in society" and the "ability to successfully achieve in classrooms taught in English" with no linguistic support. The student must also demonstrate the "ability to meet the state's proficient level of achievement on state assessments" in academic content in English.

Immigrant children and youth are defined in ESEA Title III as "individuals who are 3 through 21; were not born in any state; and have not been attending one or more schools in any one or more states for more than three full academic years." Note that not all immigrant students are ELLs.

The terms often used to describe "language minority children and students" in grades preK–3 or ages 4–8 are ELLs, **English learners** (ELs), and LEP. It is important to remember that in order for a child to be identified as an ELL, EL, or LEP, the student must have been administered a state-approved language assessment that follows specific criteria to determine English language proficiency. Each state and local school district has its own list of requirements and assessments that help school administrators identify a student who qualifies for instruction in preK–3 language instruction education programs.

Definition of Dual Language Learners

According to the National Head Start Act of 2007, **dual language learners** (DLLs) are defined as "language minority children ages 2–5, where the heritage or **primary language** spoken at home is a language other than English." The term DLL is used in early childhood, Early Head Start, and Head Start programs for a child who is learning two (or more) languages at the same time (**simultaneous language acquisition** and development), or a child acquiring or transitioning to a second language—English—using primary language support in early childhood and Head Start classrooms while continuing to develop the primary or heritage language at home and in the community. DLLs also includes key groups of children served in American Indian/Alaska Native (AI/AN) and Migrant and Seasonal Head Start (MSHS) programs, as well as AI/AN or MSHS children served in programs located in federal regions not under the auspices of AI/AN Head Start or MSHS, and children served in programs in Puerto Rico and U.S. territories.

DLLs in Head Start programs must also be identified by a valid and reliable language proficiency assessment and provided primary language support while acquiring a second language, English, or participating in a **dual language development program**.

C. What terms do states and practitioners use to describe young children who speak different languages?

■ *Karen N. Nemeth*

Administrators may encounter a confusing array of terms when attending meetings or reading guidance about working with young children who have home languages other than English. In addition to the officially sanctioned terms used in conjunction with federal funding and assessment initiatives, other terms arise from state policy, local tradition, and other factors. The National Association for the Education of Young Children (NAEYC) has joined with the Office of Head Start to use the term **dual language learner** (DLL). In their 2010 position statement, TESOL begins with the traditional term **English language learner** (ELL) but uses learners of English who are speakers of other languages (ESOL) throughout the document (TESOL, 2010). In this way, TESOL differentiates between ESOL learners and **English as a second language (ESL) programs** or ESL-certified teachers. Also in 2010, the Council for Exceptional Children Division for Early Childhood released their position statement; in their guidance for early childhood special education practitioners, they used the term DLL to refer to children who are growing up in homes with diverse non-English languages.

ELL and **English learner** (EL) have become the terms we see most often in school districts, whereas DLL is the term we see more often in preschool programs. This disjointed terminology highlights some important differences between these two types of programs. In most cases, state educational code determines the criteria that must be used by a district to identify a student as an ELL or EL, and this usually involves some kind of assessment. As you will read in later sections, the identification of ELLs usually includes a determination of their English language proficiency (ELP).

Because almost all states have no requirements for serving children who are new to English in preschool, the terms used to describe them are more a matter of choice than of assessment results or regulations. Many states do, however, offer suggestions for teaching preschool children who are DLLs. Many states and programs have come to the realization that, for all intents and purposes, children under the age of 5 are all ELs—they are all still working on their use and understanding of the English language. Identifying some children as DLLs has less to do with their ELP than with recognizing that they are growing up with different language input and cultural milieus that need to be acknowledged. In fact, many policies now say that any preschool child who speaks a language other than English at home should be considered a DLL and given the appropriate supports in the **home language** and English.

It is important to understand that although the terms we use to describe children may sound similar to the terms we use to describe teachers or programs, they are not the same. For example, a dual language immersion program is one subset of programs that fall into the **bilingual education** program. Children who are DLLs do not necessarily attend that type of program—and may not be receiving any specified services at all. Because the contributors to this book come from different aspects of our field, you can expect that they will use different terminology to describe the children who are the focus of our writing. In the editorial sections of the book, we use ELLs/DLLs to bring them all together.

The term bilingual is sometimes used to describe the language abilities of a person, or the endorsement or certification of a teacher, or a type of educational program. This term is also likely to lead to confusion. The dictionary defines a bilingual person as someone who is fluent in two languages. A very young child is not really fully fluent in any language. Some locations, such as New York, include it in the term **emergent bilinguals**, which they use in place of DLLs for young children. Research talks about the similarities and differences in language development between simultaneous bilinguals, who are growing up with two or more languages in the home from birth or soon after, and sequential bilinguals, who begin life with one language at home and then move or enter school and begin to learn a second language.

A teacher may be bilingual, but that does not mean her multiple languages are used in her job. A teacher who is certified or endorsed as a **bilingual education teacher** must be fully bilingual and will teach using her non-English language. Bilingual education programs offer significant portions of instruction in the non-English language, but the proportion of one language to the other varies greatly from program to program.

Confusion about the terms we use to describe students who come to school with a different home language certainly adds to the complexity of our work. This confusion also reflects the deeper complexity of sorting out which programs, teachers, and assessments are needed for any given population. Administrators can be more effective when they have a strong understanding of the different terms in this field and their implications.

D. How are preK children and K–3 students alike and different?
■ *Karen N. Nemeth*

There is an important shift in cognitive development between the ages of 5 and 6. Before the age of 6 years, all children are still working on the development of their first language so, technically, every child in that age range in the United States could be considered an **English language learner** (ELL). After age 5, when they have completed the basic language development process, the path to acquiring a second language and developing fluency is not part of the early language development arc and begins to draw on other cognitive abilities. Meanwhile, there is a shift from preoperational thinking to concrete operational thinking around the ages of 5–6 years that will control how well learners respond to different kinds of tasks and experiences. In addition, children who are 5 and under are unaccustomed to the conventions of deportment expected at school; they do much better when allowed to play, explore, and discover.

Because children under the age of 6 are in a different cognitive and language development stage, the way they learn best is quite different from what works with older children. Taking lessons and activities from the older grades and drilling them into preschool children will almost always meet with failure. Unfortunately, because many teachers and administrators are accustomed to working with older children, they may believe that taking the same types of lessons and doing them more slowly or more frequently will somehow make the little children learn. Working more on inappropriate tasks neither helps to build language skills nor helps to achieve academic outcomes.

Children over the age of 6 are gaining skills and abilities that will lend themselves to more traditional mode of teaching and learning (not the least of which is being able to sit at a desk and concentrate for more than a few minutes). They are more likely to show what they know and can do using traditional methods of assessment than younger children, who are very unpredictable when asked to perform on demand for assessment purposes. Changes like these do not happen at the flip of a switch—or at the date of a child's birthday or the first day of school.

We know that preschool-aged children learn best with a combination of play-based discovery learning and developmentally appropriate direct instruction that is similar to, but not the same as, the instruction used in older grades. These methods should be seen in grades K–3 as well, but the balance of time spent on each one will shift as the level of direct instruction and the complexity of content grow.

All preK–3 children should be experiencing learning in the following ways:

- Hands-on exploration
- Use of real objects to build context for learning words and concepts
- Opportunities to explore, observe, and discover
- Being read to by adults while also learning to read independently
- Authentic, multi-turned conversations and discussions with peers and adults
- Opportunities to make choices and follow interests
- Using hands to build fine motor strength and skill with substances like paint, clay, scissors, and snap blocks
- Problem-solving activities

The changes made as children progress from year to year will be reflected in how much time they spend on these activities compared to the time spent on more teacher-directed activities. Children under the age of 6 should never face ditto sheets (or computer games/apps that look like ditto sheets), teacher-controlled craft projects, flashcards, passive TV, or meaningless rote memorization in school. These techniques may be used in older grades but should be kept at a minimum.

E. How are preK and K–3 curricula models alike and different?

■ *Theresa Roberts*

Comparing preK and K–3 curricula requires a distinction between traditional preschool curricula and new preschool curricula. The traditional approach to curriculum in preschool has been for teachers to select and prepare a variety of activities and materials based on their professional judgment and the needs and interests of the children in their classrooms. They may use several sources in this development, including commercially purchased programs, websites, and materials from trainings and workshops. Traditionally, preschool teachers have developed curriculum materials designed to address the social-emotional and physical development of children, as well as the cognitive outcomes that are emphasized in K–3 curricula. Traditional preschool curriculum planning has focused a great deal on preparing an engaging classroom environment that allows children to apply and hone exploratory and meaning-making endowments for self-development. In more recent years, these informal and teacher-centered curriculum development practices have been complemented with very general curriculum philosophies that identify broad categories of the types of activities children might engage in across various domains. They are fairly unstructured and offer little detail about specific instructional routines, particularly in important school readiness domains such as literacy and math. Creative Curriculum is one example of this type and is widely used in Head Start classrooms.

The use of comprehensive curriculum materials that specify units or themes of study, sequential learning activities, expected learning outcomes, and accompanying assessment and support materials is an emerging practice in early childhood. Themed units of study that provide integrated activities across math, social studies, science, music, and art domains are a typical feature of the new preschool curricula. These emerging preschool curricula are more similar to those of K–3 than traditional preschool curricula because they include an enhanced focus on school readiness skills, particularly literacy and math, and an increased call for explicit teaching, frequently referred to as intentional teaching by preschool professionals. Early childhood teachers and administrators may have questions about the suitability of these materials for young children or feel that they are not sufficiently individualized for the interests and needs of children in their classrooms and programs. Preschool teachers need evidence, time, and support to help them understand and adapt to changing curricula designed to benefit the children they teach.

Another way in which preK and K–3 curricula differ is that the identification of independent and center activities that encourage a significant amount of child choice and play is robustly featured in both traditional and new preschool curricula. In recent years these types of activities have almost disappeared from the K–3 curricula used in public schools. The value of the play component is supported by evidence of a positive association between mature dramatic play and language development.

The degree of emphasis on family engagement and collaboration is another way in which preK and K–3 curricula differ. Both traditional and emerging preschool curricula explicitly plan for family collaboration. Although K–3 programs may also contain ways of connecting home and school, it is more likely to be seen as ancillary practice than are the practices for family collaboration specified within preschool curricula. Bear in mind when obtaining or planning a preschool curriculum that income-eligibility programs (the bulk of publically funded preschool education) often require documentation of family engagement in program reviews and that preschool educators are committed to the importance of it. Therefore, the quality of the family engagement component is an important feature of a preschool curriculum and provides an opportunity for fostering development of **English language learners** (ELLs) to the extent that these components are culturally responsive and meaningful and enacted collaboratively with families. They merit careful consideration when selecting and supporting implementation of curricula.

One important limitation of many of the emerging comprehensive preschool curricula is that while they may provide instruction in important areas identified in current research as promoting development, they often do not have a very detailed or clearly reasoned scope and sequence of activity. They may be more loosely structured than K–3 programs. For example, recent analysis suggests that the literacy instruction recommended in many of these comprehensiveness programs is too brief, contains too many different activities, and needs to more effectively provide language support and scaffolding that enable ELLs to access what is being taught. These analyses are supported by multiple sources of evidence that implementing comprehensive curriculum programs alone does not ensure positive cognitive growth of preschool English only (EO) or ELL children. This is similar to findings for K–3. Curricula likely to be effective will embed important details about how children learn into instructional routines and learning experiences. Large differences in children's learning can be accounted for by these details in instruction.

The differences between preK and K–3 curricula reflect the (1) characteristics of the children and (2) purposes and emphases of the programs they are designed for. The nature and learning processes of the children who will engage with a curriculum and the goals and purposes of the program they are being selected for should be the starting point and a primary consideration for curriculum selection. When preschool programs are housed within school districts, there may be a desire to select the preK version of the program already selected for grades K–3 on the assumption that continuity between the preK and K–3 curricula is beneficial for children's learning. There is no current research evidence supporting this assumption. It is not necessarily the case that the preK and K–3 versions of a curriculum will be equally effective for both preK and K–3 children. The very beginning level of English proficiency characteristic of many preschool ELLs is a very important factor that may reasonably favor those curricula that have a clearly articulated and rich language development strand with effective language scaffolding practices built into each instructional routine. A preschool curriculum should be selected on its merits for promoting learning specifically for preschool children, including **English learners**, and as such the quality of the language development component within it warrants intensive evaluation.

The recommendations in the following list will help in choosing the appropriate curriculum model.

1. Select curriculum considering the following factors:
   - Are the themes, materials, and activities likely to be engaging and interesting to preschool children?
   - Is a scope and sequence that outlines the nature and order of what is included in the curriculum provided?

- Are the instructional routines specific enough to accomplish stated goals?
- Are supporting materials provided? Are these materials culturally responsive?
- Are there specific practices for using first languages?
- What is the quality of the family engagement component?

2. Provide professional development that engages teachers in exploration, practice, and analysis of the curriculum materials.
3. Articulate clearly how the curriculum is to be implemented.
4. Clarify how the new curriculum is to be orchestrated with other materials/programs already in use.
5. Analyze very carefully the strengths and weaknesses of the instruction within the curriculum and modify so that instruction captures the important details leading to effective learning.

F. How are preK children's and K–3 students' language learning and development needs alike and different?

■ *Patton Tabors*

Certainly the most critical need that young children (preK) have in terms of language learning is the development of the oral language foundation for their later literacy acquisition. This is true for all children, but particularly important for young **English language learners** (ELLs) who have not had extensive experience in English. What does this mean in terms of curriculum for young children?

This need means that the classroom environment should be extensively infused with oral language at *every* opportunity. PreK children should be learning six to ten new words a day in order to build the conceptual vocabulary they will need when they embark on literacy activities. For ELLs, this means doubling up their vocabulary in two languages, although they may be learning different words in each of their languages. In bilingual classrooms, vocabulary building will need to always be a two-way street so all children are gaining the same concepts in at least one language. The following sections provide examples of how this works.

Circle Time

Circle time is usually the main organizational grouping of the day in preK. Circle time in a classroom with ELLs can be particularly useful for them if there is a set routine and material is presented in a way that they can understand. In other words, the presentation of theme material or activity options should be short, simple, and as visual as possible. By being explicit about vocabulary, teachers can provide ELLs with the necessary words to participate in the activities being offered.

It is also a time when many teachers use music and movement to engage the children. They should choose songs with highly predictable words and coordinated movements. Introducing the words first without the music can help ELLs catch on more quickly. In addition, giving children many opportunities to return to their favorite songs reinforces their learning. Frequently, ELLs find their voice for the first time in their new language while singing at circle time.

Activity Time

In many classrooms, activity time is when children are engaged in hands-on activities that introduce them to materials, concepts, and vocabulary. This is a perfect opportunity for teachers to use *running commentary*, explaining what they are doing as they demonstrate an activity or as they talk about what the children are doing. This technique provides children access to *context-embedded language* that provides vocabulary and syntactic structures in English.

Book Reading

Don't make book reading an endurance contest! Keep it short; choose books carefully so children hear the same words repeatedly. Talk the story in simpler words if the text is too advanced. Read books more than once so children can show off their growing understanding of the vocabulary, and give them a chance to read to each other or work in small groups tailored to their level of English acquisition.

Snack and Lunchtimes

Teachers need to be involved in conversations during these critical times to help develop vocabulary. It is easy to start by discussing the food items available, but then the conversation should expand to include the children's interests. If children bring snacks from home, there may be some interesting items that will provide vocabulary in more than one language. Teachers should use every opportunity with ELLs to encourage the use of **home language** in the classroom. This is also a time when teachers can place students in groups that will help with English acquisition by having English speakers and ELLs interspersed at tables to encourage child-to-child conversation.

Outside Time

Organized outdoor activities can also ideal times for vocabulary development. Many large-group games (e.g., Duck, Duck, Goose; Red Rover) have repetitive linguistic features that are easy for ELLs to key into and start using themselves. An effective way to encourage child-to-child language help is to partner ELLs with English-speaking children and have them work together throughout a cooperative game. Once these play relationships are developed outside, they may well lead to social play inside the classroom as well.

Words, Words, Words, Words

The more words children know, the more vocabulary they will have available to connect to the letters and sounds that they will discover in print when they start reading. Teachers help children develop their vocabulary by *intentionally* presenting new words for them to learn as part of every activity in the classroom, by using and explaining new words in conversation with them, and by reading new words to them and helping them understand their meanings. A preK classroom where the teacher is aware of the children's vocabulary needs and is always explaining, defining, or showing them what a word means will be a supportive classroom for both English-speaking and English-learning children.

G. What skills and dispositions are needed by teachers of English language learners in early childhood?

■ *Luz Marina Cardona*

It is a profound ethical responsibility for early childhood education (ECE) teachers, administrators, and policymakers to reinvent practice so that linguistically diverse young children can achieve their fullest potential. An educational philosophy with equity and justice at its foundation is necessary to meet the educational needs of a diverse community of learners in classrooms where minority and dominant cultures and languages collide. Developing such a philosophy requires a spectrum of knowledge, skills, and dispositions grounded in a pedagogy that examines the challenges of facilitating the development of identity and the construction of knowledge in linguistically diverse children.

A major challenge requiring examination is the dominant culture's practice of homogenizing the cultural and linguistic diversity of children and families with whom ECE teachers work. The belief that linguistically diverse preschoolers get a head start toward academic success by speaking English before they enter kindergarten results in an unfair trade for immigrant families who are "gaining a preschool and losing a language" (Fuller, 2007, p. 128). Though beyond the scope of this piece, it is also worth mentioning that another byproduct of the homogenization process is all that's lost, or simply never gained, by linguistically nondiverse children who rarely have the opportunity to learn new languages and cultures.

Another challenge that ECE teachers encounter is the push for formal academic instruction in the preschool years, derived from an emphasis on improving standardized test scores at the elementary school level. The underlying goal of improving scores in the primary grades by emphasizing the development of academic skills in preschoolers through structured and didactic literacy and numeracy lessons affects children's preschool experiences through a "one-size-fits-all" school readiness program. Overcoming challenges such as these calls for ECE teachers to be equipped with sound knowledge in child development, in addition to critical thinking and comprehensive communication skills.

Working with immigrant and linguistically diverse children thus demands an understanding of language development as well as substantial knowledge related to the children's backgrounds. ECE teachers also need to have an advanced knowledge of the processes involved in language teaching and learning and an understanding of sociolinguistics, or the role of language in daily life (Wong Fillmore & Snow, 2000). To avoid glossing over fundamental issues of exclusion and discrimination and falling into the trap of simply celebrating diversity, an understanding of the more evolved "affirmation, solidarity, and critique" level of multicultural education is required in order to move beyond the "monocultural, tolerance, acceptance, and respect" models, which are distinguished by an unconcerned and/or romanticized view of diversity (Nieto, in Shor & Pari, 1999, p. 26). Additionally, in order to reverse the social and economic inequality that linguistic minorities are historically subjected to, ECE teachers need to have a working knowledge of the principles and practices of anti-bias education (Derman-Sparks & Olsen Edwards, 2010) and of the social-reconstructionist approach to multicultural education (Sleeter & Grant, 1999).

More than sound pedagogical strategies that demonstrate expertise in language education–related issues, affirming the culture of linguistic minority students and supporting the development of the **home language** by using it as a legitimate vehicle for learning is indicative of teachers' cultural competence. The National Center of Cultural Competence defines this competence as "an ongoing process that involves self-assessment, managing the dynamics of difference, adopting and institutionalizing cultural knowledge, and adapting to the diversity and cultural contexts of the individuals and communities served" (Sareen, Visencio, Russ, & Halfon, 2005, p. 5).

To be culturally competent, ECE teachers must continually engage in a critical analysis of topics pertinent to cultural and linguistic diversity issues. Such critical analysis involves reflecting on the history and future of linguistic minorities from the standpoint of anti-bias education and of the "affirmation, solidarity, and critique" approach to multicultural education mentioned previously. Inherent in these approaches is an unwavering solidarity with the struggle of language minority children and of their families who constantly take risks to overcome the linguistic and cultural barriers that prevent them from having a voice in educational and other social contexts. Their resilience and courage in the struggle to maintain their language, to affirm their cultural identity, and to belong in an English-dominated environment deserves the support and action of teachers, administrators, and policymakers in charge of providing equitable educational opportunities and comparable learning outcomes.

The ECE field has had to incorporate "the explosion of knowledge in the science of child development" (Bredekamp, Isenberg, & Jalongo, 2003, p. 16; Whitebook, Bellm, Lee, & Sakai, 2005, p. 3). This knowledge presents the perfect opportunity for preschool teachers, administrators, and child advocates to educate policymakers, school officials, and community members on the "basics" of child development and cultural competence. It is now widely accepted that the preschool years lay the main groundwork for academic success. Thus, the attention that the ECE field is receiving in light of this knowledge is pivotal for the professional advancement of teachers and, not least of all, for the academic, social, and economic advancement of the linguistically and culturally diverse populations with which they work, thereby fulfilling the moral compulsion for social justice in communities and in society at large.

H. What is developmentally appropriate practice for grades preK–3?

■ *Janet Gonzalez-Mena*

Developmentally appropriate practice, as seen by the National Association for the Education of Young Children (NAEYC), is based on a concept of ages and stages and their effect on teaching and learning. The NAEYC has created a framework that promotes young children's optimal learning and development based on child development research. This framework provides a knowledge base regarding effective educational practices and as such helps teachers understand the implications for promoting growth, maturation, and learning in children during the first eight years of life.

The image is of children passing through a series of stages, each of which focuses on particular tasks that involve mind, body, and feelings, as well as social skills. Each age group has its own developmental challenges. The age groups are: infant–toddler, 0–3 years of age;

preschool, 3–5 years of age; kindergarten, 5–6 years of age; and primary grades, 6–8 years of age. The teacher's job is to meet children at their current level and help, even challenge, them to move toward appropriate and achievable goals in all developmental domains. The developmental process may be easier for some teachers to see and grasp in the first three years of life than it is in the primary grades; however, the concepts and implication for teaching practices apply throughout the first eight years.

Certain principles guide developmentally appropriate practice:

- Children learn and develop in a variety of ways.
- Development moves toward ever greater complexity.
- The "whole child" concept is important and must be considered because mind, body, and feelings are intertwined and are all important to development and learning.
- The rate of development and learning varies from child to child and depends on a combination of physical, mental, and emotional maturation and experience.
- Development is a growth process in which skills, abilities, and knowledge build on what children already know and can do.
- Early experiences affect development and learning and are part of the child's social and cultural contexts.
- Relationships are important. Secure, consistent relationships with responsive adults lie behind optimum development, as do positive relationships with peers.
- Children's experiences (e.g., persistence, initiative, and flexibility) shape their dispositions. They also shape their motivation and approaches to learning, which can affect development.
- Play is an important vehicle for learning and development and increases self-regulation, as well as competence in language, cognition, emotional, and social skills.
- There are optimal periods for certain kinds of development and learning to occur.
- When children are challenged to achieve at a level just beyond their current mastery and encouraged to practice their new skills, development and learning advance.

I. How should we interview and hire effective staff for preK and K–3 children who are English language learners?

■ *Laura C. Morana*

Shaping the lives of our students so they are ready to compete in this global society begins with the identification and nurturing of teachers, whether they are novices, experienced, or new to a school or a district. As administrators, hiring staff is the most important decision we engage in on behalf of our **English language learners** (ELLs).

Recognizing that programming for ELL students must be responsive to their diverse needs makes the hiring process multifaceted, and at times challenging. The process begins with the screening of applications jointly by the principal and the bilingual/English as a second language (ESL) education supervisor, who can be considered the preliminary interview committee. The committee considers legal certification requirements. In New Jersey, candidates must be certified in **bilingual education** and/or ESL and, depending on the grade level, must meet content-area highly qualified teacher requirements.

Hiring criteria must be defined and communicate the district's expectations for teaching and learning. These include criteria for planning, classroom environment, instruction, and overall professional responsibilities. A set of powerful questions guides the interview process so that ability, passion, and commitment to working with a diverse population are recognized.

The screening process I recommend culminates with the identification of prospective teachers who will advance to the "demo lesson" phase. A hands-on approach allows the teacher to show his or her ability to plan, demonstrate creativity and flexibility, and engage students in a meaningful lesson as agreed on by the classroom teacher and the administrators. Two successful candidates are then selected to advance to the interview with the superintendent. The two candidates are regarded as strong competitors who are equally competent and ready to serve as a high-quality teacher.

As a superintendent, I take this process very seriously. The two candidates are each engaged in conversation to gain an understanding of content and pedagogy and how they will make modifications to meet the varied needs of ELLs in their classrooms. One of the critical questions that I raise is in regard to the students they met as part of the demo lesson at the school level. This allows me to learn about the prospective teacher's plans to understand students' backgrounds, cultures, skills, language proficiency, interests, and special needs from a variety of sources.

This conversation regarding the students' knowledge is very revealing because candidates frequently make reference to how bright, polite, cooperative, and eager to please the students were throughout the brief demo lesson. Frequently, a sense of optimism and the use of a strengths-based perspective are conveyed through the response to open-ended questions. Knowledge of resources that will allow them to reach parents who may not be English proficient is another area that is addressed through the interview process.

Another aspect of the interview process is a simple question that can be revealing too: What did the candidates learn through the interview process at the school? As a superintendent, I believe that it is important for the candidates to have a clear understanding of the expectations for teaching and learning as introduced by the principal and supervisor who will be directly involved in the observation and evaluation of their performance.

J. What do staff in linguistically diverse programs need to know when they start working?

■ *Laura C. Morana*

There is not yet an agreed-on most effective approach to provide language instruction to **English language learners** (ELLs) and very few studies have directly examined the impact of language of instruction for preschool children and beyond. Therefore, we believe in augmenting the **home language** throughout the early years of development.

Establishing a culture for learning characterized by high expectations and a genuine commitment to the teaching and learning process is at the core of the framework that further defines how to best maximize our students' potential and **native language** proficiency. Our district has established a **transitional Spanish/English bilingual program** that supports students along the second language acquisition continuum from Spanish to cognitive **academic language proficiency** in English. The English language arts framework defines how the native and target language are to be used to deliver instruction. Spanish is used as the main vehicle for instruction in the preK and kindergarten classes. A dual language model defines the frequency of the use of the native and target languages.

The district is fortunate to be able to offer a high-quality preK program to all interested 3- and 4-year-old ELLs who are eligible for either a bilingual class or an English-only class, depending on their English proficiency as determined through the home language survey. Spanish speakers demonstrating ability in English as well as ELLs who speak languages other than Spanish are clustered in a targeted English-only class. Technical support is provided to the bilingual and general education classroom teachers by the district's preschool master teachers and the bilingual/English as a second language (ESL) supervisor.

PreK, **dual language learners** (DLLs) participate in a bilingual model that includes instruction in English one week followed by instruction in Spanish the next. The kindergarten program transitions students to educational settings with English as the primary language of instruction. In kindergarten, students are grouped by ability and receive focused English instruction from a certified ESL teacher. Intensive language supports across the school day help all DLLs enter grade 1 with a wider repertoire of English-language skills. A decrease in the use of Spanish is observed as students gradually transition into all English by the end of grade 2.

The district's framework for teaching and learning defines expectations for students to remain highly intellectually engaged in significant learning throughout the lesson. They must make concrete contributions to the lesson, as teachers adapt it as needed to meet the academic and linguistic needs of individual students and to be responsive to the students' culture.

Students in grades 1–3 with lower English proficiency levels are placed with a certified **bilingual education teacher** who promotes English language acquisition by providing native language support. The goal of the program is to build a foundation in literacy and academic content that facilitates English language and academic development as students acquire the new language. The program is designed to allow ELLs a smooth transition from the bilingual program to a general education classroom within a few years.

Teachers are encouraged to provide first language support whenever possible and necessary, especially to help students with key ideas and concepts. In addition to using techniques to make oral input comprehensible, teachers are encouraged to organize the curriculum around thematic units to help students develop the needed academic vocabulary for different content areas.

The primary goal of the ESL program is to offer ELLs an educational program that allows access to the core curriculum content standards and opportunities for **English language development**. An ESL program, as defined by the New Jersey Department of Education (2013), means "a daily developmental second language program of up to two periods of instruction based on student language proficiency which teaches aural comprehension, speaking, reading, and writing in English using second language teaching techniques, and incorporates the cultural aspects of the students' experiences in their ESL instruction" (p. 4). In New Jersey, ESL instruction is guided by the World-Class Instructional Design and Assessment (WIDA) Consortium's English language proficiency standards for English language learners. These are the standards and language competencies ELLs in preK programs and elementary and secondary schools must meet to become fully proficient in English and to have unrestricted access to grade-appropriate instruction in challenging academic subjects.

By grade 3, the transition continues so that most instruction is in English with native language support when needed. English language acquisition is encouraged by promoting academic vocabulary development, phonemic awareness, and grammatical understanding of English.

Recent arrivals (port-of-entry) continue to read and write in Spanish while they acquire oral language skills in English. Sheltered instruction strategies are used in all content areas, and a thematic approach is utilized to connect ESL with language arts literacy, science, and social studies.

■ *B. J. Franks*

In all honesty, all certified and noncertified bilingual or monolingual staff (administrators, school nurses, paraprofessionals, secretaries, lunch personnel, transportation personnel) who work with DLLs need professional development. All staff need to know or be aware of (1) the benefits of being bilingual and bicultural; (2) the process of second language acquisition, especially academic language; (3) cultural differences, such as values, communication styles, parenting styles, and disciplinary practices; and (4) how to tap into the students' cultural background. Teachers, in particular, need to know language and content standards and how to integrate both throughout all lessons. In addition, they need to assess first language communication skills through interviews with parents and guardians. Teachers should utilize an ELL specialist to support the needs of all students.

Many pathways exist to impart this knowledge. First and foremost, a school culture that embraces additive bilingualism needs to be in place. Other possibilities include book and lesson studies established during staff meetings, grade-level meetings, or within professional learning communities. All-day professional development sessions could be devoted to these topics with follow-up discussions or support in the aforementioned venues. Whatever the setting, the important ingredient is teacher and staff discussion and reflection of their own practice and how they integrate the new knowledge into their current pedagogy and interactions. This process must be ongoing, especially as new students arrive from different language/cultural groups.

K. How should we define the roles of the bilingual teacher, English as a second language teacher, general education teacher with diverse languages, teacher assistant, coach/mentor, principal, and supervisor?

■ *Diane Staehr Fenner*

The roles of all constituents who have an impact on **English language learner** (ELL) education are shifting as we enter a new era of education that is being shaped by many factors, including the implementation of the Common Core State Standards (CCSS) in most states. To that end, in 2013, TESOL International Association convened a group of practitioners, researchers, policymakers, and thought leaders on the role of the English as a second language (ESL) teacher during the implementation of the CCSS. The meeting was framed around these three questions:

1. What are ESL teachers' current roles in implementing the CCSS for ELLs?
2. What should ESL teachers' most effective roles be so that ELLs achieve with the CCSS?
3. What are the most promising strategies to support ESL teachers as they teach the CCSS?

In describing ESL teachers' current roles, participants shared that ESL teachers are often relegated to a seemingly lower status within their school than that of content-area teachers. One underlying reason for this perceived stratification is uneven credentialing systems, which vary widely from state to state, for ESL teachers and content-area teachers who teach ELLs. This variation creates ambiguity around ESL teachers' roles that sometimes obscures their expertise. It also means that some content-area teachers are not fully prepared to teach **English learners**. Another reason can be found in the highly qualified teacher (HQT) definitions from the No Child Left Behind Act (U.S. Dept. of Education, 2002). ESL is not recognized as a core academic content area under NCLB and is therefore not included among the HQT definitions. The HQT requirements for the TESOL field have been left up to the states to interpret, resulting in a broad spectrum of definitions that often leads to the diminished status of the ESL teacher.

Convening participants described a need to redefine ESL teachers' role so that (1) ELLs can best work with the demands of the new standards, and (2) ELLs' content teachers can use effective strategies to support ELLs. The time has come for ESL teachers to be recognized as "experts, consultants, and trainers well versed in teaching rigorous academic content" to ELLs. The convening participants proposed that ESL teachers consult with content teachers by helping them analyze the academic language demands of their content areas and providing support in designing lessons that teach academic language and rigorous content simultaneously.

Also, ESL teachers are often the practitioners best positioned to help colleagues draw on ELLs' first languages and cultures to aid in instruction. In order for a more collaborative, **consultation method** such as this to succeed, ESL teachers would need to demonstrate empathy with content teachers' complex situations; attend more content-area meetings; and engage more with content teachers at the school, district, and state levels.

Finally, administrators must advocate for ESL teachers and ELLs by making targeted changes at the school level that will elevate ESL teachers' status. Such changes include making teacher evaluation systems more inclusive of ELLs and ESL teachers and embracing the school's linguistic and cultural diversity. Convening participants stressed that administrators must fully support ESL teachers in their new, necessary role as experts and consultants as the CCSS are implemented. When administrators are aware of ESL teachers' expertise in language and culture, they are more likely to promote a school culture that includes ESL teachers and ELLs.

Some promising strategies were proposed to support ESL teachers in their critical role as implementers of the CCSS for ELLs:

- Help develop ESL teachers' leadership and voice in policymaking, particularly as it affects English learners

- Require that content-area teacher training programs include a strong ESL teaching component
- Require that all preK–12 teacher training programs include a CCSS component
- Provide ongoing, robust, high-quality professional development for all teachers of ELLs that contains authentic activities and examples
- Model effective strategies that enable all teachers to support ELLs within a CCSS framework

RECOMMENDED RESOURCES

Staehr Fenner, D. (2013). Advocating for English learners: A guide for educators. Thousand Oaks, CA: Corwin.
TESOL International Association. (2013, April). Implementing the Common Core State Standards for ELs: The changing role of the ESL teacher. Alexandria, VA: Author. Available from www.tesol.org/docs/default-source/advocacy/ccss_convening_final-5-3-13.pdf?sfvrsn=4

■ *Karen N. Nemeth*

Although the role of the ESL teacher is fairly well defined, the other teachers who work with ELLs/**dual language learners** (DLLs) may find their job descriptions a bit hazier. In **bilingual education** in most states, a teacher must have a certification or endorsement to his teaching certificate. Even with this type of certification, there is very little clear structure to the form bilingual education should take. We have seen teachers and administrators disagree about the day-to-day work that children and staff should be doing in early childhood bilingual education classes, and many misconceptions arise.

In general, bilingual education refers to programs that use the child's **native language** for instructional purposes, but program goals may be quite different. In two-way dual **language immersion programs**, the goal is to expose both ELLs/DLLs and English monolingual children to learning together in each other's language so that all of the children will grow up to be bilingual. In transitional bilingual classes, the goal is to teach children initially in their native language while supporting them to transition as quickly as possible to English-only instruction.

The National Association for Bilingual Education (NABE) provides the national perspective for this aspect of the education profession. Their position is that all children can benefit from growing up bilingual, and learning and literacy in the native language helps strengthen each child's knowledge base and supports their later transfer to English.

According to Stephen Krashen on the NABE website (www.nabe.org/BilingualEducation), "The best bilingual education programs include all of these characteristics: ESL instruction, sheltered subject matter teaching, and instruction in the first language. Non-English-speaking children initially receive core instruction in the **primary language** along with ESL instruction. As children grow more proficient in English, they learn subjects (e.g., math and science) using more contextualized language in sheltered classes taught in English, and eventually in mainstream classes."

So, depending on the grade and the location, bilingual education teachers may teach nearly 100% or as little as 10% in the non-English language. They may follow the grade-level curriculum, presenting instruction in their language, or they may create their own curricular supports in the language needed by the students. This is much more likely to happen when there are few curricular supports in a language other than English.

Often, additional expectations may creep into the bilingual education teacher's day. Identifying themselves as fluent speakers of a non-English language makes them prime candidates for extra work that may or may not be an appropriate use of their time. They may be called on to serve as interpreter for family conferences, asked to translate the school newsletter, or invited to help a general education teacher understand a new student who has started school in the general education classroom. It is important for administrators to understand that being fluent in a language does not necessarily prepare one to be a skilled translator of written materials. They also need to understand that a bilingual teacher is not necessarily prepared or the appropriate person to translate an assessment that is based on English-only data.

In some cases, particularly in preschool programs, general education teachers may be hired because they happen to speak a needed language. When this happens, it falls to the administrator to create a plan for defining this teacher's role and how she will use the two languages. As with certified **bilingual education teachers**, administrators must be careful not to add so many additional tasks to these teachers' workloads that they have trouble doing the jobs for which they were hired. For example, if a program hires bilingual speakers to serve as classroom paraprofessionals in order to meet adult:child ratio requirements, it is inappropriate to pull those bilingual aides out of their classrooms to help all over the building. When making staffing and professional development plans, it is critical that administrators plan for the real work—in class and outside of class—that these educators will be expected to do.

L. What resources should administrators be reading or organizations should they be joining to stay properly informed?

■ *Karen N. Nemeth*

There are so many organizations, websites, newsletters, social media groups, and meetings that it is hard for many administrators to keep up. Some key organizations will provide focused support; others will add to your knowledge or can be assigned to other staff. It is important to be in touch with national organizations that help administrators stay abreast of leadership positions, national trends, and critical research. State and local chapters also provide value by keeping administrators informed about what is happening locally. In most cases, a well-rounded leader in early childhood education for young **English language learners** (ELLs)/**dual language learners** (DLLs) needs both national and local memberships for his or her continuing education and professionalism.

The organizations in this section provide valuable information on their websites and in print journals and newsletters. They may offer professional development by way of expert speakers and conferences and online learning via webinars. Consider sharing an article with staff and then gathering everyone for an in-depth discussion, or making time for the whole staff to view a webinar and discuss how to implement what they learned. Make the most of your memberships by sharing information with your staff and keeping everyone's skills and knowledge up to date.

Every administrator of an early childhood education program or school, regardless of the setting, should belong to the National Association for the Education of Young Children (NAEYC). It is the primary national professional association and is at the center of early childhood education leadership. Visit www.naeyc.org to access many resources to support and guide your work with DLLs in early childhood. There are also many state and local chapters that may be useful to administrators and their staff.

Here are some additional options, depending on your background and the needs of your program:

- TESOL International Association (www.tesol.org). "TESOL International Association's mission is to advance professional expertise in English language teaching and learning for speakers of other languages worldwide." The official name of this organization no longer spells it out, but it is based on the former name, Teachers of English to Speakers of Other Languages. TESOL has chapters in many states and regions, and the national organization addresses early childhood issues in its Early Education Interest section.
- The National Association for Bilingual Education (NABE; www.nabe.org), "In a changing world: NABE stands as one nation of advocates! Supporting *all* languages, defending *many* cultures!" is the slogan on their web banner. The national organization has an Early Childhood Special Interest Group and chapters in 20 states.
- Additional language teaching and learning resources can be found via the American Council for Teachers of Foreign Languages (ACTFL; www.actfl.org) and their subgroup, the National Network for Early Language Learning (www.NNELL.org), which also has state and local chapters.
- Any preschool program administrator can find a wealth of resources for supporting DLLs/ELLs at the Office of Head Start's Early Childhood Knowledge and Learning Center website, with specialized materials created and provided by the National Center on Cultural and Linguistic Responsiveness at https://eclkc.ohs.acf.hhs.gov/hslc/tta-system/cultural-linguistic. No membership is needed. Administrators who do work with Head Start programs may also be interested in the news, resources, and professional development events of the National Head Start Association (NHSA; www.nhsa.org).
- The Council for Exceptional Children Division for Early Childhood (DEC; www.DEC-SPED.org). The DEC is a major subgroup of the National Council for Exceptional Children that is geared toward promoting policies and advancing practices for early intervention and early childhood special education. Resources from this organization will help administrators gain a better understanding about how to meet the needs of young children who may have special needs and who also speak different **home languages**.
- Similarly, the American Speech Language Hearing Association (ASHA; www.asha.org) provides specialized guidance that administrators may need as they work toward developing a collaborative and cohesive program for diverse populations.

Nonprofit and government-funded resource websites also provide excellent resources that can be invaluable for administrators, teachers, and families. Try some of these:

- www.colorincolorado.org: A free, web-based service that provides information and activities for educators and families of Spanish-speaking children who are ELLs/DLLs. It is a program of WETA public television, funded by the American Federation of Teachers.
- www.ncela.gwu.edu: National Clearinghouse for English Language Acquisition and Language Instruction Educational Programs. This is the resource website of the federal Office of English Language Acquisition.

- www.cal.org: Center for Applied Linguistics. This private, nonprofit organization produces and disseminates information for the field. Their mission is "to improve communication through better understanding of language and culture."

In addition to the preceding resources, there is a growing number of early childhood education and language development–related research journals. It would be impossible for any one professional to keep up with all of them. The national associations discussed previously can provide an excellent service by finding and summarizing the best information the field has to offer. Many also provide quick and easy access to new and important information on social media.

On Twitter, follow
    @NAEYC
    @NABEorg
    @ TESOL_Assn
    @HeadStartGov
    @NCELA
    @DED_sped
    @colorincolorado
Search for Twitter chats identified by hashtags such as
    #ELLCHAT
    #earlyed
    #ECE
    #TESOLconf14
    #NAEYCac

Many of these groups have Facebook pages as well, which you can find listed on their websites.

Some examples of LinkedIn groups to join are
    ELLs/DLLs in Early Education
    TESOL International Association
    ESL & Bilingual Teacher Professionals
    Dual Language Teacher Connection
    Early Childhood Education Network

M. What kinds of professional development and ongoing support can be effective for teachers of young English language learners?

■ *Douglas D. Bell, Jr.*

Supporting teachers of young **English language learners** (ELLs) can be an important task for a school leader or administrator. The most effective way to provide this support is through professional development. Unfortunately, there is little research on this topic for teachers of young ELLs. The one idea that is stated in the research is that teachers need professional development. Many teachers lack focused training in techniques for high-quality teaching of young ELLs (Bell, 2010).

There is a significant shortage of teachers trained to work with ELLs. Most teachers are not trained to support the development of academic language with young children (Russakoff, 2011). The level of teacher knowledge and skill is directly correlated with the quality of an early learning program that serves ELLs (Halle, Hair, Wandner, McNamara, & Chien, 2012). Teachers usually have insufficient training in linguistics, and therefore are unfamiliar with difficulties students face with academic learning in the second language (Price et al., 2009).

Professional development and training for teachers of young ELLs is best supported by using a combination of pre-service training and ongoing in-service training. Some teacher preparation programs offer a stand-alone course or multiple courses in working with young ELLs. Once on the job, teachers would benefit from workshops and training on topics related to working with young ELLs. Teachers need ongoing training in sufficient breadth and depth in the knowledge, skills, attitudes, and beliefs required to scaffold high levels of learning for all learners (Ballantyne, Sanderman, & Levy, 2008; Samson & Collins, 2012).

The workshops and in-service training are most beneficial when they are individualized rather than used as blanket topics (Walker, Shafer, & Liams, 2004). Professional development should be connected clearly to elements in teacher evaluation. Otherwise, when diversity and working with ELLs are included in assessments and evaluations, the absence of any evidence to the contrary often warrants credit for these elements. However, real and concrete ways for demonstrating the knowledge, skill, and ability can be measured, and teachers can be trained in these practices through professional development.

Part of the ongoing support that administrators can provide is mentoring and coaching. When evaluation identifies areas of need for professional development, the teacher will benefit from scaffolding by a more able peer. Support is important because unsupported teachers tend to develop negative attitudes toward ELLs and teaching them (Walker, Shafer, & Liams, 2004). This scaffolding can be carried out in a mentoring or coaching relationship and provided by a person with specialization in working with young ELLs, an administrator, or a teacher leader. If this model is to be used, and a school teacher of English to speakers of other languages (ESOL) is to provide the coaching for the classroom teacher, training in teacher leadership and coaching techniques will be required for the ESOL teacher.

■ *Judie Haynes*

Professional learning for teachers of ELLs should be a "comprehensive, sustained, and intensive approach to improving teachers' and principals' effectiveness in raising student achievement" (National Staff Development Council, 2001). One-shot professional learning programs do not provide adequate mentoring and assistance to teachers. They need ongoing support in order to implement what they have learned from university coursework or district professional development programs provided by an expert in the field.

One way for teachers to collaborate and share information is through social networking. Twenty-first-century professional learning should help teachers of **English learners** (ELs) become connected educators. Teachers can make global connections with other educators. They will learn the power of interactive platforms such as Facebook and LinkedIn, and Twitter educational chats such as #ELLCHAT.

One of the goals of professional development for teachers of ELLs should be to help them deliver curriculum and assessments that are targeted to the English language development level of the ELLs in their class. They need support and opportunities to practice preparing lessons (Zacarian & Haynes, 2012a).

It is also essential that administrators participate in these activities. Most administrators look at lesson plans, but spend very little time in classrooms. They need to know when they observe teachers that lessons have been appropriately modified for ELLs.

■ *Sonia W. Soltero*

Administrators who are visionary, knowledgeable, and committed to their students and staff produce the best results, not only in terms of student academic achievement but also in teacher and parent satisfaction. Culturally and linguistically responsive leadership is critical for young ELLs to thrive and be successful in school. The views, attitudes, and expectations of the principal or director set the tone for the entire school or center. Administrators' priorities and values are readily apparent to teachers, parents, and students by the extent to which they create positive learning experiences for ELLs.

Administrators who are involved in teachers' professional development as participants not only become well informed about ELLs, their presence also communicates their commitment to teachers and parents. Administrators' participation in teacher professional development also ensures that everyone has the same information, reducing the potential for making decisions that are contradictory to what teachers learn through in-service preparation (Reyes, 2006). A good starting point is to base professional development and curricular practices on the National Association for the Education of Young Children (NAEYC)'s Position Statement on Linguistic and Cultural Diversity, Responding to Linguistic and Cultural Diversity (1996), which offers recommendations for preparing early childhood professionals and working with young ELLs and their families. (The position statement is also available in Spanish.)

Another means of continued professional development is to allocate funds annually to attend regional (e.g., California Association for Bilingual Education and Illinois Association for Multilingual and Multicultural Education) and national (e.g., National Association for Bilingual Education Conference and NAEYC) educational conferences. Many states also hold statewide conferences for ELL parents, such as the Illinois Bilingual Summit, that can provide valuable information and resources, as well as opportunities to network with other schools and centers.

Administrators can also create opportunities for networking with other schools or centers that have ELLs. This type of networking provides support systems to share information and experiences. Although limitations in funds or time may be an obstacle to creating these networks, technological advancements offer ways to communicate and share information across cities, states, and even countries through online communities (e.g., blogs, social media), virtual meetings (e.g., video conferencing, Skype), and online pinboards (e.g., Pinterest).

Regularly scheduled time for teachers and paraprofessionals to plan and talk to one another is very important. Administrators must provide teachers frequent opportunities for curricular planning, sharing successes and struggles, and discussing student progress. Designating time and organizing frequent opportunities for teachers and staff to meet and plan creates a valuable support system for teachers. In addition, vertical articulation between subsequent grade levels provides teachers with better understanding about where students need to be academically and linguistically and also where they were previously. For example, grade 1 teachers meet with kindergarten teachers one month and with grade 2 teachers the next month. For preK teachers it is important that they meet with the receiving kindergarten teachers as well. The purpose of these cross-grade level meetings is to communicate and clarify specific grade-level expectations and curriculum (Soltero, 2004).

Administrators can also support teachers by allotting adequate funds for essential and supplemental resources to help with young ELLs' educational needs. Instructional resources should include culturally and linguistically diverse materials, in particular children's literature and music. In addition, interactive media and technology tools should be carefully screened and selected to avoid rote, low-level types of engagement, such as worksheets on the internet. For young ELLs, who are not yet proficient in English, interactive media may be an effective way to provide **comprehensible input** because of the audio-visual support. However, the NAEYC Position Statement (2012) on technology and interactive media cautions about inappropriate overuse of this medium, given that young children, especially ELLs, need to develop and learn through interaction with other children and adults.

One final important point is for administrators to ensure that the message about **bilingualism** and the role of the first language sent to parents and families is based on research rather than individual beliefs. The most detrimental recommendation that many well-intentioned teachers make to ELL parents is to speak English at home to their children, sending the message that the native language is not important. There are many problems with this kind of advice: parents who are not fluent in English are not good language models for their children; the child-parent bond is at risk because parents are not able to fluidly communicate with their children in English; authority is eroded because parents cannot fully impart values and norms to their children in a language in which they are not yet proficient; important family and cultural knowledge is lost because parents are not able to sustain extended conversations with their children in English. In addition, parents of ELLs have two common concerns: the fear that their children will be confused because they are developing two languages, and the worry that their children will not develop English if they receive native language instruction and support. Administrators and teachers need to provide correct and factual information, based on extensive research, that points to the benefits of bilingualism and how a well-developed first language provides the best bridge to acquiring English (Garcia, Jensen, & Scribner, 2009).

N. What do general education teachers need to know to work effectively with the English language learners in their classrooms?

■ *Douglas D. Bell, Jr.*

General education teachers have many duties and require a great deal of knowledge. However, most general education teachers are largely untrained in working with **English language learners** (ELLs; Cho, 2012). Teachers themselves sometimes report that they feel inadequately trained for working with young ELLs (Reeves, 2006). Teachers need training to help them meet their ELL students' language and learning needs (Samson & Collins, 2012). Accomplishing this requires training in many specific areas.

An understanding of child development is crucial to all teachers in an early childhood classroom. Often, literature speaks about working with ELLs from a strategic or technical viewpoint. Teachers are effective when they keep in mind that their students are *children* who have different developmental needs and characteristics at various stages.

Keeping child development in mind, the next area of understanding the general education teacher needs when working with young ELLs is cultural diversity awareness. Although this awareness is increasing in teacher education and training programs, many teachers are still unfamiliar with the impact of cultural diversity on development in and out of the classroom (Walker, Shafer, & Liams, 2004). Supporting teacher understanding of race, ethnicity, culture, bias, and their educational implications can be helpful. Teachers can then use this knowledge to support the intentional inclusion of the child's language and culture into the curriculum (Halle, Hair, Wandner, McNamara, & Chien, 2012).

Knowledge of linguistics and language development is also necessary for general education teachers to work effectively with young ELLs (Price et al., 2009). Teachers of young children need a basic understanding of how language works, how sounds develop and are formed, and how general oral language develops (Halle et al., 2012). The classroom teacher should also have a solid understanding of the second language acquisition in young children and the theory and practice of bilingual development. Additionally, this knowledge should be connected to literacy and areas of reading: phonological awareness, phonics, vocabulary, comprehension, and reading fluency.

Finally, the general education teacher needs to know how to apply classroom practices in ways that benefit young ELLs. Although learning specific methods is helpful, the learner benefits more if the teacher is aware of and sensitive to learner needs and uses that information while tapping into a variety of teaching skills (Pica, 2000). General education teachers need to know a variety of adaptation and support strategies useful to children who are learning the language. Also, incorporating learning strategies that are useful for any language into lessons can be very helpful (Burchinal, Field, Lopez, Howes, & Pianta, 2012). Finally, teachers need to know how to assess young ELLs in ways that are authentic, valid, and reliable (National Association for the Education of Young Children, 2005).

■ *Jennifer Mata*

In order to work effectively with ELL students, general education teachers need to either be certified **bilingual education teachers** or certified English as a second language (ESL) teachers if they are not bilingual. ELLs need to maintain their **native language** (L1) while they are learning English. This will help them transfer the knowledge and skills they have already learned in their L1 and facilitate the process of acquiring English.

The ideal situation for an ELL student of any proficiency or grade level in general education is to have a bilingual teacher who speaks both English and the student's L1 proficiently. In this ideal scenario, the teacher implements a **bilingual education** program known as a two-way immersion program (Peregoy & Boyle, 2008) or **developmental bilingual education program** (Christian, 1994), in which a certain percentage of the content is taught in English while the remaining content matter is taught in the ELL's L1 (Lindholm, 1990; Lindholm & Gavlek, 1994; Lindholm-Leary, 2001; Peregoy, 1991; Peregoy & Boyle, 1990). Both ELLs and native English speakers benefit from learning both languages (the **minority language** and English), as they continue to learn the target content matter for their grade level through their native and second languages.

Yet this ideal scenario is rarely found in classrooms. The second-best case scenario is to have an ESL-certified teacher in the classroom working with all ELL students, regardless of their L1, as well as native English speakers. This teacher teaches all content matter in English, providing scaffolding for the ELLs' proficiency in English. Because of her ESL training, she would also be using sheltering techniques to ensure that ELLs comprehend and learn content pertinent to their grade level while learning English (Peregoy & Boyle, 2008).

Some truths about ELLs that will surely help guide any teacher working with these students include the following (Chumak-Horbatsch, 2012):

- ELLs are not confused by learning two languages. They are quite capable of learning English while maintaining and continuing to make progress in learning their L1, if they have sufficient exposure, support, and guidance in both languages.
- ELLs require a language-rich environment and meaningful interactions to acquire a second language.
- Using the L1 helps ELLs make progress acquiring the target language, English, because language and literacy skills can be transferred across languages, even when the two languages are quite different.
- Any student who learns two languages is enriched by being exposed to two cultures and being able to communicate with and understand two different populations.
- ELLs who maintain their L1 are able to understand home-taught values and maintain close relationships with relatives who only speak their native language, building a linguistic foundation for the child and setting him/her up for success (Cummins, 2001). They also demonstrate better cross-cultural communication skills and earlier mastery of meaning, including cultural nuances (Bialystok, 2001).
- Students who become bilingual demonstrate advanced cognitive and linguistic skills, develop "agency" earlier, and are more successful academically and socially (Beach, Campano, Edmiston, & Borgmann, 2010). First grade bilinguals have been found to possess creativity, inquiry, and problem-solving skills akin to those of university graduate students (Schecter & Cummins, 2003).
- ELLs use code-mixing as a valuable communication strategy. This usage requires talents and skill and should not be corrected; it reflects ELLs' cultural hybridity and biculturalism (Pandey, 2012a).

O. How can administrators support effective collaboration and planning among staff who work with young English language learners?

■ *Ellen Hall and Alison Maher*

Boulder Journey School, a full-day, year-round preschool located in Boulder, Colorado, welcomes children ages 6 weeks to 6 years and their families. The Boulder Journey School Teacher Education Program, in partnership with the University of Colorado Denver and the Colorado Department of Education, offers an opportunity to earn a master's degree in educational psychology. Intern teachers participating in the year-long program join a permanent faculty of 25 mentor teachers. The philosophy of education and pedagogy of Boulder Journey School are inspired by the schools for young children in Reggio Emilia, Italy, and the ideas of Frances and David Hawkins (boulderjourneyschool.com, reggiochildren.it, hawkinscenters.org). The school's fundamental values are based on an image of children as competent and capable and as valuable citizens with inherent and irrefutable rights. Additionally, the school community gives value to contextual professional development through collaborations focused on the analysis of our documented observations.

In the renowned schools for young children in Reggio Emilia, Italy, educators work collaboratively to support the education of children and adults. The pedagogical team, composed of a pedagogista, an atelierista, and a teacher, engages in ongoing research through the process of documentation that includes observation, reflection, and curriculum projections. The pedagogista brings knowledge of learning, motivation and child development to the research; the atelierista brings knowledge of materials and aesthetics; and the teacher contributes an understanding of the children and their families and of the many relationships and experiences taking place in the classroom. Inspired by this system, educators at Boulder Journey School created a similar web of support in our context. The pedagogical team at Boulder Journey School includes studio, music, community, and technology specialists. This team has been designed to offer all educators at the school regular opportunities to meet and discuss classroom experiences, including individual and group learning, through multiple lenses and from multiple perspectives.

We think that bringing expertise in studio arts, music, community, and technology to our work can broaden and deepen the daily experiences of children and adults. Relationships among educators on the pedagogical team and with teachers are collegial and reciprocal. *The learning that is generated is our best source of professional development because it is authentic, contextual, and timely.* It is a collaboration through which all members of the school community can become increasingly knowledgeable not only about the areas of focus—technology, community, studio arts, and music—but also about teaching and learning. Together, we gain a better understanding of how to support all learners, including **dual language learners**.

Careful analysis of documented observations during daily classroom moments lies at the center of our work together. The process of documentation connects the research of the children with the research of the adults and offers educators and parents an opportunity to make connections between classroom experiences and theories of learning, motivation, and child development—thus offering professional development that is centered on the strengths and goals of each child and on the ways in which each individual can contribute to the learning of the group.

Teachers use a variety of tools to document their observations—videos, photographs, transcribed conversations, work samples, notes, graphs, and charts. In regular meetings, educators reflect on documented observations, addressing the following questions:

- What does the documentation tell us about the children's goals, strategies, and theories?
- What does the documentation tell us about the children's competencies and misunderstandings?
- What does the documentation tell us about the teachers' goals, strategies, and theories?
- What does the documentation tell us about the teachers' competencies and misunderstandings?

- What connections can be made between the documentation and theories of learning, motivation, and child development?
- How can the documentation inform future learning experiences for children and teachers?
- What resources can be made available to achieve short- and long-term learning goals for children and teachers?
- In what ways can the documentation inspire future professional development?
- In what ways can the documentation be shared with children and families within the school community and colleagues worldwide, inviting multiple perspectives and creating an even larger body of work from which to make meaning and co-construct learning?

■ *Monica Schnee*

General classroom teachers must be given the tools to support **English language learners** (ELLs) in their classrooms through collaboration, professional development, and most fundamentally, through the guidance and knowledge of the English as a second language (ESL) professional.

Young ELLs present very different challenges than those of older second language learners. The fact that young learners are just beginning to develop language and concepts and that they are **dual language learners** is crucial in understanding how to effectively support the collaboration and planning among the staff who work with them.

In my experience, collaboration and planning are successful when the following practices are put in place. The general classroom teacher and the ESL teacher should have a schedule that respects each other's instructional goals and objectives. An ideal time for the ESL professional to work with ELLs is during the literacy block when strategies specifically focused on second language acquisition can be modeled and implemented by the ESL teacher. It is also important for the ESL professional to be able to observe these learners at play to get to know them outside the academic realm, to connect with them in a natural, noninstructional situation in order to support them as they acquire a new language in a different setting.

In my years teaching kindergarten ELLs, I have come to the conclusion that at this age, pull-out instruction should be kept to a minimum. All children are developing language and social skills. Pulling ELLs out for small group instruction is only beneficial when the student is too low-functioning, too shy, in "culture shock," or if the demands in the general classroom are too high and the student becomes frustrated or isolated. Another great benefit of a model of co-teaching or team teaching is that both teachers get to observe each other's instructional methods. They both learn to take advantage of the other's strengths to build a more robust instructional setting for all learners.

Administrators should be mindful of scheduling common preparation time for the general classroom teacher and the ESL teacher. There is immense value in being able to discuss common goals, to strategize ways in which instruction should be differentiated for ELLs, and to share struggles and successes.

During common planning both professionals are able to share benchmarks and expectations that have a common and consistent language. Time working together brings about an understanding of how to integrate instructional, behavioral, and emotional goals. During this planning time, both professionals are also able to discuss materials and resources that are age and culturally appropriate for these learners.

Communication with parents is another main factor that influences the success of all learners, particularly ELLs. Therefore, providing time and resources for collaboration optimizes the parent-school connection, resulting in a more cohesive and culturally aware approach to parent involvement.

Allowing professionals to share weekly time to brainstorm, plan, and discuss instruction should be a priority to ensure effective collaboration that will lead to greater support for ELLs and all learners.

P. How can administrators effectively supervise staff when languages don't match?

■ *Karen N. Nemeth*

This question really raises two key concerns:

1. How can you know if a teacher is doing a good job if she speaks a language some students don't understand?
2. How can you know whether a teacher is performing well or not when she speaks a language you don't understand?

In the preschool and early elementary years when students have just begun to work on developing literacy, so much of their learning is supported by oral language. Most specifically, young children learn a lot from what teachers say to them. When observing a teacher in a multilingual classroom, it is important to watch more than her behavior. For example, if the teacher very clearly says a safety rule, you might be tempted to give her credit. If, however, you take into account how many of her students would not understand her words, you would also want to look for additional ways that she gets her point across.

Looking for adaptations and supports to communication such as visuals, props, demonstrations, and body language helps you see that she is being more effective in communicating key information to students who are **dual language learners** (DLLs). Most classroom observation tools, such as Early Childhood Environment Rating Scale-Revised (ECERS-R), Early Language and Literacy Classroom Observation (ELLCO), Classroom Assessment Scoring System (CLASS), have not been fully adapted for the multilingual classroom. The responsibility falls on the shoulders of the administrator to go beyond the standard English-only assessments and observe how well the teacher's behaviors actually fit the students in her classroom.

When teachers are speaking a language that helps them communicate with the non-English speakers in the classroom, there may be a lot of valuable learning taking place, but the administrator has a hard time knowing how well things are going. You can begin by looking for signs that students are engaged with the teacher and the tasks at hand. Are the child and teacher looking at each other when they are talking? Can you see the student acting in response to what the teacher said? Is the tone in the room positive and comfortable? Do you see a lot of learning going on? These are all things you can look for when observing a teacher who is not speaking your language.

And, of course, sometimes the best way to assess how a teacher is doing is to ask her. Practice good coaching techniques that encourage the teacher to keep good notes on her classroom practices so that she is able to discuss them with her supervisor when needed. Although this may not be the most objective form of observation, it certainly can be a good way to open up mutually beneficial conversations between teacher and supervisor.

Resources and Questions

SELF-ASSESSMENT CHECKLIST

☐ Are you confident in using the various terms needed in different contexts to talk about children who are learning in two languages?

☐ Can you explain to staff and parents how the developmental needs of preK and K–3 children are alike and different?

☐ Are you aware of the differences in appropriate curricula for grades preK–3?

☐ Can you explain specifically the similarities and differences in language development across these ages?

☐ Are you aware of the skills and dispositions needed by teachers of ELLs in the early years?

☐ Can you define truly developmentally appropriate practice for grades preK–3 according to NAEYC?

☐ Have you adapted your interview procedures for bilingual candidates?

☐ Have you created an orientation plan to support new bilingual teachers coming into diverse classrooms?

☐ Have you created an orientation plan to support new teachers who are *not* bilingual or who do not speak the languages of the children?

☐ Have you updated the job descriptions of educators working in various settings with children who are learning in two languages?

☐ Have you revised your own professional membership and development scheme to fit the demands of supervising a diverse program?

☐ Have you updated your professional development plan for staff who works with children learning in different languages?

☐ Have you changed your plan for supporting general education teachers so that they are more effective with linguistically diverse groups?

☐ Do you have an updated plan for supporting collaboration among staff and administrators?

☐ Are you ready to supervise teachers who may be teaching in a language you don't understand?

QUESTIONS FOR REFLECTION

- What challenge is most pressing when you think about the work your school is doing to teach children who are English learners in grades preK–3?

- What aspect of your program do you think is most effective in teaching young children who are English learners?

- How has reading the information in this chapter changed your answers to the first two questions?

- What will you try to learn in the remaining chapters of this book?

CHAPTER 2

Identification and Planning

Key Considerations for Language Plan

- Our language plan will use research-based decisionmaking strategies to identify potential **dual language learners** (DLLs) and assess their home and English language proficiency in order to make appropriate placements for them.

- Our language plan will describe exactly how each service option for DLLs will be planned and implemented, and on what criteria decisions will be based.

- Our language plan will show how adaptations can be made in schoolwide policies and practices to be inclusive of our young DLL students.

- Our language plan will tie the planning decisions we make with the standards we must follow.

C hapter 2 assists administrators in setting up the programs and services they will provide for young children who are DLLs/**English language learners** (ELLs). The overarching questions for this chapter are: Who are your ELLs/DLLs? What options should you consider when planning the types of programs and services you will provide for them?

Administrators face specific challenges in planning programs for preK–3 ELL children. These students are not only new to your school, they also are new to the whole school experience. Their early stage of cognitive development makes them less predictable subjects for screening and assessment. The variety of languages and the appearance of low-incidence languages make it more difficult to make language-appropriate placement and staffing decisions. Young children need more thoughtful support as they transition into the preK program and from one grade level to the next. To make things even more complicated, early childhood administrators will encounter an expanding array of Common Core Standards, state standards, and layers of regulations they must follow as they plan services for young ELLs/DLLs.

This chapter gathers expert advice to lay the groundwork for the planning process. The first step is to improve strategies for identifying the languages and the language learning needs of each student. Fine-tuning the identification process contributes to more effective planning for placement, services, and transitions for young ELLs/DLLs. Contributors to this chapter also provide information about all of the factors that need to be addressed in planning educational programs for young ELLs/DLLs. Subsequent chapters then offer all of the guidance needed to put effective plans into action. The planning guide at the end of this chapter gives you a way to capture the practical considerations that will make your language plan unique and help you tailor your efforts according to the factors that characterize your program.

A. How should we identify young children who are dual/English language learners?

■ *Debbie Zacarian*

Juan Carlos Rivera is 3 years old and coming to Smith Preschool for his first day of class. Picture him walking toward the school holding hands with his parents. They are excited and nervous about what lies ahead. Knowing that this book is about **dual language learners** (DLLs) and the topic of this chapter is identifying them, what assumptions might we have already made about Juan Carlos in terms of the language that he uses at home with his relatives, friends, and community? How might our assumptions be based on our personal and professional experiences as well as our work environments? These questions are critical to ask ourselves as we approach the topic of identification. That is, do we tend to identify language learners based on our own beliefs about what the terms dual or **English learner** (EL) mean, how they apply to our own particular contexts, and what we have to offer this growing segment of the nation's student population?

To explore the concept of identification a little more deeply, let's look at what we hope to accomplish in this process. Here are two global ideas to consider: As educators, we want all of our learners to succeed. As parents, we want our children to succeed. If we step back to think strategically about what helps children be successful in school, what does identifying a student as a DLL/EL mean in the "real world" of early education and care?

The Massachusetts Department of Early Education and Care conducted a survey of the state's early education and care providers. It also conducted onsite observations of seven of its sites. One of the primary purposes of the survey and site visits was to learn about the system of dual language programming so that the state could better understand and develop its policies for this population (Zacarian, Finlayson, Lisseck, & Ward Lolacono, 2010). Twelve thousand surveys were sent to providers of center-based, school age, public preschool, Head Start, Early Head Start, and family childcare programming, and 693 responded. Analyzing the findings revealed that while each site had sweeping differences in the total number of DLLs (from high to low incidences), the type of programming also varied immensely. Some children received instruction in their **home language**, others received translation support, and others received no support in their home language.

The site visits also revealed some important findings. One of particular note was that the types of programming that providers identified, such as bilingual programming, varied greatly. In some settings bilingual programming referred to a program entirely provided in a child's home language; in others it referred to some translation support when a child did not appear to comprehend. Why is this important? As we look at identifying language learners, we must think carefully about what we are trying to do. In other words, once we learn that a child is a speaker of another language, how will we use this information to help him or her succeed?

Another critical element for us to consider is the reality that some of our learners come from homes that practice high levels of literacy and prepare their children for school. In these homes, children observe literacy practices from birth. Let's return to Juan Carlos. His mother and father are both college educated, have jobs in their respective fields of engineering and education, and are fully bilingual in Spanish and English. Since birth, Juan Carlos has observed his parents reading newspapers and books and communicating via the internet. While he speaks Spanish at home, with relatives and with his community, he needs to learn English. What do you think his chances are for success in school?

Let's compare our guess with what we think will occur with that of his peer, Amanda Simmons. Amanda speaks English with her father, Spanish and English with her mother, English with her paternal grandparents, and Spanish with her maternal grandmother. Her parents dropped out of high school because they did not find it meaningful. Although they want Amanda to be successful in school and wish to support her in the best ways possible, as almost all parents do, they do not practice literacy as a way of being and acting at home.

Amanda and Juan Carlos enroll in Smith Preschool on the same day and are the same ages. What factors are critical for us to know about the two in terms of the educational programming that we will provide so that both may be successful?

Athough we need educational policies and practices at the early education level, we have to understand identification as a complex process that is not simply identifying DLLs by using assessments (e.g., WIDA ACCESS placement test, Pre LAS, and LAS Links). One potential remedy is for all of us to develop enrollment systems that devote time and assets to understanding parent and family childrearing systems in terms of language and literacy development (Genesee, Lindholm-Leary, Saunders, & Christian, 2006; Gutiérrez-Clellen & Kreiter, 2003), as well as how children understand the world around them (Zacarian, 2013; Zacarian & Silverstone, in press). Enacting this remedy involves understanding that parents and school systems are both great influences on a child's development; they are two interconnected worlds (Bartel-Haring & Younkin, 2012). It is also urgent that we consider the ways in which we build on the strengths of a child's home experience in school. Again, this involves our taking the time, at enrollment, to best identify and understand our children's sociocultural, language and literacy, academic, and thinking-to-understand-the-world development (Zacarian, 2011, 2013). It also requires that we use this essential understanding to provide programming that matches our children's experiences so that they succeed in school and beyond.

■ *Karen N. Nemeth*

There are three factors that come together in the decisionmaking process for identifying young children who are **English language learners** (ELLs) or DLLs.

1. You have to be very familiar with the regulations that govern your program, and for each grade and age level in it. You need to know the definitions that are required for your program and what assessment methods are required or allowed. Then you need to learn where the flexibility is within those rules.
2. You need to respectfully get to know each family. Many states suggest or require a home language survey of some kind. If a survey is designed to ask families what language is spoken in the home, but that survey is only in English, can you see where problems might arise? When designing a home language survey, make sure that it is conversational and approachable, rather than threatening. Ask questions that go beyond demanding an accounting of the actual languages spoken. You might ask the family to identify some family members who are important to the child and the child's favorite foods or fears; you might ask about the kinds of music the family enjoys or examples of how they spend time together on the weekends. These nonthreatening questions can open the door of

communication and understanding. And it is always a good idea to follow up written surveys with face-to-face conversations for clarificaton. In many programs—such as New Jersey Department of Education—the presence of a **home language** other than English is sufficient to identify a child as a DLL, because that state's premise is that every preK child needs support of the home language. But the state has additional requirements for testing English language proficiency for grades K–3 that must be used.

3. You may need to select a screening tool or assessment to identify students who have **limited English proficiency** (LEP). In some states, such as California at the time we are writing this book, use the home language survey to identify possible ELL students. They must be further assessed for limited English proficiency to qualify for English as a second language (ESL) services. The weakness of that system is that we cannot always be sure that families will answer the survey accurately. There have been many instances in which families feel they can prevent their child from being identified as an ELL if they just list English as the only home language—even if the child might clearly need language services. In other cases, the family just might not understand the question. Even if a young child seems fairly proficient in English when entering your program, he or she may have learned and retained many concepts and vocabulary words in the home language. Current research strongly dictates that such a child must continue to learn and to learn in their home language in order to build on that prior knowledge until they have been fluent in English for several years. This premise may not, however, be supported by your state or local regulations, so it is important to go back to step one as the key to your language proficiency identification plan.

Identification is only the first planning step. Placement decisions are based on the identification made and the services you have available. Continuity is very important. K–12 districts should work closely with Head Start and other private preschool programs so that young DLLs don't get jolted among widely disparate types of programs. To support continuing growth of both language development and academic learning, the preschool, kindergarten, and upper-grade services must be coordinated and smooth transitions must be supported.

B. How are placement decisions made?

■ *Wayne E. Wright*

Placing a young **English language learner** (ELL) in the most appropriate classroom and program type is a critical decision that has an enormous impact on the student's academic success and life. Federal and state laws require that ELLs be identified at the time of enrollment and that parents be informed of the program placement options. Initial identification is typically made through the use of a home language survey. At a minimum, the survey asks questions to determine (1) what language(s) is spoken at home, (2) what language(s) the student first began to acquire, and (3) what language(s) the student uses most often. If the answers to any of the questions include a non-English language, the student is designated as primary home language other than English (PHLOTE).

To determine if a PHLOTE student is an ELL, an English language proficiency (ELP) test must be administered. If the test determines the student is **full English proficient** (FEP), the student may be placed in any classroom. Those below this level are officially classified as ELLs. They are legally entitled to be placed in classrooms with teachers certified to work with ELLs and that are part of specialized programs designed to address their linguistic and academic needs. The test results also provide a specific ELP level that must be considered in placement decisions. ELP assessments must be given annually to monitor student progress and to make subsequent placement decisions until the student is reclassified as FEP. Although unnecessary, some schools also assess the student's proficiency in the **home language**.

Administrators must be aware, however, of the limitations of these language proficiency tests. Although such tests may be effective in identifying ELLs at the lower levels of English proficiency, they are less effective at determining which students are indeed sufficiently proficient to handle mainstream English-only instruction. Thus, after initial placement, classroom teachers and ELL specialists should closely monitor their students and carry out additional, more authentic assessments to determine if classifications are accurate and if the most appropriate placement decisions have been made. Extreme caution must also be used when interpreting home language proficiency test results. For example, it is not uncommon for test results to designate Latino ELLs as both non-English and non-Spanish speaking. Except in cases of severe cognitive development disorders, it is absurd to suggest that there are children with no language. Such designations are the result of poorly designed tests that only measure a narrow range of items within a specific standardized variety of the language. Results suggesting low proficiency in the home language should never be used to justify placement in nonbilingual programs.

Other factors must also be considered in placement decisions, such as the students' prior educational background. And, of course, appropriate placement decisions can only be made if a school has appropriate classrooms and programs for ELLs to be placed into. The varieties of potential programs are described in other sections of this book. Parents must be informed of the different placement options. But it is not enough to simply run down a list and force the parents to make a quick, uninformed decision. With such a critical decision, time must be taken to fully explain each option and make the parents aware of the benefits and limitations of each program type. Some districts have produced short videos in different languages with clips from various program types that can help parents make an informed decision. With good information, proper guidance, and effective options, parents and schools can make the best placement decisions to ensure the academic success of ELLs.

RECOMMENDED RESOURCES

Crawford, J., & Krashen, S. (2007). *English learners in American classrooms: 101 questions, 101 answers.* New York: Scholastic.

Hamayan, E., & Freeman Field, R. F. (Eds.). (2012). *English language learners at school: A guide for administrators* (2nd ed.). Philadelphia: Caslon.

MacSwan, J., Rolstad, K., & Glass, G. V. (2002). Do some school-age children have no language? Some problems of construct validity in the Pre-Las Español. *Bilingual Research Journal, 26*(2), 213–238.

Wright, W. E. (2010). *Foundations for teaching English language learners: Research, theory, policy, and practice.* Philadelphia: Caslon.

C. What are the best ways to assess language proficiency during early childhood (preK–3)?

■ *Sandra Barrueco*

Early childhood assessment (preK–3) has been a historically difficult undertaking, particularly with multilingual children. The issues and questions on hand abound for this age group at the individual, classroom, and program levels: How can typical and atypical language development be differentiated? Is this child's language progress typical for one developing multiple languages, or could a disorder (or other issue) be present? How can we track growth in English, in the **home language**, and across the two to understand how well a child is developing proficiency, and/or to understand how our classroom or program approaches are working for these children? And, as discussed in a prior section, how can young children be identified as ELLs for specialized instructional approaches?

Answering these questions is complicated for early childhood professionals, given the tremendous range of development seen in young children, the variability of backgrounds and experiences that multilingual young children and families have had, and a paucity of empirical knowledge about young multilingual children in general. A dearth of well-developed assessment approaches for this age range has complicated matters further. On a positive note, the tide is finally turning as more focus is placed on early childhood and the country's demographic shifts. For example, much more is now known about early language development among **dual language learners** (DLLs).*

Progress is also underway within the early assessment field, particularly for the two most frequently spoken languages in the United States. My colleagues and I recently reviewed all the language and literacy measures for young children available in both English and Spanish (Barrueco, López, Ong, & Lozano, 2012). Our analysis focused on each assessment's linguistic, cultural, and psychometric strengths and weaknesses. The positive news is that most of the recently developed or updated measures are adequate in many respects. This is quite a change from 10 to 15 years ago. However, there are quite a few (and frequently used) measures that have significant gaps, which can inadvertently cause inappropriate referrals, misclassifications, and incorrect estimates of program effects. We are in dialogue with measure developers and publishers across the United States to continue to support efforts in the assessment front. In the meantime, it is recommended that professionals who are deciding on assessment approaches and measures be aware of the key questions to consider and which characteristics to look for when developing their protocols, whether for individual child assessment purposes or for systemic use. Authors such as Gutiérrez-Clellen, Peña, Restrepo, Lonigan, and Anthony are developing solid assessments for DLL children. We describe these considerations in our own works (Barrueco, 2012; Barrueco et al., 2012).

RECOMMENDED RESOURCE

Center for Early Care and Education Research–Dual Language Learners (CECER-DLL). http://cecerdll.fpg.unc .edu/

---

*See works by Castro, Genesee, Goldstein, Guitérrez-Clellen, Hammer, López, Páez, and Tabors reviewed on the Center for Early Care and Education Research–Dual Language Learners (CECER-DLL) website, http:// cecerdll.fpg.unc.edu.

D. What do administrators need to know to plan for appropriate service models that work with different populations?

■ *Sonia W. Soltero*

For administrators to support the most effective collaboration and planning among staff, they must be well informed and knowledgeable about all aspects of **English language learner** (ELL) education. In order for them to be effective leaders, they must also understand the factors that affect, positively or negatively, the education outcomes of young ELLs (Delfino, Johnson, & Perez, 2009). In particular, principals and other school leaders must be knowledgeable about second language acquisition theory and pedagogy, multicultural and bilingual education principles, appropriate instruction and assessment practices, and effective curricular planning. In-depth and extensive professional development for administrators, teachers, paraprofessionals, and other support staff should also include a deeper understanding of culture, family, and community participation.

Because language is so closely tied to all aspects of a child's development in the early years, ignoring their **native language** significantly impairs teachers' ability to fully assess and promote young ELLs' language and literacy development. Misconceptions about early **bilingualism** often lead teachers and administrators to believe that young ELLs do not need specialized language instruction because young children "pick up language easily" (Soltero, 2011). The lack of English language proficiency is not the only aspect that affects ELLs' education outcomes. Factors that contribute to ELLs' achievement gap include parents' limited schooling, parents working low-paying jobs with long work hours or with multiple jobs, family residency status, and limited access to health care and other social services.

There is a need for administrators and teachers to understand that young children benefit cognitively from learning more than one language. For ELLs, moving from their first language (L1) to English before they have a strong foundation in their L1 can have long-lasting negative academic and linguistic effects. Preschool ELLs who are taught in English-only classrooms or transitioned to English instruction before they have solid oral language abilities in their L1 often do not achieve high levels of English fluency and do not do as well as those who have opportunities to learn in two languages (Genesee, Paradis, & Crago, 2004). Research shows that on standardized tests in English during the middle and high school years young ELLs with extended learning opportunities in their L1 from ages 3 to 8 consistently outperform those who attended English-only programs (Garcia, Jensen, & Scribner, 2009).

Early childhood administrators and teachers should understand that acquiring more than one language does not delay the acquisition of English or interfere with academic achievement in English when both languages are supported. Neuroscientists and psycholinguists point to the positive effects of learning two languages during the infant–toddler years and also to the human brain's broad capacity to learn multiple languages. In addition, young children learning two languages have more neural activity in the parts of the brain associated with language processing. This increased brain activity can have long-term positive effects on cognitive abilities, such as those that require focusing on the details of a task and knowing how language is structured and used (Bialystok, Craik, & Ryan, 2006). Research on children who acquire English after their L1 has been developed shows that they have the capacity to learn more than one language during the primary school years and that this bilingual ability offers long-term academic, cultural, and economic benefits (García & Frede, 2010).

Research points to the relationship between high-quality preschool programs and higher academic achievement in school, lower special education referral rates, higher rates of high school graduation, and increased college attendance. All these factors result in economic and social benefits later in life. The planning and use of appropriate education practices is especially relevant for young ELLs. For administrators and teachers, it is important to recognize the research-based principles of educating young ELLs. Garcia, Jensen and Scribner (2009) reflect other research findings and conclude that

- Academic support for young children in their L1 improves long-term English acquisition.
- Young ELLs who are immersed in English instead of participating in bilingual or **English as a second language programs** show decreases in reading and math achievement, higher high school dropout rates, and lower test scores.
- Neuroscientists and psycholinguists assert that oral language is the foundation for reading acquisition and that reading skills must be built on a strong oral language base.

On the basis of these principles, early childhood educators can provide the necessary language and academic foundations to better prepare ELLs to be successful in kindergarten and beyond. For ELLs, linguistic and culturally responsive preschool education must be an essential part of the overall improvement efforts of schools.

RECOMMENDED RESOURCES

Bauer, E. B., & Gort, M. (2011). *Early biliteracy development: Exploring young learners' use of their linguistic resources.* New York: Routledge.

Crawford, J., & Krashen, S. (2007). *English learners in American classrooms: 101 questions, 101 answers.* New York: Scholastic.

Garcia, O., & Kleifgen, J. A. (2010). *Educating emergent bilinguals: Policies, programs, and practices for English language learners.* New York: Teachers College Press.

Genishi, C., & Haas Dyson, A. (2009). *Children, language, and literacy: Diverse learners in diverse times.* New York: Teachers College Press.

Gonzalez, V. (2009). *Young learners, diverse children. Celebrating diversity in early childhood.* Thousand Oaks, CA: Corwin.

Howes, C., Downer, J. T., & Pianta, R. C. (2011). *Dual language learners in the early childhood classroom.* Baltimore, MD: Paul H. Brookes.

Nemeth, K. N. (2012). *Basics of supporting dual language learners: An introduction for educators of children from birth through age 8.* Washington, DC: National Association for the Education of Young Children.

Roberts, T. A. (2009). *No limits to literacy for preschool English learners.* Thousand Oaks, CA: Corwin.

Tabors, P. O. (2008). *One child, two languages: A guide for early childhood educators of children learning English as a second language.* Baltimore, MD: Paul H. Brookes.

E. How can administrators plan appropriately for successful transitions of young English language learners into the program and from one year/program/service/environment to the next?

■ *Laura C. Morana*

The principal is the primary instructional leader and manager of a school. As such, he or she is in a unique position to establish, implement, and evaluate the effectiveness of a coherent instructional framework that supports and responds to the diverse academic and linguistic needs of **English language learners** (ELLs). The further recognition of the complexity associated with the teaching of ELLs makes being responsive to the needs of teachers, paraprofessionals, certified support staff, and parents critical. The school principal must be the catalyst for collaboration with district administrators and a wide range of constituents in implementing a coherent instructional program that guarantees success for all ELLs.

To support school principals, our district created a handbook that outlines the **bilingual education** and/or English as a second language (ESL) process from the determination through programming, exiting, and supporting students as former ELLs. The process begins with the determination of English language proficiency through the administration of multiple assessments. The WIDA (World-Class Instructional Design and Assessment) MODEL (measure of developing English language) assessment is used in grades K–3 on entry into the district to determine students' eligibility for ESL–bilingual and/or ESL services. To measure student achievement of Common Core State Standards (CCSS), students are administered the New Jersey Assessment of Skills and Knowledge (NJASK) at the end of grade 3. Every ELL must take the NJASK, and first-year Spanish speakers may take the language arts literacy assessment in their **native language**. First-year ELLs who speak a language other than Spanish may be exempt from the language arts literacy section of state assessment.

The handbook also provides a description of the instructional framework that includes grade level curricula, assessment, instruction, and scaffolding strategies that are rigorous and focus on all four language skills: listening, speaking, reading, and writing. Furthermore, the curriculum outlines classroom environment expectations that include a culturally diverse library or collection of authentic fiction and nonfiction literature and leveled reading materials in a variety of genres and of sufficient quantity in both to support the curriculum.

Students' classroom academic performance is assessed using multiple criteria. The results serve also as an indicator for allowing students to exit the program. Annually, bilingual, ESL, and/or general education teachers collaborate to provide the data for the multiple criteria chart, completed early in June each year. Teachers' input and recommendations also contribute to the determination of whether a student should continue or exit the program. Parents are notified in writing if their child is no longer eligible to receive services. Examples of multiple measures to determine eligibility for exiting the program include

- English language proficiency: ACCESS composite score of 4.5 or higher—speaking, listening, reading and writing skills
- Academic performance: teacher recommendations based on student's class work, homework, test scores, and report card grades

- Reading level based on DRA2
- Performance on standardized assessments
- Performance on district benchmark assessments
- Time in the bilingual/**ESL program**

Bilingual/ESL program staff strategically monitor the progress of students who have entered the general education program by means of the monitoring report, which is completed by general education program teachers quarterly. Students who have recently exited who are not progressing in the general program may be considered for reentry to the bilingual/ESL program. Reentry is based on a comprehensive review of report cards and benchmark assessment results to determine academic progress. If an ELL is underperforming, the ESL teacher/master teacher/supervisor will consult and offer general education teacher strategies to implement during instruction. For any persistent concerns regarding former ELLs' academic performance, teachers may access the support of the schools' intervention and referral services (I&RS) team.

■ *Monica Schnee*

Administrators who understand the needs of ELLs and the different services and supports they benefit from should maximize planning so ELLs may successfully transition from one year to the next. There are some critical and essential elements that must be in place in order for ELLs to have as seamless a transition as possible. In my experience, the following considerations must be taken into account:

- Articulation of goals and objectives shared between two grade levels is essential for instruction. When there is a scope and sequence that delineates what learners should be taught within a given time frame, administration and faculty are able to plan collaboratively so that learners' needs are supported and met.
- These goals and objectives should be based on a set of attainable benchmarks that will result in the successful performance of all learners.
- How these benchmarks are assessed is an important part of the discussion and planning among outgoing and incoming teachers and administrators.

One way of supporting ELLs in the classroom is by making sure that placement is carefully planned and balanced so they can be part of an optimum learning environment.
Placement of ELLs should include the following criteria:

- When possible, pair learners who speak the same language. If this is not an option, pair learners who share a similar culture, for instance, a child from Ecuador and a child from Bolivia, or a Gujarati-speaking child and a Tamil-speaking child. This deliberate kind of placement allows children to feel more comfortable as they have a "buddy"; it shows cultural respect and sensitivity.
- Although it is difficult to foresee the success of any classroom composition, it is advisable to place ELLs together in small groups of five to eight students per class in an ESL setting. It is also good practice, when possible, to assign teachers who are more experienced in working with ELLs because they are more flexible, give more wait time, and are aware of cultural differences.

- Another advantage of placing ELLs of similar backgrounds together is that it encourages their parents to participate in school activities. It also provides a comfort zone for parents of ELLs as they all share the experience of learning in a new country. Administrators should also plan to inform parents about the routines and expectations of school because many of them are joining the public school system for the first time.

In conclusion, the successful transition of young ELLs has to include more than efficient scheduling, rigorous academics, and effective instruction. It has to support the learners in a positive and welcoming environment where the affective filter is lowered and their social and emotional needs are taken into account, so that school becomes a positive experience in every domain.

F. How are decisions made for exiting or entering a service or program?

■ Barbara Tedesco

Many states have guidelines on these critical decisions. Most require a home language survey to be completed on registration. This survey should indicate the **primary language** spoken in the home as well as the language(s) used by the child. Children in grades K–3 should then be screened to determine if a formal assessment should be completed. For students entering kindergarten, checklists and observational records completed by the preschool teacher should be utilized to support the placement decision. If young children are assessed by strangers, they often do not respond fully and are sometimes misplaced for language services. Therefore, the teacher who is familiar with the child's language performance should be consulted and his/her recommendation strongly considered. Of course, this individual should be knowledgeable about second language acquisition and not have a bias towards one program design over another. A best practice for entry should also include a native language screening. It is critical to know what a child can do in the **native language**. When determining language knowledge at a young age, teachers should assess what a child knows in both languages and consider a combination of the two languages to obtain a clearer picture (Tabors, 2008).

When transitioning students out of the program, multiple criteria should always be utilized. In addition to standardized summative assessments, other recommendations include teacher recommendation from all teachers who come in contact with the student, review of benchmark tests, checklists for milestones, and observational notes or anecdotal records. Many schools have considered implementing a transitional process to provide support while the English learner is moving into the general education class.

G. How can administrators establish effective services for small numbers of English language learners or those who speak low-incidence languages?

■ *Judie Haynes*

School districts are challenged when a family speaks a language that is low-incidence in the school district. If you have only one Albanian student in your school, for example, and he or she does not have an extended family or cluster of speakers in the community, the school acculturation process is more difficult for the family. They may have limited access to interpreters and translated materials, which will hinder their communication with the school. However, resources for low-incidence languages may be available in other communities in your state. Find out where the family goes to church or where they buy ethnic food. Network with teachers of **English language learners** (ELLs) from other school districts in your state. This may help you find other speakers of the language.

You can find native-language resources on the internet. Help the parents of your young ELL access these resources so that they can help their children in school. Wikipedia has a simple English version and translations in over 50 languages. Google supports 104 languages and has a version of their search engine for 115 countries. Use your smartphone or tablet to record information with the help of bilingual community members.

If you find community members or parents to translate documents, make sure they are written in simple English. Do not use educational jargon or your message will be lost.

Teachers need to have reasonable expectations for ELLs who are linguistically isolated. In order to acquire academic language, ELLs need information presented to them that they can understand. If you do not have a translator, an interpreter, or native-language resources from the internet, providing that information will be difficult for the school district. All school personnel should learn to provide oral messages that are comprehensible to families. Use charts, graphs, pictures, videos, and body language to communicate your message.

H. What accommodations in emergency planning and other program policy should be made for children who are English language learners?

■ *Karen N. Nemeth*

The school's emergency preparedness plan often overlooks the needs of children who are new to English. Something as simple as a fire drill can be terrifying to young children who don't know what is happening. One of the most important steps you can take is to create a video for each emergency procedure for the new students and their parents. Then be sure to practice slowly and patiently. Make sure you have an effective way to reach each parent, even if they speak no English, in case of emergency. Create very simple and clear policies with a minimum of words to make the procedures easier to understand. Some programs assign more experienced children to act as buddies to **newcomers** during emergency procedures.

Visuals are very important cues to help young children—no matter their language—to follow emergency procedures. The languages of the child and family should be listed with the contact information so they can be provided if there is an accident or health emergency. It is also important to encourage teachers to have conversations with families about the emergency procedures and to ask about their past experiences with the types of disasters included in your plan. It might be important to know that a child from a refugee camp may have experiences with fire or explosions that make him more fearful than other children. Also, always take the time in advance to use multiple means of communication with families and children about emergency procedures. It may be difficult to remain calm or patient with **English learners** during a crisis, but they need that consideration even more than children who understand your words.

I. What are early language development standards for dual language learners and why are they important?

■ *Margo Gottlieb*

Early language development standards are descriptive pathways of linguistic milestones for **dual language learners** (DLLs) at particular age ranges, generally specified from the onset of measurable comprehensible language at 2.5 years to 5.5 years of age, when DLLs enter kindergarten. In essence, early language development standards are a set of expectations whose criteria can help constituents, including family members, teachers, and educational leaders, understand what DLLs can do with language. DLLs' receptive input and expressive output can be interpreted with these criteria in their **home language** and in English to ascertain their overall language proficiency and to monitor growth over time.

There is tremendous variability in DLLs' language development captured in language standards. One consideration is whether the children are simultaneously learning two languages at home or whether they are learning languages sequentially, being introduced to English in a school setting. Another variable is the age of these young children and its impact on their linguistic, cognitive, physical, and socioemotional development. The following figure depicts the range of language development across levels of language proficiency (from 1, the lowest, to 5) in relation to age. Specifically, it illustrates the developmental span of language between Lisa at language proficiency level 3 and Luis, approximately one year older, at level 5.

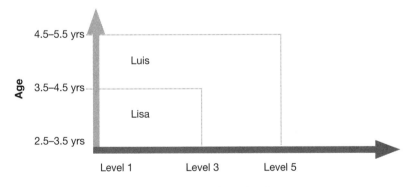

The range of language development for DLLs by age and language proficiency. (Adapted from Gottlieb, M., & Ernst-Slavit, G. [2013]. Academic language: A foundation to academic success in mathematics. In M. Gottlieb & G. Ernst-Slavit [Eds.], *Academic language in diverse classrooms: Promoting content and language learning* [pp. 1–38]. Thousand Oaks, CA: Corwin.)

The standards movement of the last two decades has been felt in the early childhood world and subsequently, many states have designed early learning standards. For the last decade, World-Class Instructional Design and Assessment (WIDA) Consortiuum has been crafting language development standards that now extend to DLLs. These draft early language development standards, in English and Spanish, are shared in the following table.

WIDA's Early Language Development Standards for Dual Language Learners, Ages 2.5 to 5.5 Years		
	Standard	**Abbreviation**
ELD Standard 1	DLLs *communicate* information, ideas, and concepts necessary for success in the area of *social–emotional development*	The *language* of social–emotional development
ELD Standard 2	DLLs *communicate* information, ideas, and concepts necessary for academic success in the content area of *early language and literacy*	The *language* of early language development and literacy
ELD Standard 3	DLLs *communicate* information, ideas, and concepts necessary for academic success in the content area of *mathematics*	The *language* of mathematics
ELD Standard 4	DLLs *communicate* information, ideas, and concepts necessary for academic success in the content area of *science*	The *language* of science
ELD Standard 5	DLLs *communicate* information, ideas, and concepts necessary for academic success in the content area of *social studies*	The *language* of social studies
ELD Standard 6	DLLs *communicate* information, ideas, and concepts necessary for academic success in the content area of *physical development*	The *language* of physical development

2013 draft, available from www.wida.us/standards/eeld.aspx

Early language development standards contribute to a developmentally sound framework for supporting instruction and assessment of DLLs. By offering the continuity of WIDA's K–12 language development standards while corresponding to states' early learning standards and the Common Core State Standards, these early language standards provide the backbone and direction for helping to educate this country's ever-increasing numbers of DLLs.

J. What are the connections between states' early learning standards and early language standards?

■ *Ruth Reinl and Erin Arango-Escalante*

States' early learning standards (ELS) outline developmentally appropriate expectations and skills that *all* children should possess on entry to kindergarten—including children who are **dual language learners** (DLLs). As such, states' ELS act as a fundamental guide for curriculum planning, assessment, and instruction of all children during the preschool years. However, a strong potential for inaccuracy still exists when using standards-based curricula for assessing, supporting, and instructing young DLLs. This is partly because of the "disconnect" between DLLs' linguistic variations and the performance benchmarks or indicators of many states' ELS, which may have been developed with monolingual learners in mind (Espinosa, 2012; Scott-Little, Lesko, Martella, & Milburn, 2007). It is difficult to accurately assess DLLs' progress using many states' ELS without a means for ascertaining how their level of **English language development** affects and relates to their performance in the different content areas. It is equally difficult to support and instruct DLLs if practitioners lack guidance about the social and academic language these children are able to process and produce at differing levels of English language development within the content areas. Using *language standards in conjunction with ELS* can help fill this linguistic gap when supporting, instructing, and assessing young DLLs.

Early Learning Standards

States have incorporated into their ELS, to varying degrees, the five major dimensions of children's development identified by the National Educational Goals Panel (NEGP): approaches to learning, physical well-being and motor development, social and emotional development, language and communication development, and cognition and general knowledge (BUILD, 2012; Scott-Little, Kagan, & Stebbins Frelow, 2005). These recommended dimensions for development and learning are depicted in the following figure.

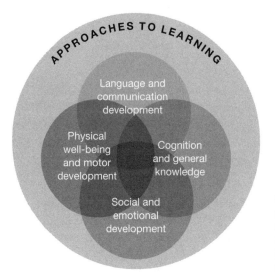

Visual representation of the National Education Goals Panel's five dimensions of children's development that are linked to their school readiness and later success. (Courtesy of World-Class Instructional Design and Assessment Consortium.)

Early Language Standards

Early language standards identify and describe the social and academic language that DLLs need to process and produce in order to succeed in meeting states' ELS. Simply put, language standards always refer to "the language of" early learning standards (e.g., "the language of social–emotional development"). Because language standards and ELS directly correspond, they can be used in tandem to help identify and support the language needs of DLLs within all areas of development and learning during instruction and assessment. In short, using language standards in conjunction with ELS helps practitioners concretely connect the linguistic variations and needs of young DLLs across *all* content areas of standards-based curricula and assessments.

The World-Class Instructional Design and Assessment (WIDA) Consortium has created six early **English language development** (EELD) **standards** for DLLs that correspond to NEGP's major dimensions of development and learning. These EELD standards include "the language of" social–emotional development, early language and literacy, cognitive development (mathematics, science, social studies), and physical development, as depicted in the following figure.

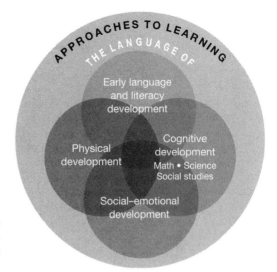

Visual representation of the early English language development standards. (Courtesy of World-Class Instructional Design and Assessment Consortium.)

Just as ELS encompass varying levels of specificity to describe the skills and knowledge children need to meet important benchmarks within each standard, so too the EELD standards framework includes various components to describe the social and academic language DLLs may encounter within each standard. Using the EELD standards framework components, practitioners can determine the level of linguistic complexity and language usage for DLLs in their program. The following table depicts the correspondence between the different specificity levels in State A's ELS and some of the EELD standards framework components.

Correspondence between Specificity Levels in ELS and EELD

	Standard	Domain	Guideline	Example	ELS and EELD Standard Together
State A ELS	Mathematics	Shapes and spatial sense	10. Investigate and identify materials of various shapes, using appropriate language	Sort parquetry blocks by one or more attributes Place unit blocks on top of their silhouettes Feel and describe parquetry blocks; then try to identify them without looking	Provide specific examples of expressive and receptive language in content area at three levels of English language development to help support, instruct, and assess dual language learners in meeting learning guidelines Level 5: *Bridging—With a partner, sort geometric shapes by their properties according to oral directions with a visual model* (e.g., "Put the square blocks together." "Put the round blocks together." "Put the blocks with three sides together.") Level 3: *Developing—Find geometric shapes by their properties, based on simple questions/statements with verbal and visual models* (e.g., "Where is the round block." "Find the triangle block?") Level 1: *Entering—Respond to yes/no questions about geometric shapes with verbal and visual models* (e.g., "Is this a square?" "Do you want a circle?")
	Standard	**MPI Topic/ Content Stream**	**MPI Cognitive Function**	**MPI Example Context for Language Learning**	
WIDA EELD Standards	The language of mathematics	Geometric shapes	Children at all levels of English language development *understand* the properties of geometric shapes	Children create structures and figures by using blocks and/or manipulating various shapes	

EELD, early English language development; ELS, early learning standard; MPI, model performance indicator.

As shown in the preceding table, DLLs at different language levels (levels 1, 3, and 5) are able to process language and demonstrate understanding in the standard of mathematics at varying levels of complexity and with different language supports. For example, within the state learning guideline, *investigate and identify materials of various shapes, using appropriate language,* DLLs at level 3 (developing) are able to process simple questions/statements related to properties of geometric shapes and then demonstrate understanding by finding the corresponding shape. DLLs at levels 1 and 5 are able to process and demonstrate understanding of less or more complex language respectively.

Although DLLs display varying levels of English language development, they are still able to access the language of ELS and demonstrate concept knowledge and understanding given the appropriate language supports afforded in the EELD standards. More information on WIDA's EELD Standards Framework can be found at www.wida.us/standards/eeld.aspx.

Resources and Questions

PLANNING GUIDE

To support effective planning, create your own DLL planning grid with the following features:

- What languages do the children in your program use?
- What languages do their families use?
- What is the way the families want to be reached?
- What are the languages spoken by staff?
- What languages can be supported by your volunteers?
- If some of the home languages will be supported by bilingual paraprofessionals and volunteers, what will their roles be?
- What languages are available via qualified interpreters?
- Create a crosswalk listing the key program guidelines your program needs to address for general education, bilingual education, preschool/child care, Head Start, and special education.
- What budget and space considerations must be considered in your planning process?
- Which staff members can contribute effectively to your planning process, and how can you get them involved?

QUESTIONS FOR REFLECTION

- What is your ideal plan to serve the population of ELLs that comes to your program?
- What are the mismatches between your current plan and your ideal plan?
- What changes do you need to make in your program to update policies and procedures and to meet the various requirements that influence early childhood education programs?

CHAPTER 3

How Young Children Learn in Two or More Languages

Key Considerations for Language Plan

- Our language plan will include professional development goals to ensure that staff is familiar with processes of first and second language or bilingual development.

- Our language plan will state our position on the role of home language learning in supporting English development.

- Our language plan will state our position on the importance of oral language development to reading and writing in both the home language and English.

This chapter focuses on early language and cognitive development to provide the critical foundation of knowledge necessary for planning and implementing an early childhood education program that is developmentally appropriate and effective. Our expert contributors make it clear that there are important differences between preK children and K–3 students; yet there are similarities that must also be considered.

In the early childhood years children are still in the process of developing language. They may be learning two languages simultaneously, or they may start with one **home language** and begin a new language at school. When they enter school, they are at the beginning of their literacy learning career as well. Recent research has helped to clarify the role of first- and second-language development in the learning and literacy progression of young **English language learrners** (ELLs)/**dual language learners** (DLLs). Contributors to this chapter explain what is currently known about how language development takes place and how differences in language development affect decisions about how to teach children to read and write.

Our experts shed light on one of the most important factors that sets early childhood education apart from the older grades: the critical importance of supporting the home language for young learners to succeed in learning both their home language and English. Answers about the importance of family culture and home literacy practices help administrators gain deeper insight into the home–school connection that enable them to assess their students more effectively and plan accordingly. Contributors also summarize recent research that shows key behavioral and cognitive advantages to being bilingual. When administrators build their depth of knowledge and understanding about the characteristics and development of young ELLs/DLLs, they are better prepared to lead their staff with effective planning and implementation of programs and strategies for teaching them. The language development chart at the end of this chapter helps readers engage staff and peers in discussion and professional development on these basic foundations of knowledge needed to plan and implement effective early education for DLLs.

A. How do young learners develop first and second languages?

■ *Patton Tabors*

We may think of language learning as confined mostly to the earliest years of a young child's life. However, the language learning process, which begins at birth—or perhaps even before, given the sounds a child can hear in utero—is a lifelong process. It varies in intensity, depending on circumstances such as exposure and use. Learning a new language can be undertaken at any age, and new language elements—such as vocabulary—are added throughout a lifetime.

However, the first five years of a child's life are a very intense time of language learning. Language learning begins at home in interaction with family members. Many children are born into households where only one language is spoken. Unless they undertake learning another language as a foreign language or move to a place where another language is used, they may remain monolingual throughout their lives. Other children, however, are exposed to two (or more) languages from birth, or may learn one language as their family language and then be exposed to a societal and/or school language when they are older. If these children continue to use both languages they will be bilingual.

During those first five years, children learn the basics of their family language or, if they are being raised bilingually, of their two languages. These basics include phonology—the sounds of the language(s); vocabulary—the words of the language(s); grammar—how words are put together to make sentences in the language(s); discourse—how sentences are put together to tell stories or make an argument, for example; and pragmatics—the social rules about how to use the language(s).

So, how does this work? Let's use learning English as an example, but remember that this process is similar for other languages as well.

The sounds that the baby hears are the important starting point. These are the sounds that the baby needs to reproduce in order to start communicating in the family language. At first, babies use their voices to babble a wide variety of sounds, but over time they begin to restrict their sound production to the sounds of the language they hear. Common early sounds start with a consonant followed by a vowel, like *ma, ba,* or *da.* Often they are strung together: *mama, baba, dada.* Between 12 and 18 months most babies produce their first words (*doggie*), followed by two-word utterances (*my doggie*), and finally whole sentences (*my doggie is black*). Although this process may seem almost effortless, it is a major cognitive challenge for infants and toddlers. The process is extensively influenced by the input that children receive from those close to them. The more words they hear, the more sense they will make of the language they are trying to learn.

Children who are learning two languages at the same time may take a little longer sorting out two phonological systems, two sets of vocabulary, and two different grammar systems. It has been shown, however, that the process of acquiring two languages from an early age, rather than causing confusion, can in fact have both cognitive and social advantages.

Throughout this process, young children understand the language(s) being used around them before they are able to use the language(s). This means that *receptive ability* precedes *productive ability.* This is true for first, second, or subsequent languages.

The process of second language acquisition is different for young language learners. Young children who have already gained some competence in a first language are able to bring their language-learning skills to the new language. They do not need to relearn what language is all about; they just have to learn what this *new* language is all about. They start with careful listening to hear the sounds of the new language and careful watching to begin to understand how the words and phrases in the new language are used. During this non-verbal period, they may even practice the new sounds and words under their breath before saying anything out loud.

The older the child is, the more cognitive experience can be brought to the task of learning a new language. This ability means that children who are 3, 4, or 5 years old when they start to learn a new language can memorize chunks of language ("I'm a good idea") and then deconstruct those chunks to build their understanding of individual words and grammar. It is important to understand that these memorized chunks do not often represent actual understanding of vocabulary and grammar, but merely an understanding of how a phrase is used in a social context. Eventually, they will construct original sentences from this material, arriving at the productive stage of second language acquisition.

Learning a second language is a riskier business than learning a first language because social context and individual characteristics can play a much larger role in the process. Three underlying factors—motivation, exposure, and personality—have been identified as having an impact on how well and how quickly second language learners progress.

Motivation plays a role in second language acquisition because children have a choice of whether and when to embark on the task of learning a new language. Some young children may choose to remain in the nonverbal period in a new language as long as their needs are being met and/or they can find playmates who speak their first language. Others may learn a few high-utility words or phrases but not undertake the full second language learning process. Only when children are sufficiently motivated by social or contextual circumstances do they truly make the necessary effort to learn a new language. Parental attitudes, family plans, availability of preferred playmates, and classroom structure may all play a part in establishing motivation.

Exposure, of course, refers to the amount of time, and the surrounding circumstances, in which young second language learners are introduced to their new language. Occasional exposure to another language may result in some receptive learning, but in order for consistent progress to be made children need to be placed in circumstances that are frequent enough and motivating enough to encourage them to move beyond receptive understanding to productive use of their new language. The more time these children spend in an environment where they can learn their new language, the more progress they are likely to make. Of course, this has implications for the development of their first language as well. Keeping sufficient input available in the children's first language while second language learning is also proceeding is of real concern and should be balanced with exposure to the new language.

And, finally, personality. Second language learning is highly dependent on the social relationships that children develop with those who speak the new language. Consequently, children who are more outgoing may be in a position to hear more input in the second language, thereby learning the language more quickly at first. More reserved children may take longer to mobilize their strategies for being included in communicative situations where the new language is being used. Adults in this situation can be key in providing social opportunities for these children. Assessments of second language achievement need to take into account the differences between children with more or less outgoing personalities.

How long will it take a young child to learn a second language? It is important to note that this process is a complicated social and cognitive undertaking. Gaining age-appropriate competence in a second language, even for children as young as 3–5 years, is a highly challenging game of catch-up. As the process evolves, monolingual children continue to make advances in their language abilities, and bilingual children need to continue to use not one but two developing languages at the same time. Adults who are involved in supporting this process need to be aware of these complications and provide the greatest amount of help possible.

B. How long does it take a young child to become fluent in a second language learned sequentially?

■ Elizabeth D. Peña

A challenge in evaluating children's English language skills is in knowing what to expect after a given amount of time. Children who learn a second language sequentially often use their first language as a starting point for second language acquisition. In the United States, children who begin learning English in the early school years are often still in the process of learning their first language as well. A number of factors contribute to how quickly children learn a second language. These factors include similarity or dissimilarity to the first language, how long the child has been exposed to the second language, and amount of current exposure to the first language.

Some languages are similar in vocabulary and structure, which may facilitate learning in the second language. For example, Spanish and English share a number of **cognates**— words that are similar in meaning and phonology (e.g., elephant and *elefante*). These similarities may help children to develop comprehension skills relatively quickly. Grammatically, English and Spanish also share ways in which plurals are marked with an -s or an -es. In contrast, Mandarin and English share few cognates and mark plurals in different ways.

Children who have been exposed to their second language for a longer time often demonstrate better mastery of that language compared to children who are more recently exposed to it. Children who have more daily exposure to the second language also seem to demonstrate higher levels of mastery. However, the particular language domain interacts with linguistic experience in different ways.

In **sequential language learning** it seems that children acquire receptive vocabulary knowledge more quickly than expressive vocabulary knowledge (Gibson, Peña, & Bedore, 2014; Kohnert & Bates, 2002; Kohnert, Bates, & Hernández, 1999). Thus, some children in the early stages of second language learning demonstrate gaps between their receptive and expressive knowledge. In the lexical–semantics domain focusing on depth of vocabulary knowledge, children seem to use their first language knowledge to gain knowledge in the second language to quickly understand relationships among words. Within a relatively short amount of time (1–2 years), children using Spanish at home demonstrate receptive vocabulary knowledge in English that is comparable to bilingual children exposed to English and Spanish at home (Hammer, Lawrence, & Miccio, 2008). In the grammatical domain, children seem to need much more experience with the second language in order to perform similarly to English-dominant children (Bedore et al., 2012; Bohman, Bedore, Peña, Mendez-Perez, & Gillam, 2010). For children to gain deeper knowledge of the nuances of English grammar, they need to both hear it and practice the different constructions. As they learn the second language, children may overextend the rules of English on irregular verbs, for example, which demonstrates productive knowledge of English (Jacobson & Schwartz, 2005). Thus, it is not unusual for children to persist in making some grammatical errors in English, even after they have mastered semantic skills comparable to monolingual peers.

RECOMMENDED RESOURCE

www.2languages2worlds.wordpress.com

C. What factors influence the development of first and second languages in early childhood?

■ *Anita Pandey*

Three factors are essential for successful language acquisition and/or learning in the **native language** (L1) and second or subsequent language acquisition:

1. **Comprehensible input** (CI)
2. Interaction
3. Scaffolding (feedback-based)

CI is essentially *understandable* language. It is the basis for *interaction*, dialogue, or *meaning negotiation,* which in turn enables *scaffolding* (see Pandey, 2012a). Scaffolding (i.e., language support) can take different forms, including the following:

- Provision of an example or template (e.g., "Ask for a turn by raising your hand." "Remember to say *'excuse me,'* please!")
- Direct or indirect feedback (e.g., "Say /y/, not /j/." "What do you say?")
- Positive skills reinforcement (e.g., *Bravo!*).

The more opportunities we provide children to engage with others using CI and to receive feedback, the more we enable language learning, a cyclical process diagrammed in the following figure.

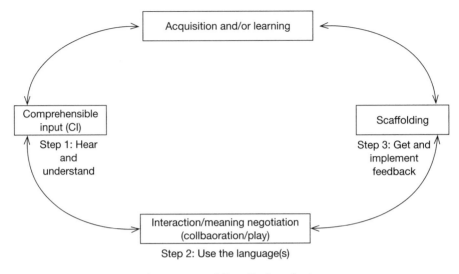

Language acquisition: Key ingredients

These language-facilitating factors work in tandem; they are not so much linear phases as interconnected steps. Exactly how much of each step a learner needs is unclear, however, because each individual is unique. Nevertheless, evidence suggests that the more of the input a child encounters, the more comprehensible it is. Also, the greater her opportunities to use the language (i.e., collaborate), the faster and more likely she is to master it.

Evidence suggests that CI alone is insufficient for language acquisition. If it were, children would master language relatively easily by simply listening to others or the radio and watching television. As the old adage holds, "Use it or lose it!" In short, to learn a language, one must use it in whole or in part (e.g., through code-mixing). Collaboration is another key component. Note that dialogue is also a vital reasoning and organizational tool, hence the high value accorded it (i.e., performance) in the Common Core State Standards (CCSS). When you use a language, however rudimentary or incorrect your usage, you are more inclined to infer its component parts and patterns. Even infants and young children interact with their caregivers and others, although their level of interactivity depends on a number of factors, including the *age* of the interacting party and differences in childrearing/socialization practices. For instance, some babies and toddlers are coaxed to respond (non)verbally through repetitive questions and imperatives, while others are encouraged to listen to music, stories, exchanges, and more, and to participate nonverbally (e.g., periodically signal their understanding via directives like "*Baila Papi! Baila!*" [Spanish for "Dance, Papi! Dance!"]). The language adults employ with infants and children generally ranges from directives to egalitarian interactions, and the nature of the participation expected of children is culturally variable.

Monitoring children's language use in different settings gives you a fuller picture of a child's language competence—including their vocabulary in different content areas—so that you understand how best to maximize each child's language acquisition/learning, varying the tasks, context, and perhaps even their conversation partner(s) as necessary. Carefully monitor all sources of CI, dialogue, and feedback children receive, using a checklist, audio and video clips, and/or diary entries. Monitor how children "perform" with different partners. You might find that they are more vocal with some than others. A checklist is a handy tool to keep track of and evaluate progress in language and associated content in the classroom, in the cafeteria, on the playground, and elsewhere. An example that you could use and/or modify appears in Pandey (2012b, p. 32).

Finally, children, like adults, learn best when they receive continued and timely feedback. This input helps them make necessary modifications (not always instantly) and advance their language skills relatively quickly. Direct feedback works better for some children, indirect for others. For example, when my 7-year-old observed, "They're a little more clearer," I provided her with indirect feedback. "Yes, they are clearER!" I responded, stressing the final syllable and suffix. She promptly self-corrected. However, she has continued to vacillate between *more/-er* and *-er* forms, suggesting that she understands and has learned the comparative *–er* form, but not when to delete "more."

To modify her language use, a child must be cognizant of (1) what constitutes problematic language, and (2) how to phrase it in clear, grammatical, and/or acceptable terms. Many younger children and **dual language learners** (DLLs) are able to identify incorrect and/or unacceptable language; however, they are unable to rephrase such language because doing so is more cognitively and linguistically demanding. When my 7-year-old observed, for instance, that her friend was "allergic to trees," I explained that "allergies" was a broader term and that "allergic" was restricted to consumables. She looked confused, but when I asked her which two statements (out of three) made "the most sense," she promptly identified the correct ones.

Exactly how much feedback children need is unclear. It's a good idea to provide as much as possible. It also helps to monitor the presence of these and other language-facilitative factors in each child's interactions—both inside and outside the classroom—by way of a checklist or other handy tool (see Pandey, 2012a and b).

The relatively *unconscious* nature of L1 acquisition, as opposed to the *conscious process* that characterizes much of classroom-based language learning, has prompted researchers such as Krashen (1982) to distinguish between *language acquisition* and *learning*. Krashen also contends that interactions with individuals (and, one could add, with interactive e-applications) who are more fluent in the language are generally more instructive, as you are more likely to learn something new through such exchanges. He terms this language-facilitative trigger $i + 1$ (i stands for *interaction* and the $+1$ refers to the slightly higher competence of one's partner, which serves as the catalyst). We would do well to keep this guiding principle in mind when we pair and team up students because groups are only as effective as their membership.

Peers and young adults are valuable second language and literacy aides (Pandey, 2010), so the more opportunities we provide children to interact with their peers and others (through group work and play, for instance), the better. In summary, all children must *hear* and/or see language (e.g., sounds or other units from one or more languages) to make sense of it. They also need to *use* it.

To reiterate, best practices that facilitate language mastery include the following:

- Provision of CI
- Teamwork or collaboration
- Use of engaging and relevant instructional resources
- Scaffolding
- Continuous monitoring of your own and children's language—for instructional planning and assessment purposes

With regard to the final bullet point, plan to periodically monitor your and your teachers' language and instructional practices (see Pandey, 2012a, for guidelines). Reflection questions for teachers and administrators include the following:

1. Does each child receive enough CI inside and outside the classroom?
   - How do I/we monitor CI?
2. Do I/we provide ample opportunities for interaction inside and outside the classroom?
   - When and where?
   - For how long, and what has been the outcome?
   - How do I/we determine this?
3. Have I and/or others at school and in the child's home or community observed her negotiate meaning and/or receive and respond to feedback?
   - What form(s) did these processes take?
   - What was the outcome?

Don't be afraid to employ multimedia. Technology is a valuable partner in providing CI, fostering interaction, and, in many cases, providing instant feedback. Remember that lights, camera, and action do attract. Even newborns respond to lights, music, and differences in accent, voice, tone, and pitch. Age-appropriate multimodal technology (Pandey, 2012a) introduces excitement. Indeed, children can interact with computers and encounter CI online and on their own. Tap these and other avenues of *autonomous language learning* and/or computer-mediated instruction (Pandey, 2012a) to supplement classroom-based instruction.

D. What is the role of home language learning and maintenance in supporting successful outcomes in English language learning and literacy?

■ *Anita Pandey*

One's **home language** (HL) is typically one's **primary language** (Pandey, 2010). Some HLs are, in fact, dialects, and many are underestimated and unfairly stigmatized (Pandey, 2000, 2013b). It embodies valuable cultural capital and is an integral part of a child's identity; it mirrors who she is, where she came from, and where she is headed. It represents the comfort zone essential for learning, especially in the early years when children latch on to the familiar. Children, like adults, learn best when they are relaxed. Stress interferes with learning and prompts misdiagnoses. Notice how many **dual language learners** (DLLs) use language frequently associated with learning disabilities, when in fact their high(er) anxiety might account for their language (mis)use.

Children need the familiar as a bridge to the unknown. Continued use of the HL and/or another language enables children to connect with more people. The HL is the primary means through which children make sense of their world and connect with others—acquiring vital content through new words and other language units relatively easily, while engaging in meaning-making and mastering culture-specific politeness norms such as turn-taking (Pandey, 2012a). Indeed, it literally expands their circle and enables them to comfortably navigate both their primary culture and the (secondary) school one. It also stimulates more neurons and neuronal connections, yielding expanded cognitive skills—what some researchers term higher-order thinking or **executive functioning**. This translates to enhanced memory and problem-solving skills, superior intercultural and interpersonal skills, and reduced dementia and incidence of Alzheimer's disease (Pandey, 2013a).

Research shows that continued use of the HL actually facilitates acquisition of subsequent languages, including English (Pandey, 2012a). When we think about this, it makes sense that we learn more about our primary language (and culture) in the course of learning another because we inadvertently compare the other language to ours. A child feels lost—uprooted—when her HL is discontinued. The best analogy I can think of is a plant. Put a stem in water and you are likely to find that 10% might take root, but the vast majority will wilt and dry. In his essay "El Arbol," Dr. Eugene Garcia cites a powerful Spanish *dicho* (proverb) that his father shared with him in his childhood. This proverb, "*El árbol fuerté tiene raices maduras*" (A strong tree has mature roots), sums up the value of the HL in every child's life. As Garcia observes, for many so-called **limited English proficient** students in the United States, "Their roots have been either ignored or stripped away in the name of growing strong . . . . [M]any have suffered that fate of the rootless tree—they have fallen socially, economically, academically, and culturally" (quoted in Pandey, 2012a, p. 136).

Overlooking the value of the HL in our children's academic and personal growth and success—by excluding it from the curriculum and/or overtly or covertly discouraging the use of languages other than English at school—causes a number of additional problems. Among these problems are misdiagnosis, as was noted earlier, and undue pressure on the part of children who speak other languages to perform in English-dominant or English-only schools.

Failure to mention other languages is a form of linguistic exclusion. Such emphasis on English constitutes ideological manipulation. As I note in *Language Building Blocks*, "What we do not say speaks volumes" (Pandey, 2012a, p. 93). The needs of second dialect speakers and DLLs are frequently misdiagnosed at English-only and English-dominant schools. Many are assumed to have special needs when, in fact, all they need is continued access to their HL. Readiness for U.S. school culture is often conflated with capability, when, as we know, school readiness is a culturally variable behavioral practice (i.e., with a different set of expectations associated with schools, teachers, parents, and even with children in different settings). Unfortunately, some children "begin to conform" or display traits commonly associated with specific "special needs" (Pandey, 2013b).

Use of just English with DLLs often contributes to low self-esteem or identity crises, leading to a high dropout rate—all of which bode badly for a nation with a predominantly aging population that is dependent on its youth. We must, therefore, make every effort to stop failing our children—and use of the HL and a language-building-blocks approach that embraces other languages and associated cultures, including the HL, is exactly what we need

(Pandey, 2012a). Such an approach is particularly beneficial for culturally inclusive vocabulary instruction, which is key to reading and content mastery.

As most of us know, language diversity is a child's passport to participation in the global economy. Even a working knowledge of another language allows us to appreciate and convey unique and culturally significant meanings. It also helps us to understand why many DLLs *seemingly know fewer words* than their English-speaking counterparts when they might simply be drawing on a more compact HL vocabulary to convey both concepts that are familiar or shared and culturally unique. Their HL enables children to hear, see, feel, and taste concepts for which another language might lack words or equivalent meanings. Indeed, everything valued in a culture is encoded in its language.

Vocabulary is an arbitrary language unit that is culturally variable in form. Most languages have words and/or expressions that lack exact English equivalents. English and its dialects in use around the world also differ. For example, in Indian English, "foreign" means "promptly" or "right away," and "no" means "yes" when used in a tag question (e.g., "It's good chai, no?").

Some words have added meanings in other languages (i.e., they are not exactly equivalent). In Spanish, for instance, in addition to book-based learning, the term *educación* refers to manners or positive demeanor. One could be schooled, yet have *poco* or no *educación* in this primarily oral culture that prizes respect and positive language use. Thus, by focusing on the HL, we gain valuable insights into key cultural (i.e., literacy) practices that account for students' success (or lack thereof) with literacies emphasized at school. Specific sounds, too, are meaningful in different languages/cultures (Pandey, 2012a). Examples include the long *a* (/aa/), the informal term for "come (over)" in Hindi, Punjabi, Gujarathi, Marathi, Bengali, Urdu, and related languages.

Because English lacks words for key concepts in many other languages (Pandey, 2013c), inviting your staff and students to co-inventory cultures by listing language and dialect-specific sounds, words, and (non)verbal expressions could greatly enhance global understanding at your "scul" (i.e., *school* in Bosnian, Croatian, and Serbian) and community. We look to DLLs to help us better understand their languages, cultural nuances, and literacy practices. A greater understanding of literary practices can come through homework assignments, such as inquiring about the everyday translation engagements that require use of their HLs. This includes talking with students about the other language varieties (including dialects) they understand, speak, read, and/or write. Indeed, to fully understand and meet the needs of DLLs, we must first and foremost be investigators and collaborators.

For children who speak heavily Latinate languages such as Spanish, the HL is their most vital vocabulary and content tool available, because the bulk of grades 3–12 math and science vocabulary is Latin-based (Pandey, 2012a, 2012c). As my 5-year-old rightly observed, "Mama, carné makes more sense than *meat*. Carnivores eat *carne!*" Indeed, all children stand to benefit from exposure to other languages.

HL use, through its artful integration in vocabulary and reading exercises, and even in math and science lessons (see Pandey, 2012a–c), also enables all children to expand their thinking and engage in cultural ways of conceptualizing (i.e., bi/multicultural thinking), which is essential in this day and age. So continued use of the HL is the best medicine for ensuring the overall health of all children—not just DLLs. It is a sure way to attain the CCSS career-readiness objective.

Use of HLs also adds excitement to the classroom, facilitates recall, and builds community, as children learn to be creative—to experiment—and language becomes the clay that they craft to convey and create unique content. In the process, many develop a creative or "salsaed" language that differentiates them.

The following are two challenges to HL instruction that you should seek to address:

1. The cultural dissonance between children and staff—for instance, the predominantly minority and relatively young student population taught by majority-monolingual and older (over 35) white females. This mismatch in race, age, language, pedagogy, and gender is further exacerbated by differences in social class and culture.
2. Concerns about the cost, curricular fit, and availability of quality HL (both knowledgeable bilingual instructors and instructional resources) and opportunities for English advancement.

Strategies for HL use that I recommend include these two:

1. Public recognition of children's HLs and/or bilinguality (e.g., through medals, certificates, and/or on report cards and progress reports), so DLLs feel validated and all children develop an interest in and a love for languages
2. Integration of other languages in the classroom and through out-of-class projects that simultaneously bridge the *school and the home* (see Pandey, 2013c)

In summary, the HL is the foundation for successful mastery of the second language. It must, therefore, be carefully and strategically advanced, alongside English, given the bidirectional impact of primary and secondary acquisition.

E. What is the role of oral language in first and second language acquisition in the early years?

■ *Anita Pandey*

Don't underestimate the power of words (i.e., speech). Oral language development (i.e., fluency) is the first step toward successful primary (L1) and secondary (L2) acquisition— and *literacy*. If you are wondering how speech and writing are connected, and how the former drives the latter, remember that writing is merely our attempt to record speech. Several languages still in use lack a conventional orthography. Examples include indigenous languages of Mexico and Guatemala as well as pidgins, spoken languages used primarily for trade and other service encounters (Pandey, 2005). The fact that many Indian languages sprang from the rich poetic and vedic (i.e., math-, astrology-, and philosophy-infused) oral Sanskrit tradition of the *Ramayan* and the *Gita* is reflected in the frequency of rhyming words and word pairs for opposites, synonyms, and other lexical categories in Hindi and related Indian languages (see Pandey, 2012a). Because rhyme facilitates recall (i.e., learning), we can see how pidgins and other so-called "nonstandard" dialects like Black English venacular (Pandey, 2013b) are musical and especially instructive for speech. They employ reduplicatives or repetitive rhyming forms. Children who speak languages that are rarely or never written tend to use compact, musical, and easy-to-recall forms such as these, and most have an easier time decoding words and recalling information. This is because brevity, coupled with rhyme and feedback (e.g., via the call-'n'-response strategy), facilitate learning. How else do we explain how even adults rap along effortlessly and recall 3,000-verse poems like the *Ramayan* relatively effortlessly?

To bypass or cut short the natural order of development of oral language in a bid to jumpstart and/or accelerate reading and writing is inadvisable (Pandey, 2012a). It could, in fact, cause developmental "delays" and/or a number of language and learning issues in both the L1 and the L2.

We must emphasize oral language in the early years, especially in preschool, because speech and dialogue, as we saw in section C of this chapter, promote interaction—a key ingredient in vocabulary development and overall language and content acquisition. Ensure that your staff provides multiple opportunities for children to hear language and to speak—through play, debate and other oral language—facilitating activities that, in turn, grow their receptive language skills. This way, they steadily and rapidly increase their vocabulary and other oral language skills—the foundations for all learning, including writing and core content. Children need to increase their vocabulary by roughly 1000 words per school year (Pandey, 2012a). If we were to rely on classroom instruction alone this rate of language growth would be nearly impossible, which makes it all the more important for us to get children to talk as much as possible, with as many individuals as possible.

Emphasizing reading and writing too early (as in preK–1) instead of first ensuring that all children—even **dual language learners** (DLLs)—have a firm grasp of basic, high-frequency terms (including idioms, the hallmark of spoken American English, which tend to confuse DLLs), puts the cart before the horse. In short, we set DLLs—and ourselves—up for failure. We must first work on providing interactive contexts for children to add to their oral language skills, particularly their vocabulary. We must also give them ample time to master the basics of interpersonal communication, such as rules of politeness that vary from situation to situation. For some children who take longer to warm up to outsiders, this could take up to six years. Through play and other avenues for language extension, children (like adults) advance their language skills (i.e., increase their vocabulary more each school year) and their critical-thinking and problem-solving capabilities much faster. They are constantly engaged in linguistic computations, ranging from code-mixing to translation. Such engagements are essentially exercises in equivalency. We can hypothesize that these children have an easier time connecting speech to writing. In short, they look for familiar words in print and are able to read and comprehend faster and more easily. After all, you can only read what you understand and can decode.

Children who start school after age 6 or 7, as in Finland, India, and much of Africa, have an *oral advantage*. This might very well explain why children in predominantly oral cultures outperform those from economically privileged U.S. families in math, music (through their ability to instinctively rap or creatively string together rhyming words), verbal repartee (witty comebacks), and even oral presentations. Remember that strong oral language skills are also a predictor of self-confidence and other forms of academic success. For this reason, encourage your staff to stimulate dialogue inside and outside the classroom. By providing environments rich in oral language, we foster in our most vulnerable young minds the ability to reason, organize, and apply key concepts and theories, as well as the skills of reading and writing.

A home that is seemingly low in conventional literacy resources (e.g., books, technology gadgets, and 24-hour high-speed internet access) might not be as impoverished in the oral language domain. By the same token, a child who has one or more siblings and who resides in an extended family home—with many individuals to interact with on a daily basis—is arguably more *linguistically privileged* than a single child in a suburban nuclear family setting.

In summary, listening and speaking are acquired first, and reading is contingent on fluency. Most children's phonological development is more or less assured and will be unobstructed by a *critical* or *sensitive period*; the same is true of their semantic, grammatical, and discourse skills (Pandey, 2012a). Early instruction should prioritize phonemic awareness and vocabulary development. Indeed, knowledge of the process and mechanics of L1 and L2 acquisition could help us teach letter recognition, basic literacy, and content more effectively in the early years. By expanding children's opportunities for oral language enhancement in the L1 and L2 through in-class and out-of-class collaborations, teachers also, if unintentionally, increase children's reading and writing skills and global understanding through their functional bilingualism (Pandey, 2012a).

F. What is the role of culture in language learning?

■ *Lisa M. López*

Language, by nature, is embedded in culture. Therefore, it is difficult to learn language or function within a language without an understanding of the role of culture on language. Brisk (1998), in describing the best bilingual educational programs, emphasizes the need to respect the cultures represented by the families of the children in the program. Part of respecting a child's language, an important ingredient in successful second language acquisition, is respecting their home culture. This respect for the family's culture helps establish a positive teacher–child relationship, a crucial aspect of quality programs. Research has shown that teachers who respect the language and culture of the family have students who excel academically (Tabors, 2008).

Dual language learner (DLL) children, in the process of becoming bilingual, must also become bicultural. Assimilation research has shown that as families become more assimilated into U.S. culture, they lose their **home language**. For example, families who have lived in the United States for a long period of time, as well as second- and third-generation families, are less likely to maintain their home language and instead choose to speak only English. Additionally, as children get older and understand the dynamics of speaking two languages versus one (i.e., English has more capital, and it is perceived to be easier to learn only one language), they choose to speak more English and less of the home language. In addition to losing a language, they are also losing their cultural identity. This, in turn, affects their long-term development. Sociologists have found that the high dropout rate of Latino students in high school is linked to this phenomenon (Pew Hispanic Center, 2009). Children no longer identify with their family's culture because they no longer speak the language; however, they have not fully assimilated and do not quite identify with the American culture. This cultural limbo triggered by language loss results in larger than normal dropout rates. Therefore, it is important to respect and acknowledge children's home culture and language from an early age while introducing English and the culture of the society in which the family is now living.

G. What are the best ways for an English language learner to learn to read and write, and what factors should go into that planning?

■ *Theresa Roberts*

Research has established that **English language learners** (ELLs) and English-only (EO) children learn to read using the same general learning processes. Fast and accurate word decoding and strong comprehension processes lead to skilled reading by both ELLs and EOs. Therefore, it comes as no surprise that the essential preschool foundations for conventional reading and writing include alphabetic knowledge, phonemic awareness, and oral language competence. It is increasingly recognized that preschool development of these skills is possible, as well as meaningful and engaging to young children. Getting off to a good start in learning to read in preschool is important. However, many preschool teachers have not had the opportunity for the coursework, instructional practice, and experience using data to evaluate instruction and learning that underlie effective literacy teaching for preschool ELLs. A very important factor to consider is how preschool teachers can be supported in developing the group instructional skills to effectively and efficiently teach these foundations and to evaluate the extent of each child's learning of what has been taught. Expectations that they do so are an important part of this support.

Emerging evidence documents that what may appear to be small variations in instructional detail can substantively influence what and how much preschool children learn about these important literacy foundations. Key features of high-quality instruction for each of the three foundations include the following:

- Identifying clear goals for lessons
- Sharing this goal with children
- Providing sufficient practice with what is being taught
- Providing extensive opportunity and expectation for children to y participate orally
- Relating what is being taught to meaningful and authentic literacy experiences
- Extending what is taught into other areas of classroom activity where children have opportunities for self-regulated application of their new knowledge and competencies

Opportunities for becoming literate should be planned throughout the program. Examples of these opportunities include writing names and stories; labeling; telling and retelling stories; and participating in dramatic play to encourage use of new vocabulary, pretending, and complex thinking.

The suggestion that oral participation is important for ELL's literacy learning warrants comment. Many early childhood educators have been taught that a period of silence, or nonverbalness, is a typical feature of second language acquisition and that children learn language during this silence. Yet oral production aids many areas of language-related learning, of which literacy is clearly an example. Recent re-examination of the evidence that silence is typical and beneficial to language learning has raised doubts about these claims (Roberts, in press). For these reasons, literacy instruction that calls for and motivates the linguistic participation of ELLs is what I recommend.

Another aspect of high-quality literacy instruction that is valued by preschool teachers and happily is associated with better literacy learning is positive socioemotional conditions for learning. Targeted, well-organized, efficient, and skill-focused instruction accompanied by positive emotional relationships between teacher and children, where teachers consistently respond to individual children, work together to create strong emerging readers. PreK literacy foundations align perfectly with the essential literacy skills needed by K–3 children but should be taught in a way that is sensitive to the cognitive, attentional, and social-emotional needs and characteristics of young children. Literacy learning experiences and instruction should be focused, engaging, participatory, and full of good feeling.

An important contextual variable that bears on literacy instruction is that most preschool programs are half day and have a mandate for and embrace the practice of equitable attention to cognitive, socioemotional, and physical development. Time is limited, and there is much of importance to be accomplished. Allocating (but not *over*allocating) the necessary time for instruction and learning of literacy foundations is important. While not firmly established, good estimates are that 8- to 10-minute lessons, 3–5 days a week on the alphabet and phonemic awareness is sufficient for most children, although some children need less instruction and others more. And, of course, oral language development should occur all day, every day, during daily storybook reading of narrative and informational text, in conversations, during center and table activities, and during mealtimes and transitions.

The appropriate level of preschool expectations for alphabetic knowledge, phonemic awareness, and oral language skills that support literacy attainment is a moving target. Recent studies indicate that preK **English learners** (ELs) are capable of learning quite a bit more than might have been thought just a few years ago. For example, many preschool programs emphasize rhyming and syllable counting within the scope and sequence for learning about the sounds in words. This skill level is typically referred to as phonological awareness. Yet recent studies reveal that identifying the individual sounds in words (identify the first phoneme in "cat") and orally blending the phonemes /c/ /a/ /t/ is within the developmental capabilities of typical preK ELs. Identifying initial sounds and orally blending sounds together are early markers of the more sophisticated skill of phonemic awareness, which is most strongly associated with success in beginning reading.

The linguistic demands of English instruction for preschool children who may be experiencing their first exposure to English make high-quality literacy instruction absolutely necessary if young ELLs are to achieve the level of alphabetic and phonemic awareness skill commensurate with that of EO children. Oral language is omitted in the previous sentence; an important caveat is in order. Acquiring proficiency in a second language to a level that will support academic achievement is estimated to require four to seven years. ELL children will not typically achieve the same level of English oral language proficiency as EO children, even after attendance in an exemplary language and literacy program. Close collaboration with K–3 partners for a well-articulated and systematic oral language development program is essential.

PreK program guidelines, foundations, and performance standards often differ in a very important way from those of the K–3 system. Support and utilization of children's first language is valued and encouraged in classroom practice in preschool settings. Research over 30 years has made it clear that the continued development of the first language is an established support for English literacy acquisition. This support can and should be capitalized on in preschool programs. Recent studies have demonstrated that initial instruction in the first language, combining English and the first language in literacy practices such as storybook reading, and using more rather than less of the first language in classroom instruction is compatible with or can even increase English acquisition and the reading and writing skills dependent upon it (Roberts, 2009).

In summary, I make the following recommendations:

- Establish preschool literacy programs that include explicit teaching of the alphabet, phonemic awareness, and oral language foundations.
- Devote significant professional development to increasing the depth of teacher knowledge about each foundation.
- Devote even more professional development to helping teachers acquire the details of instructional and scaffolding skills for effectively teaching each foundation to ELLs.
- Provide classroom support.
- Establish clear expectations for teachers to consistently provide high-quality instruction.
- Include children's first language in the literacy development program.
- Develop a system for monitoring children's progress in each area, and engage teachers in analyzing the progress data for their classroom and planning for differentiated intervention based on that analysis.

RECOMMENDED RESOURCES

Roberts, T. A. (2008). Home storybook reading in primary or second language with preschool children: Evidence of equal effectiveness for second-language vocabulary acquisition. *Reading Research Quarterly, 43*(2), 103–130.

Roberts, T. A. (2013). Opportunities and oversights within the Common Core State Standards for English learners language and literacy achievement. In S. B. Neuman & L. B. Gambrell (Eds.), *Quality reading instruction in the age of Common Core Standards*. Newark, DE: International Reading Association.

■ Lisa M. López

There is a great deal of diversity in the types of ELLs entering school. That diversity informs their current and future academic abilities relating to language and literacy. When thinking about the diversity of ELLs, one must realize that **bilingualism** is a continuum of abilities in each language (Valdes & Figueroa, 1994). Strengths and cognitive abilities vary within each of the child's languages. Therefore, because of the diversity among **dual language learners** (DLLs) in relation to this continuum, there is no one way for DLLs to learn to read and write.

First, one must understand that there are different types of ELLs. Some children learn two languages from birth and are considered simultaneous bilinguals. Other children learn one language prior to school entry and then begin learning English after age 3; these children are **sequential language learners**. The language learning process differs for these two groups of children.

Additionally, if you think about the different types of DLLs along the bilingual continuum with regard to dominance types, children who may speak both languages but are English dominant often act similarly to monolingual English speakers. Therefore, some of the same strategies for teaching monolingual English speakers will also work for them (e.g., exposure to books in English, development of phonological skills, introduction to the alphabetic principle). On the other hand, children who are dominant speakers of Spanish, for example, may benefit most from literacy instruction in their **home language**. They can then be taught to apply similar strategies to English reading and writing. Children who are advanced in both languages can be taught in either, although for these children English skills typically begin to surpass Spanish skills by the end of preschool. Therefore it may make sense to begin literacy instruction in English.

Finally, the group of largest concern is those not exhibiting dominance in either language, the **emergent bilinguals**. These children will have a more difficult time acquiring literacy skills because they are still developing oral language skills. For these children it is instrumental to work on oral language skills in both languages prior to beginning literacy instruction.

To summarize, when planning a literacy curriculum it is important to think of the diversity of DLL children in the program and where they are with their language learning in both their home language and English. It is difficult to fully develop literacy without a strong oral language background.

H. What is the role of home literacy practice in supporting success for English language learners in grades preK–3?

■ *Lisa M. López*

Home literacy practice is important in the daily lives of all children. Reading books to the child; teaching him or her about shapes, colors, and numbers; and practicing writing the child's name are some examples of activities parents can do at home to help their child be successful in school. A large amount of research has identified the importance of home literacy practices, primarily shared book reading, for successful literacy development with monolingual children (Senechal & LeFevre, 2002).

A growing body of research is also identifying similar home literacy activities as important for **dual language learners** (DLLs). Specifically, shared book reading has been identified as one of the best home activities for immigrant parents to do with their children (Farver, Xu, Lonigan, & Eppe, 2013; López, Ferron, & Ramirez, 2013). This can and should be done by parents in their **home language**. In fact, shared book reading in the parents' home language has been found to be more beneficial to the child than shared book reading in a language the parents are less familiar with.

For DLLs, exposure to and use of language also play a role in early language and literacy development (Hammer et al., 2012). Therefore, in addition to literacy practices, having a rich home language environment is essential. Exposure to and use of the first language at home help build an oral language foundation, which is necessary for the development of strong literacy skills. In order to expose the child to language, it is important to encourage parents to recount stories, describe what is occurring in their daily lives, and ask the child questions about his or her day. In addition to exposing the child to language, it is important to encourage him or her to use language in communicating.

In summary, while home literacy practices occurring in English benefit children early in preschool with regard to English school readiness, home literacy practices in Spanish have long-term benefits for children's Spanish development without detriment to their English school readiness (López, Ferron, & Ramirez, 2013). In fact, strengthening the child's home language through home literacy has long-term benefits with regard to school readiness. Encouraging home literacy practices is essential as it has been documented that immigrant families often do not recognize the need to engage in such practices at home (Reese & Goldenberg, 2008).

I. What is the relationship between growing up bilingual and the development of executive function skills?

■ *Tracey Tokuhama-Espinosa*

One of the most important researchers on **executive functions** (EFs) and cognitive training, Adele Diamond of the University of British Columbia, believes the three core EFs are (1) refined working memory, (2) inhibitory control (self-regulation and perseverance), and (3) cognitive flexibility (Diamond, 2013). Diamond strongly argues that EFs are the key to success in the 21st century. The main skills for survival in modern society, not only in school but also in the workplace, revolve around creative problem solving, making good choices, and being able to stay on task—all EFs.

Benefits beyond the Classroom

In a 32-year-long study, Moffit et al. (2011) showed that people who as children displayed less inhibitory control grew into adults with poorer health who earned less and committed more crimes than those with more inhibitory control. In another study, Diamond claims that "reasoning would not be possible without working memory" (Diamond, 2013, slide 18), meaning the benefits of EFs go far beyond the classroom and influence health and well-being across the lifespan.

"Effortful control" (Rothbart, Ellis, Rueda, & Posner, 2003; Rothbart & Rueda, 2005) is another way to label the ability to manage the temperament to which one is genetically predisposed, and to accomplish inhibition and self-regulation. All of the EF subelements—working memory, inhibitory control, cognitive flexibility, and effortful control—are closely related but are actually found in slightly different neural networks in the brain (Bobb, Wodniecka, & Kroll, 2013), meaning they are generally stimulated by different activities. Whereas working memory and inhibition are developed early in life, cognitive flexibility appears years later, according to Diamond (2013). There is now evidence to show that EFs are enhanced because of **bilingualism** or multilingualism.

How Does Growing Up Bilingually or Multilingually Improve Executive Functions?

Growing up with more than one language has been shown to improve EFs (Bialystok, 2011; Poulin-Dubois, Blaye, Coutya, & Bialystok, 2011), and it now appears that the cognitive development of bilingual children is superior in many ways to monolinguals (Barac & Bialystok, 2011). Bialystok et al. have shown that there are clear advantages in executive control by bilinguals (Bialystok & Viswanathan, 2009; Greenberg, Bellana, & Bialystok, 2012). Improved executive control begins in childhood but extends into adulthood (Bialystok & Feng, 2009), meaning developing these skills early on has long-term benefits. Executive function improvements in bilinguals have been shown in a variety of tasks, including word mapping (Bialystok, Barac, Blaye, & Poulin-Dubois, 2010), perspective taking (Greenberg, Bellana, & Bialystok, 2012), general language proficiency (Bialystok & Feng, 2009), and attention (Garbin et al., 2010; Robinson, Mackey, Gass, & Schmidt, 2012; Yang, Yang, & Lust, 2011), as well as global **metalinguistic awareness** (Sanz, 2012).

Working memory means being able to hold information in mind while working with it, usually to complete a process. For example, working memory is used when a student sees a math formula on the board, copies it down, and remembers what steps to take in which order. Working memory "is critical for making sense of anything that unfolds over time" (Diamond, 2013, slide 16). Working memory is improved by bilingual practices (Gass & Mackey, 2013), which often occurs in a spiral of cause-and-effect situations. For example, we know that learning languages is easier when a person has good working memory (Andersson, 2010), but it is also true that learning languages improves working memory (Morales, Calvo, & Bialystok, 2013). Memory improvements are shown in lexical access (finding the right word in your head) (Sunderman & Fancher, 2013) and verbal working memory (Wodniecka, Craik, Luo, & Bialystok, 2010). Additionally, it has been shown that working memory helps with associating ideas, relating what was just learned with previous information, as well as understanding cause and effect.

Inhibitory control means being able to self-regulate and discipline oneself to stay focused on a specific task requiring focused attention. In many ways this is the same as self-control. Improved inhibitory control related to executive process on nonlinguistic interference tasks (Hilchey & Klein, 2011) and auditory comprehension (Blumenfield & Marian, 2011) in bilinguals is well established as are general inhibition abilities (Gass, Behney, & Uzum, 2013). This appears to be the case in both rehearsed classroom activities and spontaneous speech (Friesen & Bialystok, 2013; Pivneva, Palmer, & Titone, 2012) and relates not only to inhibition, but also suppression of stimuli (Luk, Anderson, Craik, Grady, & Bialystok, 2010). As with overall EFs, it appears that the benefits of bilingualism remain, independent of the age of acquisition (Gold, Kim, Johnson, Kryscio, & Smith, 2013). That is, a person who became bilingual early in life will retain the benefits of inhibitory control into old age (Finger, Billig, & Scholl, 2011). Inhibitory control seems to be something that bilinguals themselves are quite aware of (Bobb, Wodniecka & Kroll, 2013).

Cognitive flexibility means being able to demonstrate intellectual empathy for other views and see things from a different angle. It also relates to the ease with which one switches perspectives and focuses attention on different things around the learner in order to take in the right types of information needed for problem solving. Though the real fruits of cognitive flexibility aren't seen until middle childhood, there is evidence of significant cognitive gains even before a bilingual reaches the first year of life (Kovács & Mehler, 2009). This cognitive flexibility is seen in a bilingual's ability to task switch faster than monolinguals (Prior & MacWhinney, 2010), use vocabulary (Ibrahim, Shoshani, Prior, & Share, 2013), and even drawing (Adi-Japha, Berberich-Artzi, & Libnawi, 2010). Numerous studies using modern brain scans demonstrate the actual changes in the brain because of expanded cognitive flexibility (e.g., Adesope, Lavin, Thompson & Ungerleider, 2010; Kuipers & Thierry, 2013).

It seems that the bilingual brain is stretched well beyond the general capacities of a monolingual brain, and the results are improved EFs, which have benefits that extend to other subject areas and into 21st-century skills. Activities as simple as developing age-appropriate skills—vocabulary building, speaking, reading, and writing—are enough to reap these great benefits. If this is the case, one has to ask why more school systems fail to incorporate foreign language instruction earlier. Hopefully the evidence now being shared with teachers and policymakers about bilingualism and improved EFs will turn the tide in favor of more bilingual school programs.

Resources and Questions

LANGUAGE DEVELOPMENT GRAPHIC

For discussion purposes only, this chart can be used to engage staff in conversation about how they understand first (L1) and second (L2) language development.

First Language	Comparison	Second Language
Stages that begin at birth	*Comparable elements of L1 and L2 development*	*Starts any time additional language is introduced*
0–6 weeks: Crying (hard for parent and child to understand each other)	Nonverbal cues help	Home language only (doesn't match language in classroom)
6 weeks–6 months: Cooing (vowel sounds)	Child listens to/observes the language around him	Observational period (common, but not universal)
6–12 months: Babbling (practices sounds she hears, responds to requests with actions)	Child demonstrates understanding before able to communicate verbally	Responsive period (child shows receptive language via actions)
12–18 months: One word at a time 18–24 months: Two to three words together	Selects key words or phrases to communicate	Formulaic speech (chunks of frequently heard words used to communicate)
24 months and up: Emerging fluency	Simple sentences, focus on the here and now	Informal fluency (speaks well in L2, but may still think and learn in L1)
5 years: Mature language	Expressive and receptive language skills ready to learn in school	Formal/**academic fluency** and language in L2

QUESTIONS FOR REFLECTION

- What coursework or personal professional development have you undertaken to learn about the developmental needs of children under the age of 9 years?

- What learning have you done regarding your planning for the education of young children who are learning in two or more languages?

- What plans will you make to fill in the gaps in your own knowledge and to support professional development on these topics for the staff that work for you?

CHAPTER **4**

Developing Instructional Programs for Young Dual Language Learners

Key Considerations for Language Plan

- Our language plan will outline the formats used for teaching young **dual language learners** (DLLs) and the staff expectations within each format.

- Our language plan will describe the procedures and behaviors expected of teachers and paraprofessionals as they teach young DLLs.

- Our language plan will list types of materials for DLLs that should be in each classroom.

- Our language plan will cover when and to what extent English and other languages are to be used within each format.

- Our language plan will specify collaborations expected among staff working with young DLLs.

- Our language plan will explain our view on strategies for differentiating educational programs to meet the learning needs of students with different languages and different abilities.

Chapter 4 describes the components of a highly effective educational plan so that administrators can unify these individual components into a cohesive, seamless approach that leads to the most successful outcomes for young **English language learners (ELLs)/DLLs**. This unified approach is crucial for the success of a program and for the success of each student. All young children who are growing up with two languages have learned some information in each of their languages and continue to need the support of both languages in order to be at their best in school. Their success depends on a comprehensive approach to education that provides the most effective environment, curriculum, and teachers while they are receiving specialized **bilingual education** or English supports, as well as when they are in the general education classroom and as they transition out of those specialized supports. Ideally, every member of the staff will be prepared to interact with and support all of the young children in the program.

This chapter is filled with information that administrators need to identify each aspect of their educational program that should be included in their planning process. Contributors have provided concise guidance in manageable chunks to assist in this planning process. A key advantage of the format of this chapter is that it makes it easy for a director to delegate sections of the planning process and to be confident about moving forward with the guidance of so many specialists in the field.

The beginning sections of this chapter identify the different types of program formats that may be used to support ELLs/DLLs in early childhood education. Administrators can learn about options for deciding what will work best for their school. Advice about choosing and adapting curricula and equipping classrooms appropriately will enhance the planning process. Topics that are trending in the media, such as using technology to teach young ELLs/DLLs, enhanced focus on explicit vocabulary instruction via interactions, and differentiated instruction, are covered by our experts. Detailed answers to common questions about ELLs/DLLs with challenging behaviors or special needs are provided as well.

The assessment grid at the end of this chapter enables the reader to gather information about the assets, resources, and unmet needs that form the next step in the language plan development process. The information provided in this chapter equips readers to recognize how their program's assets and resources can be matched appropriately and supplemented to meet the needs of students and staff.

A. What are bilingual education, English as a second language, and special or related services? How are they alike or different?

■ *Karen N. Nemeth*

Bilingual education, English as a second language (ESL), and other special or related services may be required by state and/or federal education code. **Bilingual education** means any program that provides some instruction in English and some in the child's **home language.** The balance of time spent on English and the other language is often determined by the local school or teacher. **Transitional bilingual education** is meant to be a temporary solution to help students continue learning content in their home language while their acquisition of English is accelerated so that they can transition into English-only instruction as soon as possible. Dual language immersion, on the other hand, is designed to provide continuous, balanced support for both English and another language. This allows speakers of both languages to learn each other's language throughout the program. ESL education is provided by a teacher certified in that specialty and uses English only, with multiple supports, to help ELLs learn English while also keeping up with content learning as well as possible.

In most states, bilingual education code specifies how either of these options must be provided for K–12 students who are designated as having **limited English proficiency.** Research tells us that all **English language learners** (ELLs)/**dual language learners** (DLLs) in early childhood education are still in the process of mastering their home language and should have ongoing support to learn their home language and learn *in* their home language. Most of the leading researchers would like to see all young bilingual children taught in bilingual classes. K–12 schools have to follow their state regulations, which may prohibit this bilingual approach. Preschools are often not subject to the K–12 bilingual education code, although they are included in the Illinois and New Jersey codes. Most states also have a waiver process whereby a local education agency or school can avoid offering bilingual education if they do not have staff with the right languages.

Most bilingual education code also contains a provision for special services when bilingual education or a certified ESL teacher is unavailable. In those cases, the school must provide at least some specialized support for ELLs.

B. What are some research-based program models?

■ *B. J. Franks*

SIOP (**sheltered instruction observation protocol**) is a research-based model of education for **English language learners** (ELLs) that depends on effective teacher training. The training should be a hands-on experience, conducted over several days. Whenever possible, they should be noncontiguous to avoid information overload. Teachers need to process information and have opportunities to practice the instructional strategies. To that end, a coaching model to support the teacher in the implementation is highly recommended. In the beginning the SIOP/ELL specialist could team teach and gradually release responsibility to the classroom teacher.

I have found that when teachers have the opportunity to participate in the activity/strategy, they are more likely to implement it in their classes. They obtain first-hand experience and can better integrate the theory and practice into their repertoire. Teachers should be able to visit one another's classrooms and have post-discussion time using the protocol. Because it is overwhelming to try to implement all 30 features at once, teachers should be encouraged to choose a few at a time. Some schools or grade levels have chosen to focus on certain features each year and provide support for their implementation.

■ *Margarita Calderón*

In 2003–2008, the Carnegie Corporation of New York funded the project Expediting Comprehension for English Language Learners (ExC-ELL). This preK–12 research and development project was embedded in educational practices in schools by working with teachers, principals, coaches, and students to deal with actual implementation problems, issues, and successes. ExC-ELL (in English) and ExC-ELLito (in Spanish) are

- Professional development designs with strategic teacher support systems
- Research-based 10-component lesson templates for integrating vocabulary, reading comprehension, and writing skills into core content instruction
- Technology-based coaching and observation protocols to determine to what extent the components are present in the delivery of a lesson, with a rating/summary portion to tally the results and impact on student achievement.

Teachers used the ExC-ELL/ExC-ELLito strategies to strengthen students' word knowledge, basic reading comprehension, English (and/or Spanish) fluency, discussion skills, grammatical knowledge, and writing skills. They integrated these elements into math, language arts, science, and social studies lessons:

- *Depth and breadth of tier 1, 2, and 3 words* that correlate with reading proficiency (Kamil & Hiebert, 2005)

  Tier 1—Basic words (e.g., smart, toothache, shy) ELLs need to communicate, read, and write

  Tier 2—Information processing words and phrases that nest tier 3 words in long sentences—polysemous words (power, trunk), transition words, connectors (therefore, moreover, over the course of), more sophisticated words for rich discussions, and for specificity in descriptions (declare, precise, ire)

  Tier 3—Subject-specific words or clusters that label concepts, subjects, and topics; infrequently used academic words (osmosis, fractional, ebb)

The lesson delivery components include strategies to explicitly select and teach words that pose difficulty for ELLs before, during, and after reading (Calderón, 2011a; Carlo, August, & Snow, 2005). Strategies for fostering word consciousness (Graves, 2006), which accelerates word learning and reading comprehension, are also included.

- *ELLs need early decoding/fluency practice* to recognize words and comprehend a text at the same time (Nagy, 2005). Because phonics-only programs do not work with ELLs (Kamil & Hiebert, 2005), word recognition and word meaning are integrated into teacher read alouds and student reading.
- *The strategic processing of text*—comprehension skills and cognitive strategies engage students in text comprehension before, during, and after reading math, science, and social

studies texts. Teachers learn to model and monitor partner and team practice of comprehension skills (Dashler, Palinscar, Biancarosa, & Nair, 2007). Techniques that enhance comprehension include self-monitoring for understanding; using semantic, graphic, or conceptual organizers; answering questions; and obtaining immediate feedback; formulating questions about the text and obtaining immediate feedback; becoming aware of the genre characteristics/text structure; and summarizing the content or retelling a story with peers (August & Shanahan, 2006; Calderón, 2011a; RAND, 2002).

- *Focusing and anchoring content knowledge* are accomplished through cooperative learning strategies and guided interaction. Cooperative learning strategies set a safe context for language practice for ELLs (Calderón, Hertz-Lazarowitz, & Slavin,1998; McGroarty & Calderón, 2005). Teachers use these interaction strategies to consolidate knowledge and language proficiency.

    ELLs need modeling of every type of writing. Teachers learn a variety of content-area expository and narrative writing genres and the text structure of the targeted genre. They also integrate practice on language mechanics, editing in content-area projects, and portfolios that include academic writing (Calderón, 2011b; Graham & Perin, 2007).

Schools making the greatest gains have two things in common: (1) site administrators participating and supporting teachers; and (2) teachers and administrators use the protocol for multiple purposes—reflection, peer coaching, and tracking student performance.

RECOMMENDED RESOURCES

Calderón, M. E. (2007). *Teaching reading to English language learners, grades 6–12: A framework for improving achievement in the content areas.* Thousand Oaks, CA: Corwin.

Calderón, M. E. (Ed.) (2012). *Breaking through: Effective instruction and assessment for reaching English learners: An anthology.* Indianapolis, IN: Solution Tree.

Calderón, M. E., & Minaya-Rowe, L. (2003). *Designing and implementing two-way bilingual programs: A step-by step guide for administrators, teachers, and parents.* Thousand Oaks, CA: Corwin.

Calderón M. E., & Minaya-Rowe, L. (2011). *Preventing long-term English language learners: Transforming schools to meet core standards.* Thousand Oaks, CA: Corwin.

■ *Maria N. Trejo*

The general tenets and framework of ExC-ELL have been adapted to support the particular instructional issues and needs faced by preschool teachers serving ELLs. This program is often referred to as ExC-ELLito.

Young ELLs come to school with some of the same issues, such as having to learn English and the expected grade-level content, as native English speakers. In preschool, children have the added dimension of still developing their home language and while simultaneously acquiring English. Research on early brain development maintains that children are capable of learning multiple languages simultaneously (Society for Neuroscience, 2008); however, staff are often very confused and torn when they plan programs. Selecting the language of instruction is often the most debated component. Key questions in preschool continue to be, "Do I introduce literacy in the primary language or in English?" "If the child's parents do not read or write in the primary language, do I still teach preliteracy concepts in the home language?" "Is decoding learned in the same manner and sequence in a primary language as it is in English?" ExC-ELL for preschool helps answer these questions and provides strategies for improving instruction and child outcomes.

Child rearing practices are important considerations in preschool. The role and involvement of parents is crucial (Booth & Dunn, 1996). Parents are expected to be highly involved, but their culture and language backgrounds play a big role in their involvement or lack of participation. Just as there is wide diversity in the ELLs attending programs, so there is in their families and the goals they hold for their children. When parents are uninvolved, educators may erroneously assume what parents want for their children and design programs based on those assumptions. For example, educators often believe that the best-designed programs are those where instruction and activities are presented totally in the home language. Although this may be true in some specific settings, in publically funded preschools parents often want their children to learn English and want most instruction in English. ExC-ELL for preschool personnel helps with processes for parents. Strategies are provided on how to determine the wishes of parents, how best to involve them, how to explain program services to them, and how to tap their skills and contributions (Calderón, 2011a).

Bilingual personnel are quite special in preschool programs. Children and their parents are much more dependent on teacher skills and expertise than in regular programs. Parents expect staff to know much more than the school curriculum. Bilingual staff members are often called on to advise and help with a variety of community issues, such as immigration, immunization requirements, child abuse issues, and health concerns. Preschool teachers may start providing tutorial services to older siblings (California Department of Education, 2009). ExC-ELL institutes address these needs and provide guidance for teachers and staff on how to meet those added roles.

Educators and administrators are challenged to reduce the emerging preK–K readiness gap. This early gap is unecessary and can be prevented with targeted interventions. Strong and consistent professional development for all staff and coaching support for teachers is a major intervening step. ExC-ELLito provides multiple day institutes to address key skills and strategies essential for instruction of young ELLs. Its major components include the following:

- Understanding the developmental process of beginning literacy in two languages
- Identification and selecting of **biliterate** personnel
- Modeling language of instruction to expedite the acquisition of formal school language
- Strategies for enhancing parenting skills and early literacy development support by parents
- Sequencing and presentation of preliteracy skills to expedite vocabulary development and early reading development
- Implementing successful preschool programs for young ELLs
- Coaching, modeling, evaluation, and feedback to teachers and staff to improve programs

RECOMMENDED RESOURCES

Calderón, M. (2012). *Breaking through: Effective instruction and assessment for English learners.* Bloomington, IN: Solution Tree.

Espinosa, L. M., & Garcia, E. (2012, November). Developmental assessment of young dual language learners with a focus on kindergarten entry assessment: Implications for state policies. Working paper #1. Center for Early

Care and Education Research-Dual Language Learners (CECER-DLL). Chapel Hill: University of North Carolina, Frank Porter Graham Child Development Institute. Available at http://cecerdll.fpg.unc.edu/sites/cecerdll.fpg.unc.edu/files/imce/images/CECER-DLL_WP%231_Nov12.pdf

National Association for the Education of Young Children. (2002). *Early learning standards: Creating the conditions for success*. Washington, DC: Author.

Snow, C. E., & Hamel, V. (2008). *Early childhood assessment: Why, what, and how. National Research Council Report on Early Childhood Assessment*. Washington, DC: National Academies Press.

U.S. Department of Education. (2013). Opening remarks of U.S. Secretary of Education Arne Duncan at the panel, "The Obama Preschool Initiative." Available at www.ed.gov/news/speeches/opening-remarks-us-secretary-education-arne-duncan-panel-obama-preschool-initiative

C. What are best practices for bilingual education in grades preK–3?

■ *Zoila Tazi*

Several models of bilingual instruction for young children are being implemented across the United States. Within these models, academic goals for students range from providing introductory support in the **home language** to developing **bilingualism** and **biliteracy**. Increased interest in **dual language programs**, which give access to **bilingual education** to **English language learners** (ELLs) as well as native English speakers, may signal a growing awareness that bilingualism and biliteracy are desirable goals for all children (Lindholm-Leary, 2004).

Ample research highlights the efficacy of dual language programs, yet these programs are not available to all children (Collier & Thomas, 2009). The varied political entities, policymakers, conditions, resources, or attitudes that influence the introduction of these programs into schools are precisely the areas where school leaders must assume an advocacy role as the beginning of best practice. School leaders charged with implementing a dual language program also need to consider how the nature of each program affects the range of their administrative decisions and commitment to best practice.

Access

In general, dual language programs are designed to bring together, in equal proportion, an ELL population with a common language and a native English-speaking population. This combined group learns to speak, read, and write in English and in a target language. How are the participants for a dual language program selected? In those settings where placement is an administrative decision, school leaders should safeguard access for all children. Programs that demand a selection process with entrance requirements are creating special conditions that unfairly exclude some children. Rather than conceiving of dual language programs as *advanced* or intended only for children with strong language skills, best practices call for a program that is *fully integrated* into the school curricula and services.

Long-Term Commitment

Placement in a dual language program requires a long-term commitment from the school and the home. Bilingual literacy development is not identical to monolingual literacy development (Bialystok, 2007), although analysis of outcomes over time suggests that bilingual instruction, such as is provided in dual language programs, yields greater achievement for students (Collier & Thomas, 2009). It is critical to hold teachers, administrators, and parents to a long-term commitment even when a standardized test is scheduled for a given grade level. Sometimes schools or parents abandon the dual language program for fear that children may need English instruction exclusively in order to perform well on standardized tests in English. Best practices call for a sustained approach that builds on knowledge from research and from experience supporting bilingual instruction throughout the grades.

Language Allocation and Language Use

Dual language program structures allocate times and schedules for both languages. Indeed, it is necessary for children to have adequate exposure to the target language they are learning. Some programs may dedicate days or portions of a day to teaching and learning in one language only. It is important, however, to remember the bilingual learner when implementing the language allocation structure. Strict adherence to language allocation can create an artificial situation for the bilingual learner who has two languages, not one, in his or her linguistic repertoire. More recent models of bilingualism recognize the common practices of bilingual individuals who fluidly alternate between the languages they know in order to navigate situations or make meaning. Translanguaging describes the common and natural ways in which bilingual individuals organize their own learning or their own means of communication (Garcia, 2009). The wise school leader recognizes that a more dynamic understanding of bilingualism, where all languages are present in the teaching and learning process, leads to greater engagement and achievement. This means that both languages in a dual language program are always accessible and welcome. Even if it is "English day," the other language is not forbidden; it is treated as an important learning resource.

School Context

Savvy school leaders know that no program survives in isolation. In a school where the dual language program is the only setting in which children encounter a positive embracing of multilingualism, it is likely that they will still internalize a message of inadequacy rather than empowerment regarding bilingualism. The school context can be a protective factor for young bilinguals if the environment portrays all languages as worthy and valuable. School leaders can promote multilingualism in the school environment by speaking in more than one language during announcements or meetings, prominently displaying signs in multiple languages, or exhibiting samples of student work in various languages as a means of conveying the importance of all the languages spoken in the school. Rather than focus on how complicated this can become, best practices suggest that there is an imperative to represent all languages positively within the school context if educators are to reap the full benefits of bilingual instruction. It is important to make the effort. School leaders play a very critical role in validating multilingualism in the school. They hold the keys to language allocation policies, bulletin board displays, announcements, communication with parents, letters from the principal, and so forth. If school leaders can promote bilingualism as a resource for furthering the school's goals, they are more likely to engage constituents and build the sort of environment that promotes learning.

Dual language programs may be growing in popularity among those school constituents who have a global sensibility and who see the benefit of a bilingual populace right here in the United States. A full embracing of these ideas may be decades away, however, and school leaders contend with the realities of the moment. Today there is considerable controversy over bilingual instruction. Programs teeter on the brink of dissolution, for example, over test scores or the dearth of certified **bilingual education teachers**. As with many other school initiatives or ideals, school administrators are the torchbearers for bilingual instruction. Without focus and intentionality, the torch goes out. Research and conventional wisdom agree that school leaders who uphold and protect this unique modality contribute to a cause that recognizes the more expansive definition of student potential that is inherent in bilingualism and biliteracy.

RECOMMENDED RESOURCE

Freeman, Y., Freeman, D., & Mercuri, S. (2005). *Dual language essentials for teachers and administrators*. Portsmouth, NH: Heinemann.

D. What are best practices for English as a second language/English language development programs in grades preK–3?

■ *Judy Hicks and Claude Goldenberg*

The foundations of effective early childhood teaching generally are also the foundations of early childhood teaching for **English learners** (ELs; Goldenberg, Hicks, & Lit, 2013). All young children are developing language and thus require elements of effective instruction that aid that process. These elements include appropriate and challenging tasks with very clear instructions, informative feedback, active child participation and engagement, and the application of learning and transfer to new situations (Goldenberg, 2013). Of course teaching that includes these elements is *necessary*, but it is *insufficient* for ELs.

Research suggests two types of supports for ELs in order to promote their **English language development** (ELD): (1) opportunities for ELD throughout the day, and (2) a separate block of time specifically devoted to ELD. Although research has yet to settle on the best approaches to ELD in early education settings, some elements of ELD practice have surfaced.

Throughout the instructional day, teachers can support ELD within a variety of contexts and across multiple points in time. Examples include the following:

- Encouraging and being highly responsive to child-initiated conversations during play/recess, meals, before and after school, and so forth
- Modeling pragmatically appropriate phrases
- Recognizing and responding to nonverbal requests; meeting those needs and simultaneously providing language that narrates the experience
- Reading aloud from a variety of fiction and nonfiction texts
- Making texts' connections to children's lives and experiences explicit
- Explaining target or vocabulary words and using those words in a variety of contexts
- Supplementing explanations of words or ideas with visual representations—illustrations, props and realia, video clips—and providing necessary background knowledge
- When possible and relevant, pointing out and explaining **cognates** from the child's **home language** (but not doing simultaneous translation, which research indicates is ineffective at teaching the target language)

In addition to supporting language development throughout the day, evidence favors providing a separate block of time specifically for ELD. This is true for preschool settings (Restrepo, Castilla, Schwanenflugel, Neuharth-Pritchett, Hamilton, & Arboleda, 2010), but particularly for early elementary classrooms (e.g., Saunders, Foorman, & Carlson, 2006). This block of time should provide a balance between opportunities to use English for meaningful and authentic communication and opportunities to engage in more organized experiences with instruction and feedback. The more organized experiences should help children learn specific aspects of the language, for example, vocabulary, correct syntax (e.g., adjectives precede nouns), and correct morphological forms (e.g., possessives are formed by adding an s to a noun).

Meaningful, authentic communication can occur during ELD time when partners or small groups of children engage in completing a task or an experiment together. In those situations, children negotiate roles; manage materials; and share ideas, thoughts, and opinions that are likely to require authentic communicative language. Teachers can provide additional opportunities for authentic communication by allowing ample time for discussion and questions around a lesson or activity.

Teachers can also organize more structured experiences for their students during ELD time. These experiences are intended to enhance children's communicative language, both as a goal and as a means to acquiring more language (Saunders, Goldenberg, & Marcelletti, 2013). Examples of these activities include the following:

- Engaging in role plays of particular situations
- Providing sentence frames and models of grammatically correct language
- Teaching songs and rhymes that contain key phrases and vocabulary (days of the week, months of the year, colors, numbers)
- Using graphic displays to help children organize clusters of related words
- Using labeled visual aids
- Facilitating games that require children to combine actions with new words (e.g., Simon Says)

Concurrent with supporting English, programs should consider providing a separate block of home language development. In addition to validating the child's life experience, supporting and developing the home language is linked to important cognitive and social outcomes (Genesee, Paradis, & Crago, 2004).

RECOMMENDED RESOURCE

August, D., & Shanahan, T. (Eds.). (2006). *Developing literacy in second-language learners: Report of the National Literacy Panel on Language-Minority Children and Youth.* Mahwah, NJ: Lawrence Erlbaum.

E. What do administrators need to know about the effectiveness of pull-out, push-in, and embedded intervention methods for each age group in early childhood?

■ *Karen N. Nemeth*

When **bilingual education** is offered, it is usually provided as the child's regular classroom. English as a second language (ESL) services may be provided occasionally in a variety of formats, such as the pull-out, push-in, and embedded intervention methods. Understanding the pros and cons of these formats enables the administrator to support individualized services that match the resources available to each student's needs. At this point, there is still very little convincing research to show a clear favorite among these options, so administrators need to use their own understanding of best practices.

The **pull-out method** involves the ESL specialist taking the child out of the general education classroom for a specified period of time on a regular basis. Although this separation from the workings of the regular class can provide time for the ESL teacher and the student to focus on intensive language learning strategies, this format is generally considered to be more effective for older grades than for early childhood education. Young students are less able to maintain focus during abrupt transitions in and out of the regular classroom. Also, because of the level of cognitive development in preschool and kindergarten, most of these children are unable to recall much of what they learn in isolated pull-out sessions. Because the classroom teacher is unable to see what happens in those sessions, she cannot support the child's practice and mastery of skills introduced there. **SIOP** (sheltered instruction) is a more intense version of pull-out instruction that can be very effective with older students, but is still unproven for preschool aged students.

The **push-in method** is used in some programs where the ESL specialist provides services within the child's general education classroom, usually connecting directly with the curriculum and activities that are happening at the time. This enables the regular teacher and the ESL teacher to support continuity of learning for the child and to see the strategies they are each using. Still, many teachers find this disruptive to the classroom. Push-in services can happen in a variety of ways. In some schools, it may be a visit from the ESL teacher once or twice a week; in others, it may take shape as a full co-teaching model. "Many teachers confirm that the push-in model is an effective way to meet the needs of the whole child—to succeed academically, many **English language learner** (ELL) students need to build not just English language skills, but also background knowledge" (Marietta & Brookover, 2011, p. 12).

The **consultation method** facilitates embedded supports when the ESL specialist consults with the classroom teacher about supports needed by **dual language learners** (DLLs). They plan together so that the classroom teacher can embed the supports in the regular school day, all day, every day. This can be especially useful for preschool and kindergarten learners. It is the recommended format in some states, such as New Jersey, which posts recommendations in its Preschool Implementation Guidelines that state, "Pull-out and push-in strategies are not appropriate for young children learning language" (New Jersey Department of Education, 2010, p. 35).

For additional consideration, there are options outside of the regular school day programs that can support learning for young DLLs. Some schools offer enjoyable after-school activities that are designed to enhance language learning for young ELLs/DLLs in a relaxing and play-oriented environment. Another strategy employed in some areas is a brief summer language camp or kindergarten prep camp that can be offered to incoming students to help smooth their entry into the new school and new language.

F. What is dual language immersion, and what does research say about its effectiveness?

■ *Jennifer Chen*

Dual language immersion (DLI) is also known as two-way immersion (TWI) and bilingual immersion. It is considered an **additive** and the most effective form of **bilingual education** because, when designed and implemented successfully, it fosters the **bilingualism**, **biliteracy**, and multicultural competence found to promote student achievement. DLI/TWI is an instructional approach that integrates native English speakers and native speakers of a partner language in the same classroom as they learn literacy and academic content in both languages. Launched in 1963, the Coral Way Elementary School in Miami, Florida, has been educating students in both Spanish and English and is considered the pioneering TWI public school in the United States. Since then, more than 300 public and private U.S. schools have established DLI/TWI programs, at all educational levels from elementary to high school. Although the majority of DLI/TWI programs teach in English and Spanish, other partner languages (e.g., French, Korean, Chinese Mandarin) have also steadily been incorporated into these programs.

Although DLI/TWI programs have existed for 50 years, this approach has only recently gained increased support and popularity, as more empirical evidence affirms its effectiveness. The effectiveness of DLI programs is generally defined by how successful these programs are in promoting student achievement and other outcomes (e.g., literacy proficiency, academic motivation, learner attitude). On the basis of their research with 23 school districts in 15 states and data about more than 2 million students, Thomas and Collier (2003) concluded that **dual language programs** yield educational benefits, notably the potential to close the achievement gap among various groups of students and provide higher-quality education. Of the research investigating the effectiveness of DLI/TWI programs, most has focused on comparing the academic competence of students in these programs (i.e., native Spanish speakers and native English speakers) with their mainstream counterparts in other types of programs. For instance, longitudinal studies (e.g., Howard, Christian, & Genesee, 2003; Lindholm-Leary, 2001; Thomas & Collier, 2002) and smaller-scale studies (e.g., Lindholm-Leary & Block, 2010; Stipek, Ryan, & Alarcón, 2001) have demonstrated positive academic outcomes on standardized achievement tests in English and Spanish among both native English speakers and native Spanish speakers, as compared to their peers in other programs. In addition to strong academic competence, Lindholm-Leary and Borsato (2001) found that high school participants in the TWI program achieved other positive outcomes, including higher levels of academic motivation, ambitions to attend college, and pride in bilingualism. Because most research to date has investigated the effectiveness of mainly Spanish and English DLI/TWI programs, the effectiveness of programs with other partner languages is not as widely documented.

Nonetheless, as the effectiveness of DLI/TWI programs has been substantiated by robust empirical evidence, especially concerning the Hispanic student populations, it raises the question: How do DLI/TWI programs achieve their effectiveness? First and foremost, effectiveness relies on sound design and implementation. It has been reported that factors contributing to the effective implementation of DLI/TWI programs include student population, program design, school environment, instructional strategies, pedagogical equity, qualified teachers, active home–school collaboration, a duration of bilingual instruction of four to seven years, competent leadership, and quality resource support (e.g., Alanis & Rodriguez, 2008; Howard, Christian, & Genesee, 2003; Lindholm-Leary, 2001; Thomas & Collier, 2003).

An essential reading pertaining to the effective design, implementation, and refinement of DLI/TWI programs is Lindholm-Leary's (2005) article, based on a review of research and best practices, delineating a host of features promoting the effectiveness of dual language education programs. These effective features can be grouped into three categories: (1) structure (e.g., program design, competent leadership, family and community involvement), (2) process (e.g., instructional practices, professional development), and (3) alignment (e.g., curriculum, assessment, and accountability).

G. What factors do administrators need to know to choose the best program models for the population, resources, and staff abilities they have?

■ Judy Hicks and Claude Goldenberg

There is little empirical evidence supporting a *particular* program model over others, but there is ample evidence supporting *elements* of programs. Therefore, this response describes research-supported program elements to consider.

First of all, effective programs for **English learners** (ELs) have many of the same components as effective programs more generally. Elements that the National Association for the Education of Young Children (NAEYC, 1995) supports, such as a mixture of structured and unstructured learning opportunities, positive and productive teacher–child and home–school relationships, program-wide responsiveness to culture and language, and time for teachers to reflect and plan, are the broad foundations of high-quality early childhood programs.

Striking the balance between structured and unstructured learning opportunities for ELs in early education is as tricky as it is with all children. In terms of language and literacy, some teacher-directed instruction is associated with better child outcomes on elements such as vocabulary and letter knowledge (Camilli, Vargas, Ryan, & Barnett, 2010.) The provision of time for unstructured play also is consistent with both cognitive development and desirable social and emotional outcomes (Hirsh-Pasek, Golinkoff, Berk, & Singer, 2009). That optimal balance of structured and unstructured opportunities—and if and how it shifts from preschool through early elementary school—has yet to be established in the research.

What is clear, however, is that all teachers and staff need to be trained to facilitate both more and less structured times of the day effectively.

There are three basic approaches to language use in the classroom for ELs. The first model is English immersion, in which all, or nearly all, of the instruction and teacher language is in English. The program's objective is for children to become fluent in English as quickly as possible. The second model is maintenance (or developmental), which uses both the child's **home language** and English extensively in the classroom. The goal of this program is to develop both languages. The third model is the transitional, which lies between the other approaches. In the transitional model, the home language is used to some extent—for example, to help children acquire concepts, learn how to function in preschool, and engage in all classroom activities—but the goal is not necessarily to maintain or further develop the home language. The goal of transitional programs is to help children transition to an all-English classroom environment, if not in preschool then in kindergarten or early elementary school.

Research has shown that use of the home language for ELs in preschool classrooms develops both the home language and English and does not hinder English development (Barnett, Yarosz, Thomas, Jung, & Blanco, 2007; Rodríguez, Díaz, Duran, & Espinosa, 1995; Winsler, Díaz, Espinosa, & Rodriguez, 1999). Furthermore, there is evidence supporting the intellectual, cultural, and economic benefits of **bilingualism**, suggesting that promoting bilingualism is probably beneficial for children.

For programs in which home language instruction is not possible because of the presence of many languages in a single classroom or personnel or resource constraints of one kind or another, there are ways that teachers and program models can still honor and include the home language in the classroom (Goldenberg, Hicks, & Lit, 2013). All children can be taught greetings and common words in each of the languages represented in the classroom. Teachers can supplement instruction with explanations or clarifications that include words or phrases from the home language. Additionally, classroom materials can include books in home languages, and families and community members can be invited to be involved in the classroom. If at all possible, however, having staff who are fluent in the home languages of the children is ideal.

Although all young children are still developing language skills in their home language(s), ELs face the added challenge of learning English as well as their home language. **English language development**, which provides explicit language support and opportunities for authentic and structured language practice, should be provided for ELs.

RECOMMENDED RESOURCE

Lightbown, P., & Spada, N. (2006). *How languages are learned* (3rd ed.). Oxford, UK: Oxford University Press.

H. What do administrators need to know to make appropriate curriculum selections for preK and K–3 programs serving children who are English language learners?

■ *Nancy Cloud*

Early childhood educators are well aware of the need to create responsive curricula for their learners in accordance with National Association for the Education of Young Children (NAEYC)'s (2008) position on **developmentally appropriate practice**, which urges that they provide "opportunities to support children's home culture and language while also developing all children's abilities to participate in the shared culture of the program and the community." Programs must stress respect for diversity; be safe, inclusive, caring, and respectful learning environments; and integrate culturally responsive materials and teaching practices across the disciplines (Purnell, Ali, Begum, & Carter, 2007). All of this depends on having a deep level of knowledge of the children and families we serve, as well as the sociocultural context of our communities. What follows are steps early childhood educators might take to ensure a culturally responsive early childhood curriculum.

First, find out the explicit ethnolinguistic groups represented in your ELL population. Although children may share a common language like Spanish or Chinese, their cultures may be quite diverse. For example, Guatemalan children's experiences may be quite different from Dominican or Mexican children's. Important, within-group differences also exist across various regions or according to socioeconomic status or other factors.

Once you have this information, conduct an environmental scan of your instructional setting to see which cultures are represented and which are absent. Pay particular attention to your book collections to ascertain which cultures are well represented and which need to be added. Culturally relevant stories and activities help young children connect academic lessons to their lives; they make our curricula meaningful and affirm children's cultural identities. Initiatives such as http://dia.ala.org/parents-children or http://asiasociety.org/education/resources-schools/partnership-ideas/world-childrens-literature can help us build more responsive book collections for our classrooms.

As you teach units, explore the community resources you can incorporate and partner with families to locate photographs, books, and materials that might help you teach your themes with familiar objects and images. For example, when teaching units on family or community workers, ask for photographs that portray family relationships or jobs that are most treasured in each family or culture. When teaching counting use the objects that families typically use to teach this skill, not just those that we tend to use in our classrooms, such as unifix cubes or blocks. Ask cultural informants to look at the room with a critical eye and note the themes, topics, and objects that children know well or play with but are missing from our early learning environments.

Always consider the background knowledge children and families possess, and use this knowledge when you design curriculum units. For example, when studying weather and climate, consider the unique knowledge each child may bring and ensure that they get to understand the concept of weather and climate from the experiences they have had and the conditions they or their families know best. Then introduce them to the new climate and weather conditions they are likely to experience in your part of the world. The idea is to use the strengths and assets children bring to the classroom, rather than cause them to look deficient because they do not yet know the particular conditions they are likely to experience in their new environment.

Guard against superficial and trivial presentations of culture, such as only recognizing heroes, holidays, foods, dress, or flags. These do not represent the deep values, understanding, and perspectives of a culture and create stereotypical understanding among children of one another's cultures and life experiences. Instead, show the different ways we approach the world (e.g., views of family, understanding of natural phenomena) as well as commonalities (e.g., having treasured fables and folktales to explain our experience). Pay special attention to the integration of music, dance, and the visual arts, which are culturally inspired. Consider music and art forms from the parts of the world from which your learners and their families come. Families may be able to offer resources and skills if invited to participate in the development of this culturally rich curricular area.

Ultimately, the content of the early childhood curriculum is determined by many factors, including the subject matter of the disciplines, social or cultural values of the communities we serve, and parental input. We will want to evaluate our curricula to make certain that they are equally influenced by all of these sources.

I. What are effective teacher behaviors and interaction styles to support English language learners in grades preK–3?

■ *Cristina Gillanders*

Teacher–child relationships in early childhood have important implications for children's social relations with peers and future teachers (Birch & Ladd, 1998), for school adjustment (Howes & Ritchie, 2002), and for academic achievement (O'Connor & McCartney, 2007). When teachers provide responsive individualized attention, are involved in learning with children, are consistent and firm, and support positive behaviors (Howes & Ritchie, 2002), they establish positive relationships with their students. Furthermore, predictable classroom routines, stability of the teacher and the group, cooperative learning opportunities and peer tutoring, small class size, and small group instruction foster positive relationships between children and their teachers (Howes & Ritchie, 2002; Pianta, 1999). These teacher behaviors and classroom environment characteristics are particularly critical for **dual language learners** (DLLs), for their learning in general, but also for language learning specifically.

Secure teacher–child relationships encourage the risk-taking behaviors necessary for language learning and teach social interaction skills that children can use when they interact with their peers (Baker, Dilly, & Lacey, 2003). DLLs who feel comfortable in school will be more willing to participate in the life of the classroom and to engage in interactions with peers and adults. Teachers who establish positive relationships with the DLLs in their class enhance their social status among their peers. In turn, a high social status in the classroom creates more opportunities for DLLs to interact with children who use English. Full participation in the community of the classroom allows DLLs to be exposed to the new language and to use it in a variety of contexts.

Both bilingual and monolingual teachers need to intentionally create opportunities to establish positive relationships with DLLs. For monolingual English-speaking teachers, this task might feel daunting because not knowing the child's **home language** limits their ability to communicate with these children. This can certainly be a limitation, but it is possible to create opportunities in which teacher and child make meaningful connections. For example, the more knowledge teachers have of children's experiences outside school, the easier it will be to find a common ground for one-to-one conversations. In addition, for English-only teachers, knowledge of a few words of the child's home language demonstrates their willingness to learn and helps them empathize with the process of second language acquisition. Finally, explicit statements in the classroom that underscore the benefits of **bilingualism** can help DLLs gain social status in the eyes of their peers.

School leaders have an important role in creating environments that facilitate positive teacher–DLL relationships. Administrators can ensure that effective teachers stay with the same group of DLLs for extended periods of time (through "looping"). School leaders can support teachers to provide small group instruction and cooperative learning opportunities. Administrators can arrange schedules for school lunches in which teachers can have one-to-one conversations with DLLs. School leaders also can arrange opportunities for teachers to conduct home visits and to have meaningful conversations with the children's families.

RECOMMENDED RESOURCE

Gillanders, C. (2007). An English-speaking prekindergarten teacher for young Latino children: Implications of the teacher-child relationship on second language learning. *Early Childhood Education Journal, 35*(1), 47–54.

J. What materials, supplies, displays, and resources should we see in classrooms?

■ *Iliana Alanís*

Creating an effective literacy environment that nurtures **biliteracy** development requires planning and intentionality. Materials and displays should be equitable in both languages and should be connected to the topic or theme of study. Equal status for both languages must also be reflected in the print environment. When children see both languages represented, it sends a clear message that their classroom environment honors and validates both language groups.

Labeling

One important and practical strategy is to label the classroom in the target languages (e.g., English and Spanish). Generally, labels are placed at the children's eye level and may be found in different places and on various resources throughout the classroom. Recommendations include placing labels on learning centers and materials; furniture, objects, supplies, and work areas; books by genre or language; and other significant resources. Color-coding the print on labels—for example, red for the Spanish labels and blue for the English—assists young **dual language learners** (DLLs) in distinguishing between languages. Using different colors for each language is a practical way to remind young children of the language being used and promote confidence and competence as they negotiate their print environment.

Student Work

The richness of dual language classrooms should be reflected in the samples of student work displayed around the classroom. Teachers are encouraged to post examples of authentic student work that reflects what students can do in both of their languages. Posting original student writing in both languages sends a powerful message to students that they are capable bilingual readers and writers.

Bulletin Boards

Content-area bulletin boards serve as instructional areas where children have access to key academic vocabulary in the language of instruction. For example, when studying parts of a plant, science bulletin boards can have diagrams of a labeled plant or flower with a description of the purpose for each part. Students can engage in grade-level activities that require use of this academic display.

Word Walls

Word walls should be a focal point of the classroom so that words are easily found to assist students with their reading and writing. The word wall should be at eye level so that children have visual and physical access as needed. Word walls should be separated by language. This separation helps children identify words in each language even when they cannot decode them.

Instructional Materials

Materials should be accessible to students in both languages and should be changed with each unit of study. Examples include children's literature within learning centers, posters or diagrams, word walls, and alphabets (in each language).

Peers

Peers serve as an important resource for one another and for the teacher. Teachers should partner students with mixed linguistic and academic levels; that is, children with higher skill levels should partner children whose skills are less developed. Placing children in bilingual pairs facilitates use of language skills as children develop academic concepts (Alanís, 2011, 2013). Students should engage with each other as they attempt to resolve a problem or complete a task. Partners scaffold each other's learning and reinforce the native speaker's knowledge of the language when children serve as language models and resources for one another.

Desks or Tables

Desks or tables should be arranged to promote interactive lessons. Arranging desks to accommodate face-to-face interaction facilitates understanding through facial gestures and cues as children engage in academic tasks with a partner or small group.

■ *Cristina Gillanders*

As with any kind of learning, effective teachers of DLLs build on what children already know while gradually introducing new knowledge and skills. Therefore, the materials and displays in the classroom should reflect children's experiences at home and in their community. Community field trips and home visits can help teachers identify uses for literacy and mathematics. Text samples found in places where the children live can be displayed in the classroom and help children acquire concepts of print. Texts in different languages are an excellent opportunity for teachers to make explicit the written conventions in each language and compare the different kinds of scripts. For example, they can point out that both Spanish and English are read from left to right, whereas other languages, such as Chinese, are read from top to bottom. Teachers can collect pamphlets, advertisements, storefront photographs, and signs from the community that can be used by children to make predictions about the meaning of the words.

It is important that teachers explicitly identify to the children the language of the text in the displays or books used. Children need to understand that just as they can recognize when someone is speaking a different language, each language represents the written word in a different way. Some teachers use specific text colors to differentiate between languages that have the same script. Parents can help to create signs and displays in their particular language.

Classrooms and school libraries should include multilingual books. Teachers can introduce a book by reading it in the **home language** first and then in English. Monolingual English-speaking teachers can ask parents or members of the community to read the book in the home language. These readings can be audio-recorded so that children can listen to them repeatedly on later occasions. Books in the home language should also be sent home so that parents can continue promoting the home language as well as literacy development. Several publishers of children's literature currently include multilingual books in their collections.

Storybooks should be chosen carefully. When choosing storybooks teachers should consider the following (adapted from Gregory, 1996):

- Will the story be interesting to DLLs?
- Does the story relate in any way to DLLs' sociocultural and personal experiences?
- Do the children know the vocabulary words necessary to understand the story? If not, how will the teacher teach these words prior to reading the story?
- Does the story follow a storyline that is easy to understand?
- Does the story include repetitive phrases that DLLs can memorize and read along with the teacher?
- Do illustrations reflect the text so they can support children's understanding?
- Does the story allow teachers to use props and gestures to maximize children's comprehension of the story?

Songs, poems, and rhymes in both the home language and English can be displayed on chart paper. Using these, teachers can integrate children's home culture and promote vocabulary and phonological awareness in both languages. Songs and poems also allow children to practice the pronunciation of difficult sounds and to learn "chunks of language" that can then be incorporated into everyday conversations (Gregory, 1996).

K. What are the best ways to use technology to support language learning?

■ *Karen N. Nemeth*

Technology and digital media offer an irresistible array of tools, information, and connections that are ideal for supporting learning in **English language learners** (ELLs)/**dual language learners** (DLLs) in the early years.

- Smart phones and digital cameras can be used to record young children's language to save for portfolio assessment. Be sure to have signed photo/video/audio recording release forms for all children.
- Computers with internet access allow for the use of online translations, access to literacy activities in different languages, and video examples to illustrate learning, overcome language barriers, or communicate with children or relatives in other countries.
- Interactive whiteboards and multitouch tables allow young children to create and record stories and games to build their language skills and concept knowledge.
- Tablet devices can be loaded with countless apps that are designed to teach new languages, build skills in the **home language**, play games reinforcing language learning, or create stories using the first or second language. Finding story apps on tablet devices can provide excellent experience for both student and teacher because the apps can provide bilingual stories in many different languages, with sound, so each participant can hear the proper pronunciation of the other language.

Young children need active, hands-on, discovery-based learning as much as possible, so it is better to use the technology to support naturally occurring learning opportunities rather than pull students away from their activities for specified computer time. It is generally considered inappropriate to use language teaching programs with young children because research shows they benefit more from human interactions. Technology can, however, be used effectively to enhance those interactions.

L. How can we ensure differentiation so that materials and instruction are appropriate for the various ages and stages of students?

■ *Jennifer Mata*

Knowing the age and developmental stage of each student is crucial to help teachers purposefully determine which materials, instructional styles, pedagogical strategies, activities, and content matter are appropriate. Regarding **English language learners** (ELLs) in particular, it is also crucial to determine the proficiency level the student has in the **native language** (L1) and English. For this determination, observation of the students is critical and must be done before planning and instruction can take place.

Teachers should dedicate quality time to observing students while they are completing work in small groups or individually. They can use a variety of authentic assessment tools to gather pertinent information about the students. Anecdotal records can be used to document what the students can do independently, what they can accomplish with the help of others, what they are still struggling with, and what they need further practice with. Teachers can also develop checklists to record vocabulary words and content matter students already understand and begin to use regularly, as well as develop rubrics with different levels of performance to assess the work the students complete. Documenting their progress will help inform the teacher as to what to plan next to better meet the needs of ELLs.

In terms of ELLs' proficiency levels, students can usually be categorized as beginners, intermediates, or advanced English speakers (Peregoy & Boyle, 2008). Some strategies that promote both content matter and English language acquisition for all levels of ELLs include the following:

- *Prepare new vocabulary in all/any L1s.* ELLs benefit from knowing what the new English vocabulary words mean in their L1. The teacher should identify the new vocabulary being introduced and research these words in the ELLs' L1s. A small group mini-lesson can then take place before introducing the new content matter and vocabulary words during the whole group lesson (good for both beginners and intermediates).
- *Use gestures, movement, and total physical response (TPR).* Offering oral examples and explanations of the knowledge to be acquired facilitates learning for all students. For ELLs, however, using gestures and physical demonstrations of what is being taught is paramount because they have limited comprehension of verbal explanations. Using gestures and movements repeatedly to imprint meaning as specific content and vocabulary is being introduced helps ELLs remember words (Magruder, Hayslip, Espinosa, & Matera, 2013). TPR, where the teacher provides plenty of verbal instruction and commands in English and the ELL responds using whole-body action, is another way to check for comprehension and expose the ELL to new vocabulary (Asher, 1969, 1996). With time, and after significant exposure to practicing gestures/movements, listening to English provided by the teacher and peers, and their own language development, ELLs will begin to demonstrate spoken outputs in English (especially beneficial for younger beginners, but can be used for older beginners as well).
- *Talk, talk, talk, and provide a language-rich environment.* Modeling appropriate use of English for ELLs helps them move from social or conversational understanding/speaking of English to the much-needed academic or school language. ELLs will acquire social or **conversational fluency**/conversational English within about two years of exposure (Chumak-Horbatsch, 2012). Informal chats with peers and adults and use of contextual cues, body language, and facial expressions help ELLs derive meaning from these interactions and acquire vocabulary. However, in order to be successful academically and thrive in school, academic or school language must be attained. This type of English takes between five to seven years of exposure and requires the ELL to be exposed to technical, abstract, and specialized vocabulary, which is content specific (Cummins, 1981, 2000). This kind of language is not found in social, informal interactions and must be intentionally taught and planned for by the teacher (this is beneficial for all ages and proficiency levels).

Students from all of these levels of English proficiency benefit when such strategies are used by their monolingual, native-English-speaking teachers, and noncertified ESL and bilingual teachers can also implement them.

M. What practices are developmentally appropriate for the intentional support of vocabulary development?

■ *Nancy Cloud*

Developmentally appropriate practice in language development for young **English language learners** (ELLs) reflects an understanding that second language development is occurring while children are still in the process of developing their **native language** (L1). Because of this, early childhood educators will want to develop children's English (L2) while fostering the continued development of the L1. We can also aid children in making bridges and connections between their two languages. This additive approach is supported by research showing the all-important role children's L1 plays in their overall cognitive and linguistic development as well as in promoting their psychological well-being (Genesee, 2008). If we do not speak a child's L1, we can partner with family members who can continue to use and develop it while English-speaking early childhood educators concentrate their efforts on the L2.

Within this additive framework, there are many tactics to expand the vocabularies of ELLs to prepare them for the language and literacy demands of the grades to follow.

Singing, Chanting, Performance Poems, and Rhyming

When it comes to language development, rhymes, performance poems, finger plays, and songs are all wonderful activities to use to play with language and learn its rhythms and rhymes. We can affirm children's linguistic and cultural identities by drawing on well-known sayings (*dichos*), poems, and finger plays, with caregivers performing them in the L1 while we introduce them in the L2. Each culture offers us many of these options; by incorporating them into our curricula we make the program much more familiar and responsive to our learners and give important roles to our families (see http://www.zerotothree.org/early-care-education/early-language-literacy/songsengspan.pdf).

Use music with recognizable melodies, rhythms, and tones that come out of our children's cultures and with which they are familiar (see joseluisorozco.com, www.mamalisa.com, arabicsongsforkids.com). Create a mix of these songs, as well as mainstream early childhood songs that are already part of our classroom collections (e.g., songs by Ella Jenkins or Raffi). Both provide repeated practice of words and phrases that advance language use and development.

Encourage Word Learning and Teach Children to Be Curious about Word Meaning

Think of vocabulary development as "building semantic networks," and help your learners acquire related terms in associated networks. For example, teach the words we use to refer to rocks: pebble, stone, boulder, rock chip, and fossil, along with the associated action words of finding, collecting, picking up, dropping, throwing or skipping and the descriptive words used when referring to particular rocks (e.g., speckled, sparkling, dull, bumpy).

Introduce Academic Language and Connect L1 Knowledge to L2 Knowledge

When teaching early childhood themes such as nutrition use representative foods from each culture. Introduce the appropriate terms in English that refer to foods eaten on a regular basis in each culture to ensure children's opportunities to use the words (see http://www .nationaldairycouncil.org/SiteCollectionDocuments/footer/spanish_materials/Guideto GoodEatingSpanish.pdf). Place common cooking utensils, plates, bowls, and pans into the kitchen center, introducing their new English names to children and helping them bridge from the words they know to the new words for these familiar objects.

Provide Practice Opportunities

Set up activities that promote language use. Circulate to each activity center with the explicit intention of eliciting language and providing practice of the terms and phrases you have targeted for work with each child.

Use Visuals to Encourage Language Use

Incorporate photographs of familiar people, places, and objects from the child's world for storytelling and language development activities. Target specific vocabulary you would like to develop; determine the words the students know and the words they have yet to learn to expand and refine their language.

Use other visuals that represent the stories you have been reading or the content-area themes you have been teaching. As children inspect the visuals, elicit the target language and give them natural practice.

Offer and Elicit Language during Read-Alouds

Read comprehensible books in English while introducing and targeting specific vocabulary words. Many wonderful bilingual books have become available to support us in this work (see delsolbooks.com, panap.com, and colorincolorado.org). Help your ELLs label and name the characters, actions, and objects portrayed in illustrations or retell the story using the terms and phrases targeted. Maintain your focus on particular words until they are in active use. Don't just superficially explain terms when reading and move on; mere exposure does not promote vocabulary acquisition. Ensure language use, because it is the only way to promote language learning.

Keep Track of the Terms You Teach and the Student's Progress Learning Them

Establish a system for vocabulary acquisition tracking for each child. Note the words you are introducing and make sure you teach nouns, verbs, adjectives, adverbs, pronouns, and linking words with equal emphasis.

N. How can we handle challenging behaviors of students who are also English language learners?

■ *Pamela Brillante*

Many young children who have trouble communicating with adults and peers because of a language barrier may use challenging behavior as an efficient and effective way of making their wants and needs known. Understanding the function of the challenging behaviors and helping the child learn new skills to replace them takes time and understanding.

Developing a variety of skills that increases their ability to communicate helps children learn to express their wants and needs rather than using challenging behavior (Roben, Cole, & Armstrong, 2012). Supporting the **home language** in the classroom is a primary method of preventing challenging behaviors because it reduces the need for the child to use such behaviors to communicate (Nemeth & Brillante, 2011). Effective classroom strategies for supporting the home language include increasing visual supports and environmental print, making books and materials that use the home language easily accessible to the students, and employing staff or volunteers who speak the child's language (Nemeth & Brillante, 2011; Santos, Fowler, Corso, & Bruns, 2000).

Using a system of positive behavior supports, such as the pyramid model, helps children develop their social and emotional skills and, in turn, reduces their need to use challenging behavior as a control strategy (Hemmeter, Ostrosky, & Fox, 2006). The foundational philosophy of the pyramid model is **developmentally appropriate practices**. All children need time to explore their world and engage with peers, materials, and interested adults. Using classroom time to focus on teaching preschoolers to speak and understand English in isolated experiences takes away from this critical part of early childhood development (Nemeth, 2009).

This foundational level of the pyramid model also stresses the importance of social development and social interactions among children (Hemmeter, Ostrosky, & Fox, 2006). Language barriers between classroom peers can impede social interactions in the classroom and inhibit the development of social skills. Relationships with peers who speak other languages need to be fostered by developing a common language method and teaching everyone about the language and culture of the members of the class (Nemeth & Brillante, 2011).

If these strategies do not work to develop appropriate social skills in students, teachers might need to provide direct instruction in skills such as initiating and maintaining interactions with peers, problem solving within social situations, handling disappointment and anger, and expressing emotions and feelings in appropriate ways (Strain & Joseph, 2006). The caveat to providing direct instruction in this area is that the teacher must understand the extent of the language barrier that may exist between her and the student. This situation may require the teacher to seek out assistance from an English as a second language specialist or an adult who speaks the child's **native language**.

For persistent challenging behaviors, more individualized, comprehensive interventions may be required. The top tier of the pyramid model uses a comprehensive functional behavioral assessment (Hemmeter et al., 2006; O'Neill, Horner, Albin, Sprague, Storey, & Newton, 1997). These extensive observations help the teacher understand all of the different factors that are related to the ongoing challenging behaviors. Functional assessment must focus on the role of the child's language and culture in sorting out triggers, behaviors, and solutions for children who are newcomers. It is imperative that staff members—and especially the team—are well trained to assess this situation properly.

This top tier of the pyramid model helps teachers design plans to teach new skills that replace the challenging behavior. These plans are based on extensive observations and can be implemented in the natural environments and within ongoing routines and activities of the preschool day (O'Neill et al., 1997). To be effective, they need to respect the cultural practices of the family as well as support home language needs.

O. How should programs serve young English language learners with special needs?

■ *Vera Gutiérrez-Clellen*

English language learners (ELLs) with language disabilities have special needs. Like their typically developing ELL peers, they face great challenges when they enter preschool: Most programs do not provide a focused curriculum to facilitate English language acquisition, and in the majority of programs instruction is provided in English-only, a language these children may not comprehend. Unlike their typically developing peers, ELLs with language disabilities also have limited language skills in the **home language** that affect their ability to communicate with parents and other family members. Given the fact that these children have delays and special needs in both languages, it is critical that teachers address these needs in both the home and the second language.

First, educators need to be aware that facilitating the development of the home language does not result in a delay in the acquisition of the second language. Learning a second language does not appear to delay language acquisition (see, e.g., Paradis, Crago, Genesee, & Rice, 2003), and there is no evidence that learning two languages takes longer than learning only one (for a discussion, see Paradis, 2010). In fact, the first language may bootstrap the acquisition of the second language.

Second, recent research has shown that children who are taught in both languages make greater gains in the home language than those who are taught only in English (Barnett, Yarosz, Thomas, Jung, & Blanco, 2007; Duran, Roseth, & Hoffman, 2010; Restrepo, Castilla, Schwanenflugel, Neuharth-Pritchett, Hamilton, & Arboleda, 2010). Therefore, parents and teachers should be encouraged to stimulate the home language in order to address the child's needs to improve communication skills with the family and in the community.

Third, the available research tells us that teaching these children only in their second language (English) does not result in better outcomes compared with teaching them in both languages (see, e.g., Restrepo, Morgan, & Thompson, 2013). In fact, children with severe language delays do better using a bilingual approach than an English-only approach (Gutiérrez-Clellen, Simon-Cereijido, & Sweet, 2012). These findings indicate that ELL children with language disabilities are capable of learning in both languages, provided they receive quality instruction and support in each language.

P. How should we address first and second language supports in the special education plan?

■ *Vera Gutiérrez-Clellen*

English language learner (ELL) children with language disabilities need a focused and intensive vocabulary and oral language intervention. The preschool classroom (as opposed to a **pull-out method**) provides multiple contexts and participants to learn new words and concepts that will facilitate language skills. The richer these interactions, the better the learning of language, including vocabulary, sentence length and complexity, and preliteracy skills (Cabell et al., 2011; Justice, McGinty, Piasta, Kaderavek, & Fan, 2010).

There are four preschool practices that have been shown to facilitate oral language development. First, *large and small group activities* in the preschool classroom help children engage with the words and concepts presented by the teachers and clinicians. Second, *picture book read-alouds* allow teachers to present vocabulary and language forms that are not frequently heard during common conversations. Third, preschool exposure to both *fiction and nonfiction books* facilitates the development of narrative and expository skills and academic concepts related to science and social studies. Fourth, *hands-on activities and manipulatives* help young children better understand new words and ideas, especially when they do not speak the language, are learning English as a second language (ESL), or have language disabilities. Objects, toys, and pictures serve as visual and tactile cues that engage their attention and interest.

These quality instructional practices can be easily implemented by teachers within the classroom context and adapted for ELL children with language disorders. Preschool teachers are capable of effectively promoting the language development of children with language impairments (Simon-Cereijido & Gutiérrez-Clellen, in press; Wilcox, Gray, Guimond, & Lafferty, 2011). Using a traditional clinician–teacher model, the bilingual clinician conducts lessons in the classroom without teacher involvement. In the team teaching approach, the teacher and the speech–language pathologist (SLP) co-teach the lesson. Using a team teaching model, the monolingual clinician can work with a bilingual preschool teacher or a trained SLP assistant who would be responsible for the "Spanish days." Other alternatives are to train parents as volunteers with the assistance of a bilingual paraprofessional or to have an itinerant bilingual teacher provide the lessons for 30 minutes several times a week (Restrepo, Castilla, Schwanenflugel, Neuharth-Pritchett, Hamilton, & Arboleda, 2010).

High-quality preschool programs include daily large and small group activities. These activities help the child focus on different language areas. For example, large group activities are used for dialogic shared book reading where children learn new vocabulary, introduced in the **home language** first, and stimulate listening skills. There is limited use of read-alouds in preschools attended by children from low-income families (Dickinson, McCabe, & Anastasopoulos, 2003; Neuman, 1999). This problem must be corrected because these activities are critical for vocabulary and oral language development. Bilingual fiction and nonfiction books provide a great venue for parents, teachers, and SLPs to access the children's knowledge in the two languages and to use the **native language** to learn new information.

In contrast, small group activities and hands-on activities facilitate children's participation and talking, keeping them engaged and resulting in high rates of verbal participation

(Phillips & Twardosz, 2003). We recommend that the intervention be provided in the two languages, first introducing the book and target vocabulary in Spanish followed by the same lesson in English on the next day. In the small group, children do more than practice target vocabulary. Clinicians use the name of the object and often pair the word to related words and actions. This simultaneous exposure to ongoing activities and language allows the child to map the new word to new meanings, increases word learning, and facilitates oral language practice (Gentner & Namy, 2006).

■ Pamela Brillante

Every professional involved in a child's education plays an important role in the development of the individualized education program (IEP). A collaborative team approach focuses the conversation on the individual needs of each child, taking into account the language needs as well as the disabling condition. The expertise of educators from different disciplines can highlight best practices across the different fields while proposing the specially designed instruction to be included in the IEP (Zehler, Fleischman, Hopstock, Pendzick, & Stephenson, 2003).

As a professional resource, the ESL specialist provides the special education specialists with information regarding policies, regulations, and laws surrounding the education of ELLs. The ESL specialist assists the special education evaluation team in understanding the developmental stages of second language acquisition and its potential academic impact for this student.

The ESL specialist may be able to provide a native-language assessment to assist in giving the IEP team an accurate and comprehensive look at what the child can do academically, developmentally, and functionally. The ESL specialist will most likely be able to assist in interpreting the data from the assessments that may have not been developed for non–native English speakers. The ESL specialist should be part of the team that determines if a learning disability exists or is having an impact on education. Research tells us that a true disability manifests itself in all languages a student knows (Hardin, Roach-Scott, & Peisner-Feinberg, 2007). This professional expertise also assists the team in developing the appropriate supports and services to help the student develop some proficiency in the **native language** as well as English. Some ELLs born in this country may have splintered skills in the native language, specifically a strength in oral skills in the native language over reading or written skills because they have only had formal instruction in English (Connecticut Administrators of Programs for English Language Learners, 2011).

Understanding the cultural differences surrounding disabilities and schooling for the student and families may be a complex area where the ESL specialist is exceptionally helpful. The concept of disability is not "culturally neutral"; each culture may have different views of what constitutes a disability and different attitudes towards how they treat or educate people with disabilities (Department for Education and Skills, 2006). Cultural differences may have an impact on the student's classroom behavior. Different learning styles may reflect different cultural expectations.

The role of the parents in the educational process may also have cultural implications. Several terms and concepts surrounding learning difficulties, autism, dyslexia, ADHD, and other common disabling conditions in our culture may have no easy translation or definition into other languages (Department for Education and Skills, 2006). Parents may not know what to expect about the special education process or services and may have questions and hesitations steeped in cultural experiences.

Resources and Questions

ASSETS/RESOURCES/NEEDS ASSESSMENT GRID

Classroom	Assets Already in Your Program	Resources Available to You	Unmet Needs	Plans for Change
1				
2				
3				
4				

QUESTIONS FOR REFLECTION

- How does your school/program currently handle children who have challenging behaviors and who speak a language other than English?

- How do you currently plan for students who have special needs and who also speak a language other than English?

- What training, guidance, or reading has influenced the development of your program structure?

CHAPTER 5

Policies, Accountability, and Program Effectiveness

Key Considerations for Language Plan

- Our language plan will incorporate the regulations and standards that affect our work with young **dual language learners** (DLLs) and show how our program will meet each one.

- Our language plan will provide details about formal and informal student assessments, screening, and classroom assessments, as well as staff responsible for assessments.

- Our language plan will specify how the results of student and classroom assessments and any other data will be used to improve practice.

A long with an increasingly diverse student population, early childhood administrators also face increasingly diverse regulations and requirements for their programs as well as growing pressure to gather and use data for local, state, and federal initiatives and to meet funding requirements. Chapter 5 introduces the policies administrators need to be aware of, equips them with the knowledge they need to meet accountability requirements, and offers cautions and suggestions to meet the various demands for evaluation.

Regulations and requirements specific to operating a primary school program for children who are considered **English learners** come from the Office of English Language Acquisition and from the Title III funding requirements. States also have regulations that govern the education of children who are DLLs or **English language learners** (ELLs). To complicate matters, increasing scrutiny is being given to how programs are addressing their special education regulations when they need to be balanced with the bilingual education regulations.

As more and more elementary schools offer either inclusion or general education preschool, they may have to become familiar with their state's preschool guidelines and regulations. Added concerns arise when the school partners with neighboring preschool programs. Head Start programs have broad and deep requirements they have to follow. Preschool programs in each state may be subject to specific preschool requirements, and they may also be subject to their state's health and safety monitoring or licensing. Unlike elementary schools, preschools may be privately owned as part of a chain or franchise operation, which adds its own set of rules.

Local, state, and national funding awards often come with extensive policies and accountability requirements. New initiatives have been created, such as Common Core Standards and Race to the Top–Early Learning Challenge. Several national professional organizations provide accreditations for preschool programs, and they add an additional layer of requirements that must be addressed in the planning process. Resources are provided to help readers obtain the additional support they need on this topic. The contributions to this chapter also show readers how to gather data and document student progress and classroom quality in order to satisfy accountability requirements.

Language plays a key role in all measures of student learning, teacher effectiveness, and program quality. When administrators are responsible for classrooms filled with different languages, many concerns about evaluations arise. Bilingual children may develop knowledge in one or both of their languages. Teachers may teach in one, two, or more languages—and those languages may or may not match the languages spoken by the children in their classes. The availability of assessments that measure student progress, language proficiency, program outcomes, and teacher effectiveness has not kept pace with the diversity of languages spoken in our schools. Administrators are expected to evaluate what professional development topics are needed by staff, what changes are needed to help more students read and learn at grade level, what overall practices are effective in their programs, and where changes are needed. Administrators are held accountable, even though the disconnect between the available evaluation tools and the true needs of the program can be staggering.

Many curriculum developers are working to provide materials and assessment tools in Spanish. Although Spanish is the language spoken by about 65% of ELLs/DLLs in early childhood education, there are still thousands of children in U.S. schools who speak Asian languages, European languages, and many less frequently observed languages. Unfortunately, the numbers are not favorable to convince publishers to provide evaluation tools and assessments in languages other than English and Spanish, since the next most frequent languages after Spanish each make up less than 3% of ELLs/DLLs. Despite the lag in researched and published tools for evaluating programs with diverse languages, administrators are still required to report results. Readers will need to look for improvements in the field that happen after this book has gone to print.

At the end of this chapter is a comprehensive list of professional organizations and resource websites that should be part of the early childhood educator's cultural and linguistic diversity toolkit. There is also an assessment comparison chart so that readers can compile information on the assessments they use in their early childhood program.

A. What federal laws and regulations affect early childhood programs for dual/ English language learners in grades preK–3?

■ *Karen N. Nemeth*

It is interesting to note that the U.S. Department of Education defines an **English learner** (EL), or **limited English proficient** (LEP), as an individual aged 3–21 who has a **native language** other than or in addition to English (U.S. Department of Education, Title IX General Provision 9101 [25]). Most state regulations regarding **bilingual education**, however, begin with kindergarten or grade 1 and do not address preschool. As more and more elementary schools offer or partner with state-funded preschool, the boundaries of their jurisdiction change and, therefore, their obligations should change. Illinois became the first state to fully address this change when their bilingual education regulations extended down to preschool in 2010.

The main source of national leadership on meeting the educational needs of students who speak a language other than English is the federal Elementary and Secondary Education Act (ESEA). It addresses the services that must be provided to ELs via Title I (which covers accountability and high stakes testing) and Title III (which describes how the services should be provided). Together these regulations require local school districts to identify and provide English language development services (Zacarian, 2013b). It is up to each state's department of education to interpret the federal regulations and decide how to establish their own state policies and regulations to guide school districts in meeting the federal requirements. Individual school districts are accountable to their state department of education, which in most states only address grades K–12 or 1–12. Even so, wise administrators know that they are more likely to show better outcomes for their older students if they begin addressing their language learning needs as early as possible. According to "Serving Preschool Children Through Title I Part A of the ESEA," states may choose to use some of their Title I funding to serve preschool children, particularly preschool children identified as having high needs because of their status as ELs.

The requirements for identifying students as ELs are stipulated by ESEA, but the actual tools and methods are determined by the states. This has led to great variability, and some controversy as well. Many states post a home language survey or recommend that local districts create their own. This may be insufficient to make a clear determination about a child's English proficiency status. Some parents may not understand the questions on the survey; they may be wary of causing their child to be labeled "bilingual"; they may be worried about revealing their immigrant status; or they may just prefer that their child be immersed in English. Programs that depend on the home language survey alone are likely to have a high misidentification rate of ELs. Additional assessment tools should be used to increase accuracy. This is an especially difficult issue for preschool because assessments of English language proficiency for preschool children are often called into question and may be considered developmentally inappropriate for children who are younger than 45 months old.

The federal Office of English Language Acquisition and most state departments of education do not offer clear guidance on how to identify children in preschool who may be considered ELs. Further research and development is clearly needed in this area, and administrators should watch for updates in the next few years. In the absence of solid assessment options for preschool, many programs identify any preschool child who has a **home language** other than English as a **dual language learner** (DLL; the preschool term for EL), regardless of language proficiency.

Federal regulations in Title III, Part A, Subpart 2, Section 3302 (b) provide detailed requirements for informing parents of the identification and instructional plans for their child who is considered to be an EL. Again, these are addressed in each state's regulations and policies. Each administrator needs to be sure they understand what their state regulations say and who needs to comply with them.

There have been many gaps in proper service provision when it comes to identifying and planning for EL students who have special needs. The ESEA language does not exempt students from eligibility for English language development services because of their diagnosis or designation in special education. In fact, federal regulations in the IDEA (97) state that, when writing the IEP, districts must ". . . in the case of a child with limited English proficiency, consider the language needs of the child as those needs relate to the child's [individual education program] IEP. . ." (34 C.F.R. §300.346 [a][2][ii]). Especially for early childhood education, an English-only approach to special education services for children who are growing up with two languages would be considered inappropriate (Council for Exceptional Children/National Association for Bilingual Education, 2002).

Even though state governments are lagging in terms of creating regulations that adequately address the needs of preK ELLs/DLLs, it is advisable for programs to offer developmentally appropriate services to those children to pave the way for smooth transitions and continuing grade-level success. Seamless transitions based on well-coordinated systems of support from preK through grade 3 are critical to the overall success of the school, the district, and each individual student.

B. What state guidelines and regulations do administrators need to know from the perspective of preK and K–3?

■ *Laura Bornfreund*

There are certain guidelines and regulations set by states regarding **English language learners** (ELLs) that school administrators should know and understand. These requirements typically provide guidance on how ELLs are identified, instructed, assessed, and what kinds of accommodations they are allowed.

ELL students are typically identified through a home language survey and a state placement exam, but the exams used vary by state.

Some states—such as Arizona and California—require teachers to deliver all instruction in English, while other states allow students to be instructed, at least to some extent, in their **native language**. States such as Florida and Georgia allow for multiple instructional delivery models that include **pull-out** and **push-in methods**. In Illinois, districts can select from several models to develop their ELL programs, including **transitional bilingual education** and sheltered English instruction see www.isbe.state.il.us/bilingual/pdfs/228.27_guidance _lang_svcs.pdf). Several states leave most instructional decisions to the local school district.

States also have various requirements for preK–3 teachers who work with ELL students. Illinois, for example, passed a law in 2008 to extend its ELL program to its state-funded preK program. It is one of the first states to do this. In doing so, the state instituted new certification requirements for preK ELL teachers. The state now requires the same ELL training for preK teachers as it does for K–12 teachers (see http://newamerica.net/sites/ newamerica.net/files/policydocs/Starting_Early_With_English_Language_Learners.pdf). Many other states have requirements for K–3 teachers to have pre-service or in-service training to work with ELL students.

Many states allow for some type of assessment accommodations. In most states, kindergarten students take readiness assessments, which measure students' knowledge and skills typically in multiple developmental domains. It is important to know whether and to what extent these assessments are allowed to be administered in students' native language, which research recommends for assessments such as these (see www.naeyc.org/files/naeyc/file/ research/Assessment_Systems.pdf). Children in grades 1–3 participate in various diagnostic assessments as well as assessments for school and teacher accountability purposes. Before these are administered, school leaders should consult their state's policies on allowable accommodations and delivery methods.

How students transition from ELL programs is less clear, however, and not necessarily detailed in state regulations.

C. What national guidance and regulations come into play when elementary schools partner with Head Start or other preschool programs?

■ *Karen N. Nemeth*

In many states that are enacting either state-funded or universal preschool, there is an effort to partner with existing community programs. This is a desirable path to take for many reasons. Instead of putting local community members out of business, contracting with them gives the district a way to elevate the quality of the services they provide while also building good will in the community. Using experienced preschool and childcare providers allows districts to take advantage not only of teachers but also of other staff who know the families and understand the unique challenges of working with the preschool set. Partnerships like these can also be beneficial because they allow the district to leverage existing funds and get more "bang for the buck."

With all these potential benefits also come a number of challenges that will be new to many public school administrators. In most areas, the administrator answers only to the state department of education. Preschool programs have additional bosses to deal with. In many states, preschool programs must comply with childcare regulations, even though they may also partner with a district. For example, a district kindergarten may be allowed to have 25 or 30 students with just one teacher, but childcare regulations may limit a class of 4 year olds to 20 and require both a teacher and an assistant. In some states, district-operated preK programs may be exempt from regular childcare regulations, but it is a good idea to check under which circumstances this might apply to your school.

Head Start programs are funded by the Administration for Children and Families, with additional state funding in some cases. Head Start programs serve 3- and 4-year-olds in preschool programs. They are subject to an extraordinary level of regulation and guidance from the federal Office of Head Start in order to maintain their grant funding. According to the official website, "In 2012 30% of participants spoke a language other than English at home, representing more than 140 languages" (Office of Head Start, 2013). When partnering with Head Start, supports for **dual language learners** (DLLs)/**English language learners** (ELLs) are of primary concern. Head Start programs must comply with federal requirements, such as a maximum class size of 18, an approved comprehensive curriculum, and significant family engagement activities. In most states, Head Start programs are also subject to state childcare licensing requirements. If a district wants to collaborate with these programs, administrators will need to negotiate a setup that meets all of the relevant requirements.

Head Start also has a school readiness framework that provides detailed guidance for programs about learning goals in every domain. Although these are requirements for Head Start, they are also informative and useful for any preschool program. They can be found at http://eclkc.ohs.acf.hhs.gov/hslc/sr/approach/cdelf. Head Start has a strong commitment to supporting each child's **home language** and culture.

National and state initiatives that come with preschool funding also carry a whole additional set of requirements. Is your state participating in the Race to the Top–Early Learning Challenge initiative? Has there been progress toward PreK for All in your state? What about the Promise Neighborhoods funding program? Any of these may bring added benefits, as well as added layers of accountability and requirements.

Administrators who seek to partner with local preschool providers should contact their local childcare resource and referral agency to get the most complete list of potential partners. You can find the listing agency nearest to you at www.childcareaware.org. There may be small private or church-run preschools or programs that are part of a regional or national chain, such as Goddard or Montessori schools or Educare programs. High-quality programs may participate in a national preschool accreditation such as www.NAEYC.org or www.NECPA.net. Because the individual program has to uphold the qualities set forth by their larger organization or corporation, this adds another layer of requirements to address. However, it also adds another layer of resources and experiences that are valuable to the district.

As administrators prepare to collaborate, partner, and/or contract with preschool programs, they should begin by creating a list of all the factors they expect to find or adapt in the preschool program. They should then prepare a list of questions that address curriculua choices, qualifications of teachers and paraprofessionals, services for children with special needs, class sizes, screening and assessment procedures, adult–child ratios, space requirements, meals and snacks, funding specifics, parent services, professional development plans, outdoor facilities, and plans for transitioning children into and out of the program.

The important thing to remember is that preschool programs that are already operating in your community probably know more about preschool than most people in any school district. They may also be very anxious to have access to some of the assets of the school district such as school libraries, technology resources, and professional development. Elementary school administrators should keep in mind that whether they partner with local programs or not, the children they serve will be part of the next kindergarten or grade 1 class and will certainly influence the school's level of success. Working with those community programs, especially to support DLLs/ELLs, is a wise choice for any early childhood education administrator.

D. How do special education regulations work with English language learner regulations?

■ *Pamela Brillante*

Regulations serve a common purpose to protect individuals and groups in society. Disputes, mistakes, and even incidences of poor judgment can hinder any student from receiving a quality education. Regulations are in place to make sure that nothing inhibits any student's participation in the educational system. Foundationally, the No Child Left Behind (NCLB) Act of 2001 is the federal government's primary source of educational regulations for all students. This law provides a structure to assist in guaranteeing the rights of each student, no matter what language they speak, or what disabling conditions may be present, to a quality education (U.S. Dept. of Education, 2002).

The first and most important aspect of working with children who are **English language learners** (ELLs) with potential special needs is to think outside of the separate boxes in which we place disability services and ELL services. We must recognize that these two different areas of need must work collaboratively to be successful.

Students have the legal right to both ELL and special education services. Part A of Title III of NCLB, officially known as the English Language Acquisition, Language Enhancement, and Academic Achievement Act, gives guidance on best practices in educating ELLs. This act stipulates that non–native English-speaking students must be given programs that support development towards English proficiency and simultaneously meet grade-level academic expectations (ESEA, §3102[1]). Regulations under the 1997 amendments to the Individuals with Disabilities Education Act (IDEA) stipulate that any student with a disability must have access to, participate in, and make progress in the general education curriculum through a system of specially designed instruction outlined in each student's individualized educational program (IEP; Karger & Hitchcock, 2003).

Identification of children who are struggling academically for special education services begins with the discussion of the potential disability itself. Many countries exclude children with disabilities from formal education, but a lack of instruction does not constitute a disability under IDEA (34 CFR §300.306[b][1]; 20 U.S.C. §1414[b][5]). Schools need to investigate what level of education or interventions the child has been receiving up to this point before the determination of disability is made. In addition, the practice of holding back referrals to special education until the child has been in a program learning English for a certain number of years is detrimental to the ELL students with true disabilities (Klingner & Harry, 2006).

Federal and state regulations govern the process of assessing a student to determine disabilities, and for ELLs this can be a complex undertaking. Standardized assessment may be based on native English speakers; schools should understand the implications of potential issues of racial and cultural bias and exercise caution when using these assessments to determine eligibility (34 C.F.R. §614 [b][3][A][i]).

Testing should be administered in the language the student feels most comfortable in and would likely demonstrate the most comprehensive picture academically and functionally. Comprehensive evaluations should include more than just formal testing. Multiple sources of information, including informal measures such as teacher input, structured observations, and a review of the educational history, should be used to guide the team to a decision about eligibility for special education (Klingner & Harry, 2006). Once again, IDEA reiterates that "lack of appropriate instruction in reading or math" cannot result in the determination of eligibility for special education under any disability category. The determination of **limited English proficiency** is also not part of the requirements under any of the IDEA disability categories (34 C.F.R. §614[b][5][C]).

Once a student is found eligible for special education, coordination of services between ELL and special education must be established. Parents have the right to use their **native language** to communicate and participate in decisions about their child's education. The provision of a free and appropriate public education in the least restrictive environment is established in IDEA and its supplemental regulations. The student's program should be grounded in the established best practices and include supports in the **home language** (Klingner & Harry, 2006). An IEP is developed incorporating specially designed instruction that uses a variety of teaching methods, materials, and strategies. This comprehensive program provides the student with the best chance of demonstrating academic, social, and functional success in school unless this is not feasible (34 C.F.R. §614[b][3][A][ii–v].)

Coordinating services while following all regulations is key to making sure that nothing prohibits the student from participation in **dual language learner** and special education programs as appropriate.

E. What kinds of data are needed for tracking and planning for preK–3 English language learners?

■ *Zoila Tazi*

Mandates established by the No Child Left Behind (NCLB) Act of 2001 and the national Race to the Top funding initiative publicize the academic performance of young children on standardized tests. While these public reports isolate the population of children who are learning English as a second language, identifying them as **English language learners** (ELLs), they do not distinguish differences in language proficiency or school experience that may clarify patterns of achievement for this group. Despite considerable differences in their languages, early preparation, immigration experience, socioeconomic influences, and other factors, ELLs are treated as a monolithic whole in accountability reports. Teachers, school leaders, and administrators, on the other hand, plan for the instruction of individual children and are challenged to organize data that effectively informs instruction.

One of the roles of school leaders is to develop the organizational systems that support teaching and learning. Streamlined collection and analysis of student data affects achievement by improving responsiveness to children's needs and suggesting areas for intervention. Effective planning and instruction for ELLs relies on a broad spectrum of information about children that necessarily begins with details about their home languages and particular experiences. This baseline information grounds the first decisions about placement, assessment, and services. Understanding the socioeconomic factors that potentially affect achievement safeguards the interests of ELLs in those first decisions.

The first opportunity to gather meaningful information is when children enter school. A national study on student mobility indicated that 40% of third graders had changed schools at least once since first grade (Rumberger & Larson, 1998). This figure may be even higher for ELLs (Fong, Bae, & Huang, 2010). Despite these troubling figures, it remains the case that most children spend all of their school years in one school community. This suggests that the majority of children register for school at the earliest grade level, such as kindergarten or pre-kindergarten. Gathering information about young ELLs when they register for school calls for research-based understanding of important conditions such as the following:

- *The language of documents and interactions.* One in seven babies in the United States lives with a parent who has limited English skills (Center for Law and Social Policy, 2012), fueling the increase in young ELLs entering school. If information gathering about these young children is to be meaningful at all, the registration process must include translated documents or interpretation services. Although providing these services may be a formidable challenge for many schools, particularly given the diversity of languages spoken in the United States, we need to make every effort to move toward best practices in this regard. In addition, registration is often the first contact with a family; effective communication early on is critical to engaging parents and families.
- *First screenings and assessments.* There is no validity in testing children in a language they do not understand. Given the paucity of multilingual screenings or assessment instruments for young children, many schools rely on translations or on partial administrations of English instruments. Although this may garner some information, great caution should be exercised in using the data generated from these administrations. It is inappropriate to make high-stakes decisions, such as classroom placement, based on inadequate data that can only reflect what young ELLs *cannot demonstrate*. Instead, results from first screenings and assessments should be weighed against observations over time in the child's classroom or used to gauge the need for deeper evaluation.
- *School readiness.* Young ELLs are among the children with the lowest preschool enrollment (Magnuson & Waldfogel, 2005). If a school defines "readiness" solely from an academic framework, young ELLs may appear deficient even when they are assessed appropriately in the **home language**. In some settings, this may prompt the suggestion to delay school entry, although there is research indicating that this is unwarranted (Ellwein, Walsh, Eads, & Miller, 1991). Those ELLs who do attend preschool likely receive instruction in English. This may mean that a child enters school with some knowledge of the English alphabet or of basic concepts in numeracy, which can be misinterpreted as adequate development of the English language. The personnel completing the registration process for young ELLs must be well trained in child development, first and second language acquisition, and emergent academic skills. This yields a more holistic portrait of school readiness, which is useful to the child's first teacher.

Beginning with the data collected at school entry and following the first assessment scores, school leaders can track progress for ELLs to satisfy accountability reporting and reveal effective approaches that should be sustained.

The response to intervention (RtI) framework is another mandate commonly used to outline the modality and frequency of intervention that monitors progress. Here, too, an administrator must understand the unique conditions that influence how young ELLs develop academic skills. For example, in the earliest grades, preK–3, the focus of instruction is on learning to read. Strict adherence to an RtI design meant for monolingual English-speaking children may create conditions that actually imperil progress for ELLs or bilingual children (Tazi, 2011). School leaders should consider the following:

- *Fluency skills.* Fluency in naming the letters of the alphabet or in decoding words is an important literacy skill. Fluency measures are common assessments in the early grades. However, fluency in English is precisely what ELLs *have not yet developed.* It is ludicrous to apply the same expectations of fluency for all children, yet this is how fluency measures are developed and applied. The research on literacy development indicates that vocabulary development is a prerequisite to school learning and the best predictor of achievement (Biemiller, 2006); it is also a primary focus in the education of young ELLs. In planning instruction for ELLs, school leaders should weigh the significance of fluency measures against the imperative to develop to avoid overestimating the importance of fluency measure scores. Accurately tracking vocabulary and language development is a better measure of progress for ELLs that holds more predictive validity for achievement. Likewise, a savvy administrator can be instrumental in using school data to develop local norms more appropriate for the community of students.
- *Procedural skills.* Focusing on procedural skills is a common default approach when children are struggling with instruction. This assumption often emanates from an intuitive sense that children need the "basics" before they can proceed, and it commonly occurs for ELLs. Relegated to a "skill and drill" experience, ELLs often remain disenfranchised academically and in the social context of the school. Such disenfranchisement can be seriously detrimental for achievement and it perpetuates gaps between groups (Neuman, 2006). Instruction for ELLs must be rich, integrated, and differentiated—as it must be for all children. School leaders need to counter the tendency to focus exclusively on procedural skills for ELLs by placing importance on a composite of measures that highlight vocabulary development, language development, and social development along with rudimentary skills.

Student data afford a wealth of information to inform and guide instruction. At the school level, data can form the rationale for introducing or discontinuing programs. School-wide patterns are also significant factors in accountability reports and analyses. For this reason, school leaders should zoom out of the everyday details and consider how the entire population of ELLs is performing. More than the usual accountability report of performance on one test, a careful analysis of achievement for the entire school population of ELLs draws from multiple sources such as registration documents, first screenings and assessments, classroom assessments, and feedback from teachers. Additionally, a careful analysis includes comparisons of performance in prior years in order to capture program improvements or increasing expertise. Guided by a sound understanding of the conditions impacting the achievement of ELLs, systematic data collection and analysis serves to identify the benchmarks children should reach early on to guarantee their success and the approaches most indicated to reach them.

RECOMMENDED RESOURCES

Menken, K. (2008). *English learners left behind: Standardized testing as language policy.* Cleveon, UK: Multilingual Matters.

Parker-Boudett, K., City, E., & Murnane, R. (Eds.). (2005). *Data wise: A step-by-step guide to using assessment results to improve teaching and learning.* Cambridge, MA: Harvard Education Press.

■ *Laura Ascenzi-Moreno*

In order for data about young bilingual students to be valid, assessments must be holistic. Young bilingual students learn language and learn about the world simultaneously. For this reason, it is crucial that how we assess students at this age—and the corresponding data that we collect—is *student centered*. Student-centered assessment and data have the potential to engage teachers in student-specific inquiry that provides information about students' language development as well as their learning across subject areas. Furthermore, inquiry-based data collection provides teachers with learning opportunities about their students, and thereby naturally feeds into rich integrated language and content planning for **emergent bilingual** students at this crucial age.

The best example of data collection practices that take into account the entirety of student learning was led by Patricia Carini (Carini & Himley, 2009). Carini and teachers at the now defunct Prospect School in Bennington, Vermont, developed a process called "descriptive review," which directed teachers to work collaboratively in order to deeply examine student work. Descriptive review techniques work particularly well for bilingual students because they respect the embeddedness of language within all learning experiences for preK–3 students.

The descriptive review process follows a specific format. As a first step, the presenting teacher formulates and presents a question about a student along with samples of student work to the collaborative group. For emergent bilingual students, this question can be focused on their language development. For example, the following questions would be worthy of consideration for a group studying an emergent bilingual student: "How can I use this student's social language to develop academic language during writing? How can I use the arts to support this student's language development?" As a second step, after the teacher presents the focus question and student work to the other teachers, the members of the group objectively describe the work in order to lay out all the dimensions of the student's work that may not be initially evident. During the final step, all members of the group offer recommendations to move the learning of this student forward. This process supports teachers in building student-specific knowledge and aids them in building general knowledge about emergent bilingual students.

One example of the potential of this work for bilingual students is described in detail in Ascenzi-Moreno et al. (2008). In this article, one teacher examines the language development of one bilingual student who is repeating grade 2. Through the descriptive review process, she begins to see the student as a learner who is deeply involved in meaning making from texts, but who struggles with letter–sound relationships. Through bringing her "case" to a group of teachers, she developed techniques that were attuned to this student's current literacy abilities in both English and Spanish (her languages). For example, she targeted the student's oral language and built on the stronger letter–sound relationships that this student had in her **home language**, Spanish.

Although descriptive review takes time and cannot be done with all students in a class or grade level, the descriptive review process allows a school community to develop a body of knowledge (data) about emergent bilingual students that nurtures creative and effective teaching practices for these students.

F. What do administrators need to know from national professional associations to guide best practices for serving preK–3 dual language learners in general and special education?

■ *Karen N. Nemeth*

Many of the national professional associations you belong to as the administrator of an early childhood education program have official position statements and suggested best practices for educating young **dual language learners** (DLLs). A scan of some of the key statements reveals that they are all quite similar and they make recommendations that work together. It is amazing to consider that the national organization for early childhood education, the association for English as a second language educators, and the organization for early childhood special education professionals all have positions that share common ground. This makes the job of the administrator much easier because you will not find yourself trying to navigate among conflicting viewpoints. The most likely reason for the cohesiveness of these positions is that they are all based on the best research has to offer, and recent research on the teaching and learning of DLLs in the early years paints a strong picture of what should be happening in early childhood programs.

Here are some key points from the national organizations and the web addresses for the source documents:

TESOL
Position Paper on Language and Literacy Development for Young English Language Learners (Ages 3–8) (www.tesol.org/docs/pdf/371.pdf?sfvrsn=2)
TESOL's position statement lists these key recommendations:
- Oral language and literacy development should be supported by the **native language**.
- Literacy learning in English should be an ongoing process that requires time and appropriate support.
- Instruction and materials should be culturally and developmentally appropriate.
- Literacy programs should be meaning-based and balanced.
- Assessment should be reliable, valid, and ongoing.
- Professional preparation and development regarding linguistic and cultural diversity should be continually provided for educators.

National Association for the Education of Young Children (NAEYC)
Responding to Linguistic and Cultural Diversity: Recommendations for Effective Early Childhood Education (www.naeyc.org/files/naeyc/file/positions/PSDIV98.PDF)
A highlight of this position statement says, "Because knowing more than one language is a cognitive asset, early education programs should encourage the development of children's **home language** while fostering the acquisition of English."

Council for Exceptional Children Division for Early Childhood (CEC-DEC)
Responsiveness to All Children, Families, and Professionals: Integrating Cultural and Linguistic Responsiveness into Policy and Practice (www.dec-sped.org/uploads/docs/about_dec/position _concept_papers/Position%20Statement_Cultural%20and%20Linguistic%20Diversity _updated_sept2010.pdf)

The CEC-DEC's position statement makes strong assertions about the role of home language and culture in planning and implementing services for young children in early childhood education.

> DEC strongly believes in the use of respectful, responsive, and evidence-based practices with children and families from culturally and linguistically diverse backgrounds. These practices are critical to assessment and intervention, including practices with young children who are dual language learners and those who speak various dialects of English. These practices ensure that children and families from culturally and linguistically diverse backgrounds have equal access to educational services and learning opportunities. Equally important is that access occurs without diversity being viewed from a deficit perspective. (p. 5)

Head Start
(http://eclkc.ohs.acf.hhs.gov/hslc/tta-system/ehsnrc/Early%20Head%20Start/design
-planning/program-planning/UsingtheMulticu.htm)
Head Start grants are tied to a program's compliance with many factors. Here is a summary of the requirements related to serving children who are DLLs/ELLs:

> The Improving Head Start for School Readiness Act, 2007 (the Head Start Act) plainly states that programs *must have a plan* to meet the needs of children and families with **limited English proficiency.** The Head Start Program Performance Standards (HSPPS) are clear that programs are expected to actively find ways to support and expand the home language of the child. Both of these documents stress the importance of programs striving to assist children's progress toward acquiring English. These standards further emphasize the importance of fully integrating parents into virtually every element of the Head Start experience, being respectful of their language and culture.

G. What do administrators need to know about commonly used preschool classroom assessments and measures of quality?

■ Karen N. Nemeth

Discussions about preK classrooms have slightly different focus points than those of K–3 classrooms. Perhaps this is because there is more variability in the way preschools can be run when they have not traditionally fallen under the purview of standard elementary school practice. Many attempts have been made to define a "high-quality preschool classroom" and then ascertain how well classrooms measure up. This has been a popular topic for researchers looking to connect the dots between preschool environmental factors and later school achievement findings. It is also important to states that are devoting millions of dollars to support high-quality preschool. Quality rating systems generally focus on four main categories:

1. Teacher preparation/qualification and ongoing professional development
2. Small class sizes, low teacher:child ratios
3. Family engagement and support
4. Overall learning environment (curriculum, physical environment, approach)

When an administrator is charged with evaluating the quality of a diverse preschool classroom, additional considerations are needed:

- Does the teacher have adequate knowledge about first and second language development in the preschool years and about effective, developmentally appropriate strategies to support first and second language development?
- Are the class sizes appropriate *and* supported by teachers who speak the languages of the children?
- Are families invited to participate and receive information in the language that is most comfortable to them? Do families of **dual language learners** (DLLs) participate at the same level as English-speaking parents?
- Is the overall learning environment good? *And* is it good for children who speak different languages?

It is important to keep in mind that teachers who are saying the right things and using the right materials may not be doing a good job of teaching all the students because of language differences. Just scoring the teacher's behavior is insufficient if you don't know how the DLLs in the classroom are being taught.

Because preschool-aged children are not yet reading, almost all of their learning happens through experiences supported by the adult's oral communication with them. One widely used preschool classroom quality assessment tool, ECERS-R, has 43 items, half of which specifically require that the teacher communicate with the child directly to achieve a high score. In that case, if the teacher is doing the communicating, she will get a high score even if none of the children in her classroom understand what she is saying. Another widely used assessment of quality that focuses on interactions, the CLASS, tracks teacher–child interactions. However, if the observer doesn't understand the language a teacher is using with a child, how can the observer be sure those interactions are of equal quality? And if the teacher scores well on the CLASS using only English, how much of her interactions really meet the needs of students who speak other languages?

A wonderful monolingual teacher in a well-equipped English-only classroom might get high scores for the quality of services provided—and those scores would be accurate for the English-speaking children. However, in that same room, **English learners** (ELs) who can't understand what she says are not getting the same benefits. If we really want to make changes for ELs, we have to change the way we look at quality in preschool. Quality is only as good as the individual experience of the particular child. When these circumstances arise, it may be up to the administrator to adapt how the classroom assessments are used. The official scores may not be as useful if the population in your group does not match the English-only focus of classroom quality assessments, but the items can still be used to make notes about what is observed in those classrooms. Instead of focusing too heavily on numerical scores, consider using the individual items as discussion points for self-improvement and feedback discussions with teachers.

Not all quality is equal. Making policy recommendations to improve the way we meet the needs of young DLLs depends on our ability to show real results about what will work for them. Assumptions based on English-only assessments in English-only classrooms do not reflect the true picture of diversity today. You can add to the file of notes you use to evaluate the effectiveness of each preschool classroom by recording the languages spoken by the children and adults in each class and tracking how much interactive and material support is provided for each language. Another strategy that is used with growing frequency is the process of tracking conversations. Teachers keep a list of the children in their room and note when they had a full-fledged, multi-turn conversation with each child as an individual—and in which language.

Researchers, funders, policymakers, employers, and supervisors need to understand more about the differential experiences of children who may be in the same classroom but are learning quite differently. If we really intend to reduce the achievement gap, we need to document the quality of experiences had by each child in each language. When multiple languages are present, an overall score for a classroom does not capture what you need to know to be sure that each and every child is receiving high-quality early childhood education that meets his or her needs. True quality has to be assessed with individual children in mind.

H. What do administrators need to know about commonly used K–3 classroom assessments and curriculum implementation measures?

■ *Kate Mahoney*

Commonly used K–3 classroom assessments are designed for children who *are* proficient in English. Not all such assessments are good for **English language learners** (ELLs), and careful attention should be given to the decision of whether the results of these assessments are appropriate to use with students who are *not* proficient in English. Each assessment (standardized or not) is designed for a purpose, for example, curriculum-based assessment: *The purpose of this observation is to assess oral–language proficiency within the context of a science lesson.* This type of assessment allows the teacher to use a checklist to observe the child in the context of a science lesson and focus on how the child uses his or her speaking skills. This is a good way to monitor the use and progress of academic language. Consider these six essential practices to foster better assessment environments for ELLs.

1. Choosing an assessment method should follow a process that includes purpose, use, method, and instrument (PUMI). It is important to understand the purpose, how the results will be used, what method is best, and what instrument makes the most sense. All this should be considered before administering an assessment. If administrators are requiring or recommending assessments to teachers, they should be aware of PUMI.
2. Make your assessments so *authentic* that the students don't even know they are being tested. Don't create assessments outside your instruction if you don't have to. Look at artifacts from your instruction (graphic organizers, checklists, 4-corners vocabulary) to use as assessments and to document student learning.
3. When *assessment and instruction are highly aligned*, the only way to discern the two is though documentation. Some methods of assessment may seem like instruction, and you may find yourself questioning which category a given method falls into. If you're asking this question, it's a good sign—it means the assessment looks like instruction. This indicates a strong alignment between instruction and assessment. It also indicates that the assessment method is authentic to classroom practice. Alignment and authenticity in assessment are signs of good practice.
4. *Accommodations made during instruction should also be made in assessment*, and vice versa. For example, if graphic organizers are used or language is simplified during accomodation, these scaffolds should also be present in assessment. When an ELL educator differ-

entiates instruction, then the assessment needs to be differentiated in exactly the same way. Conversely, if bilingual glossaries are used in a large-scale assessment as a state-approved accommodation, then they should also be used in instruction. This type of alignment helps students show what they really know on the assessments.

5. *The assessment method needs to be selected based on target content or language objective.* Carefully consider what your target content and language objectives are and match the appropriate assessment to them. Multiple choice as an assessment method is better for measuring skills than for measuring reasoning. Assessment methods from the essay, performance assessment, or personal communication categories are better for testing reasoning.

6. If language is the target, then methods of assessment should be selected that can show a measurement of language *over time* that is *in context* (that is, a real-world context or at least a real-classroom context). Language assessment should avoid measuring language at a single point in time with decisions stemming from that one point. Psychometric language measurement methods, such as standardized language proficiency, have a tendency toward doing the opposite (measuring language out of context and at one point in time). Good language assessment is aligned with sociocultural methods. For example, measure language through teacher observation of two students having a conversation. Use an oral language rubric (aligned with your state standards) to document the results.

I. How can student achievement data be used to evaluate and support teacher improvement?

■ *Lisa M. López*

Student achievement is an important indicator providing data on student and teacher growth throughout the school year. First it is crucial to obtain a baseline, an understanding of where the child is with regard to learning, development, and achievement at the start of the program. This helps the teacher and program staff to determine whether the child is growing and learning as his or her progress is monitored. Growth in student achievement lets the teacher know that what she is doing is working for that individual student. Growth also indicates that the student, with proper instruction, can learn and achieve.

When growth is not observed, it can be for one of two reasons: the lessons are not meeting the needs of the student, or the student needs additional accommodations. If a lesson is too easy or too difficult for a child, they may tune out and therefore not increase their achievement. Lessons that are too easy may result in a child becoming bored, and bored children often misbehave. This also means that any new information they could have learned is ignored as well. If a lesson is too difficult, the child may become frustrated. This may be common with **dual language learners** (DLLs), depending on their level of English language fluency. If they do not understand what is being said or do not understand the instructions for completing an assignment, they may get frustrated. This may lead to acting out.

In order to understand the needs of a child who does not speak English as a first language, it is essential first to evaluate that child's home language achievement. This provides some information on what the child already knows. The child's pre-exisiting knowledge can be a foundation on which to build new knowledge: use what the child already knows in the **home language** to teach new information and skills in English.

Measuring growth in DLLs can also indicate whether the strategies being used by the teacher are good ones for communicating with this student. It should be expected that, at first, DLLs will advance more quickly in English than their English-speaking peers because they start at a lower level. However, that rate plateaus once they have developed some English fluency. Continuing to assess the child in the home language, in addition to English, allows the teacher and administrator to determine whether the child is acquiring information in the home language (especially if English is developing slowly) and helps in determining whether the child is experiencing expected development. Additionally, growth in Spanish can indicate cross-language transfer of knowledge acquired in English to Spanish, a good cognitive indicator that students understand the underlying concept. Research has shown that Spanish-speaking DLL children in the United States often use cross-language transfer to help in acquiring English skills (Lopez & Greenfield, 2004). Once English fluency has begun to develop, they often use reverse transfer—they transfer their English skills back to Spanish in order to continue developing Spanish language skills (Lopez, 2012).

■ *Wayne E. Wright**

Value-added measures (VAM) claim to be able to measure students' academic growth over time. While statistically complex, essentially VAM is calculated by subtracting student test scores at the beginning of the school year from their scores at the end. The difference is purportedly a measure of the *value added* to student achievement. The great temptation is to use VAM to evaluate individual teachers based on the idea that the most effective teachers add the most value to a student's growth over time. While the idea sounds great, it is actually full of flaws and opens the way for unfair, abusive evaluations of teachers—especially teachers of young **English language learners** (ELLs). Already VAM data have been used to publicly praise and shame public school teachers by publishing rankings of teachers from "best" to "worst" on websites and newspapers—a practice denounced by testing and evaluation experts as inaccurate and unfair. Nonetheless, emphasis on VAM continues.

What are the problems with VAM? First, VAM scores are far too inaccurate to make reasonable judgments about teacher effectiveness. A teacher found to be highly effective one year may be found highly ineffective the next year, and vice versa. Second, because VAM scores grade teachers on a bell curve, no matter how good all the teachers are, half will always be below average! Third, VAM assumes that the only measure of a good teacher is her ability to raise student test scores. Sparking children's curiosity and imagination, helping them develop a love of reading, developing their creativity, building their self-esteem, helping them see themselves as lifelong learners, preparing them to be good citizens, and so on are all part of the magic of teaching that can never be measured by a standardized test. Fourth, VAM assumes that test scores are valid for ELLs, even though we still don't know how to test ELLs in a valid and reliable manner.

Another big problem is that VAM is based on the assumption that all student learning across the year can be attributed to a single teacher. But ELL students are often taught through the collaborative efforts of classroom teachers, ESL and bilingual specialists, librarians, and subject-matter specialists. ELLs also learn from their families, peers, community

---

*Shortened and adapted from Wright, W. E. (2012). *Beware of the VAM: Value-added measure for teacher accountability*. Courtesy of the Colorín Colorado website: www.colorincolorado.org/article/50576/

members, and through TV and the internet. VAM also falsely assumes that students are randomly assigned to classrooms. Without random assignment, there is no basis for accurate judgment of teachers against one another. VAM can't account for the fact that young ELLs are often placed in specialized language programs.

VAM also makes the false assumption that teachers have full control over the curriculum. Yet how many teachers are forced to use curricular programs or instructional methods against their will? Many teachers are forced to provide English-only instruction for their young ELLs because of state or district restrictions on bilingual education.

Finally, VAM falsely assumes that previous and current year tests are essentially equivalent in terms of content and level of difficulty. In several states ELLs may be tested in their **native language** one year and in English the next. VAM cannot account for ELLs who do well on native language tests but struggle a bit the first time they take the tests in English.

Given these flaws, VAM results should never be used as the sole measure of teacher effectiveness. The most effective way to evaluate teachers of young ELLs is to simply walk through their classroom doors and watch them teach! Use of observational protocols such as **SIOP** (sheltered instruction observation protocol) can help administrators quickly determine a teacher's effectiveness in employing effective instructional strategies for ELLs.

RECOMMENDED RESOURCES

Baker, E. L., Barton, P. E., Darling-Hammond, L., et al. (2010). Problems with the use of test scores to evaluate teachers. Washington, DC: Economic Policy Institute. Retrieved from: http://www.epi.org/files/page/-/pdf/bp278.pdf

Bracey, G. W. (n.d.). What's the value of growth measures? Retrieved from FairTest website: http://fairtest.org/whats-value-growth-measures

Echevarria, J., Vogt, M., & Short, D. (2014). *Making content comprehensible for elementary English learners: The SIOP model* (2nd ed.). Boston: Pearson.

Wright, W. E. (2010). *Foundations for teaching English language learners: Research, theory, policy, and practice.* Philadelphia: Caslon.

J. What are the best assessments for content learning and core content standards for students who are not proficient in English?

■ *Kate Mahoney*

Measuring Content

The best assessments for content learning are those that allow teachers to measure content without too much language interference, such as assessment using a simplified version of written or oral language, performance methods, or personal communication.

All content assessments depend on language and there is no way to avoid this, so all assessments of content learning must consider the particular language needs of each **English language learner** (ELL). The majority of assessments—no matter what the subject area—depend on language, at least for their administration and for student-provided responses. For example, when an ELL educator gives directions for a content-area assessment, the directions are typically administered orally or distributed in writing and therefore depend on language, which usually is English only. Students more than likely must read the item to discern what the answer is and sometimes write an extended answer—even in a test of mathematics. With this in mind, the most significant challenge is to use assessments that are sensitive to the language needs of ELLs. It's also critical to modify the language demands of the content-area learning and assessment—not the content itself. In other words, ELLs are entitled to the same rigor of content as non-ELLs, but with reduced language demands. By reducing the language demands of content-area assessment, you increase the chances for ELLs to reveal their strengths in content areas. Content-area assessment with too much language interference can cover up or disguise content-area strengths.

Across all grades, a major challenge in content-area assessment for ELLs is making administrators aware that language interference is almost always a partial cause of low test scores. The use of English-administered tests to make high-stakes decisions about ELLs is inappropriate and not good assessment practice. Researchers have attempted to articulate the dual nature of testing—how much of a test score is a product of language and how much is a product of content—and there is evidence in the form of reliability coefficients to support this statement.

Construct-Irrelevant Variance Warning

Content, like math or science, is the construct we want to measure—it is "relevant." Language is the irrelevant construct; it gets in the way of a true measure of content. ELL educators may not label this issue construct-irrelevant variance (CIV), but they're aware of the problems caused by it—even if others in the school setting are not. CIV is a major validity threat. If it becomes too invasive, the assessment results should not be used for any meaningful purpose and the actual assessment practice should be abandoned. All too often, CIV introduces more harm than benefit.

The essential warning for administrators is this: If the assessment method relies too much on language, and the student has not developed that language, the results may largely underestimate the content target. In this circumstance, the results should not be used in the way they are used for proficient English speakers. Social consequences of using invalid assessment results may include a lower self-esteem, a declining attitude and motivation toward school, an underestimation of teacher effectiveness, and inappropriate program changes.

K. What is portfolio assessment and why is it important for preK programs or grades K–3?

■ *Diep Nguyen*

Portfolio assessment provides a valid way of collecting information on students' growth and achievement from multiple sources over time (Gottlieb, 2006). In the early 1990s it was popularized by educators concerned with authentic assessment. Portfolio assessment was used in many content subjects by teachers who embraced performance-based evaluation and integrated teaching.

A pivotal portfolio is an organized, systematic collection of evidence of student work based on common assessments that provide authentic evidence of students' learning and achievement over a period of time (Gottlieb & Nguyen, 2007). The pivotal portfolio is a hybrid of the working and showcase portfolios with two main distinctions: (1) teachers collect data and artifacts to include in the pivotal portfolio that are based on essential common assessments used by all teachers in the language education program; and (2) the pivotal portfolio follows the student for the length of his or her career in the program. Many teachers choose to keep a working portfolio and a pivotal portfolio for each student.

Portfolio assessment is useful for teachers of younger **English language learners** (ELLs) for many reasons:

- At the early childhood education level, formative assessment is critical to monitor and guide the language, academic, and socioemotional growth of students. Because these are the early formative years of schooling, frequent informal assessment of students is most effective. Portfolio assessment allows teachers to focus on collecting and documenting individual student growth in key areas of learning: language, academic, physical, and socioemotional.

- Portfolio assessment provides an organized framework that ties instruction directly to assessment. This tight alignment helps teachers make timely instructional decisions and adjustments more effectively for young learners.

- Portfolio assessment is based on the collection of evidence of learning based on students' work. At the early childhood level, these artifacts provide information about a student's current learning level but also provide a *portrait of the child as a second language/bilingual learner* over time. This "learner's portrait" provides invaluable insights for teachers in making daily instructional decisions as well as long-range plans for their young ELLs.

- Because it is based on common assessments created or selected by teachers, the pivotal portfolio provides an opportunity for them to collaborate on essential learning targets to assess, monitor, and decide together what is most important to collect from students as essential learning evidence.

- Teachers can use portfolio information to plan instruction for individual students as well as groups of students. The pivotal portfolio allows teachers to compare individual students to peer groups and to compare subgroups of students sharing similar learning needs. This comparative analysis yields authentic and useful information for program improvement. Over time, the portfolio can serve as a historical record of student achievement used for program evaluation.

Portfolio assessment, especially the use of the pivotal portfolio, provides teachers of young ELLs with the opportunity to collaborate in implementing an authentic and comprehensive assessment system for their students that reflects both growth and achievement in all key learning areas over time.

L. How can data on student performance and classroom quality be used to plan professional development and staffing adaptations?

■ *Lisa M. López*

Professional development and staffing should be based on reflective practice regarding the needs of the children and families being serviced by the educational program. It is important to evaluate these needs—via parent interviews, home visits, student achievement scores, and classroom observations—on a yearly basis.

Home visits allow the teachers and staff to obtain a better understanding of the home environment of the children. This information can inform the types of resources one can expect from families as well as what type of resources should be sent home to enhance the child's learning. For example, if children do not have many children's books at home, programs can be developed where families check out books or the teacher sends books home with children. Additionally, parent interviews help program teachers understand what languages are spoken at home and obtain a glimpse at what the child's likes and dislikes are in order to better engage the child in learning.

Student achievement data also help teachers to understand the child's level of fluency and ability in each of his or her languages in determining where to begin instruction. Professional development might be necessary to teach educators how to use student data to inform instruction. Teachers may not know what key information to look at or how to interpret achievement data, especially if they are available in two languages. Helping teachers answer questions such as, "What do I do if the child has mastered the skill in his **home language** but not in English?" and "How do I introduce English to a child who only speaks another language?" is an important part of professional development.

Classroom observations can also be used as professional development tools. Sharing results from classroom observations with teachers can help them see what they are doing well and what needs improvement. Professional development can also be centered on the areas in need of improvement if several teachers could use help in the same area. There are numerous classroom observation measures available that measure different aspects of classroom quality (e.g., CLASS, ELLCO, ECERS, LISn). It is important to focus on several observations (not a single one) to obtain a more complete view of the classroom.

Staffing adaptations may be necessary depending on the number of children in a classroom who speak a language other than English. If a staff member speaks the language of the children, it is important for that staff member to be assigned to the classroom in which these children are enrolled. Providing some instructional support in the child's home language has been found to be beneficial in the academic development of the **dual language learner** child (Brisk, 1998). Classroom adaptations can include several different models. Some examples include (1) a dual language approach in which one teacher speaks English and the second teacher speaks the home language; (2) English with some individualized language support, where English is the **primary language** spoken in the classroom but some individual support is provided to children who may not understand what is occurring; and (3) dedicated time for the home language during which one of the teachers provides small group instruction for the children in their home language to supplement the ongoing instruction. When deciding among these and other models, it is important to understand the capabilities of the staff members involved with regard to both English instruction and home language instruction. Although a staff member may speak a language, they may not be sufficiently fluent or capable to provide instructional support in that language. Therefore, although research has found the dual language model to be most effective, it is not always a feasible option and depends on the availability of resources and staff.

■ *Margarita Calderón**

Student Performance Data Correlates with Instructional Quality

A five-year study was conducted to determine the best ways to implement and measure teacher and student development programs. The study followed a *professional development → teacher knowledge → instruction → student achievement loop*. The loop studied growth

* The ExC-ELL project was funded by the Carnegie Corporation of New York.

trajectories for individual teachers and their students' outcomes. The data consisted of observation protocols by administrators and coaches, the teachers' own reflection data, and the researchers' recorded observations. Student data consisted of students' pre–post scores on the Gates MacGinitie tests of vocabulary and reading comprehension, and results from the state's language proficiency and language arts exams. There were large gains made by students in the schools that implemented the evidence-based instructional features, professional development, and observation protocol/tools with fidelity.

What Are the Processes and Tools?

The process for effecting transfer from training consisted of a five-day institute on teaching academic language, reading, and writing in all the content areas. The follow-up consisted of experts coaching teachers in their classrooms and teachers working in their teacher learning communities (TLCs) to make sense of their data. All site coaches and administrators were required to attend the institute, plus an additional day on how to use the observation protocol by shadowing the trainers during observations.

The ExC-ELL Observation Protocol (EOP) was the key tool for supporting teachers. The EOP is a combination of a checklist and spaces for notes on teacher delivery and student use of new vocabulary/oracy, reading, writing, classroom management, and cooperative learning skills. The teachers, coaches, and administrators found the EOP useful in the following ways:

- Teachers used it as a template for planning content lessons that integrated language, literacy, and content.
- Teachers used it to record the English language learners' (ELLs') and other students' performances and track their progress.
- Literacy coaches not familiar with ELL instruction used it when they needed to coach teachers with ELLs.
- Supervisors and administrators used it for identifying quality instruction, rewarding teachers, or making staffing adaptations.
- Teachers used it to reflect on their instruction delivery and how that correlated with the students observed during that class period.
- Teachers used it during their TLCs, observing and coaching each other with the EOP to reaffirm effective practices, sustain motivation, and plan professional development.

There's an app for that! The paper EOP protocol has been adapted as an app— *iExC-ELL Coach*—for the iPad, iPhone, or laptop. A small camera can be attached to follow the microphone a teacher wears. This facilitates keeping track of progress of the students throughout the year and if the teaching is reaching them. The teacher sends us the video and we send back feedback using the EOP. This system provides immediate reports on any aspect of the instruction and gives feedback to the teacher. Notwithstanding, the simple paper and pencil version continues to be used and teachers benefit from that version.

A key principle of success was the frequent assessment of learning to give students and their teachers instant feedback on their progress toward English language development, reading comprehension skills, and course objectives. These formative measures of progress toward success on state assessments give school leaders early real-time information on whether or not the school is moving toward its accountability targets. Teachers meet in their TLCs to discuss their own and their students' learning progressions. Teachers, coaches, and administrators then determine the next professional development steps.

Teacher quality correlates with student performance when teachers are empowered to reflect on their practice; when they are provided with comprehensive training on integrating language, literacy, and content; and when they are given the time and the right tools to work on their own performance assessments.

RECOMMENDED RESOURCES

Calderón, M. E. (2007). *Teaching reading to English language learners, grades 6–12: A framework for improving achievement in the content areas.* Thousand Oaks, CA: Corwin.

Calderón, M. E., Slavin, R. E., & Sánchez, M. (2011). Effective instruction for English Language Learners. In M. Tienda & R. Haskins (Eds.), *The future of immigrant children* (pp. 103–128). Washington, DC: Brookings Institute/Princeton University.

M. How should we evaluate and support teacher assistants effectively?

■ *Karen N. Nemeth*

Many preschool programs, and some kindergartens, are addressing the increasing presence of **dual language learners** (DLLs) in their classrooms by hiring bilingual paraprofessionals. Although this may be a useful first step, we find that few programs have plans, policies, or procedures in place to train, supervise, or evaluate the work of these important assets to the educational experience of young DLLs.

Consider what you expect from bilingual paraprofessionals:

- What do you expect them to do with their first and their second language?
- When and how should they use each language?
- What do the classroom teachers understand about their collaborative role in working with bilingual assistants?
- What will you look for when observing their work?
- Do you expect them to provide supports beyond the work of the particular classroom to which they were assigned?

Your answers to questions like these will help you plan appropriate orientation and ongoing professional development for bilingual assistants. They will also help to guide you as you observe their work and provide them with feedback and support. It is important to keep your expectations in check. If a bilingual staff member is asked to help with too many other tasks, such as interpreting or translating documents, he may not be able to meet your expectations for his original placement.

Professional development materials may be available in the non-English language spoken by the bilingual staff. This is a good place to start. Certainly, if someone is hired because they bring the asset of an additional language, then it would be a good idea to support their high-quality use of that language by giving them articles, webinars, books, and curriculum materials to support their professional learning. Studying professional materials or engaging in professional learning communities in their language will not hurt the staff member's ability to use English, but if you have concerns about their English you should provide supports for that as well.

Contact your curriculum provider for guidance and any resources they may have to help you ensure your bilingual staff members are implementing the curriculum appropriately. If an assistant is the only person in the building who speaks a certain language, consider helping her connect with others who speak that language to share ideas and resources even if they are in another building or another town.

As you take the time to formalize the expectations you have for bilingual paraprofessionals in your early childhood classrooms, it is a good idea to write them down and create an orientation manual that will help to prevent misunderstandings or inappropriate teaching practices in the future. This type of handbook can be informative for the assistants as well as for the staff who work with them.

Resources and Questions

RESOURCE CONNECTIONS

Bridging Refugee Youth and Children's Services (BRYCS)
www.BRYCS.org

Center for Applied Linguistics (CAL)
www.CAL.org

Center for Early Childhood Education Research-Dual Language Learners (CECER-DLL)
http://cecerdll.fpg.unc.edu

Colorín Colorado—the bilingual literacy site
www. Colorincolorado.org

Council for Exceptional Children Division for Early Childhood (DEC)
www.dec-sped.org

Education Week's Learning the Language blog
http://blogs.edweek.org/edweek/learning-the-language/

The Foundation for Child Development (FCD)
http://fcd-us.org

National Association for Bilingual Education (NABE)
www.nabe.org

National Association for The Education of Young Children (NAEYC)
www.naeyc.org

National Center for Cultural and Linguistic Responsiveness (NCCLR)
http://eclkc.ohs.acf.hhs.gov/hslc/tta-system/cultural-linguistic

National Center for English Language Acquisition and Language Instruction Educational Programs (NCELA)
www.ncela.gwu.edu

National Network for Early Language Learning (NNELL—an affiliate of ACTFL)
www.nnell.org

TESOL (the international association for teachers of English to speakers of other languages)
www.tesol.org

U.S. Department of Education Office of English Language Acquisition (OELA)
http://www2.ed.gov/about/offices/list/oela/index.html

What Works Clearinghouse (WWC)
http://www.whatworks.ed.gov/

ASSESSMENT COMPARISON CHART

	Assessment Goals	Assessment Methods Available	Languages Available/Addressed	Gaps/Unmet Goals
1				
2				
3				
4				

QUESTIONS FOR REFLECTION

- What is your usual strategy for keeping up with the various government requirements that affect your program? How might you improve your strategy?

- Which area of policy is the least familiar to you as you are planning to build your program's services for young DLLs? What can you do to learn more?

- How are you currently measuring the effectiveness of your early childhood education program?

- How do you currently address any mismatch between your assessment methods and the teacher/student languages in your program?

- What are your top priorities for improving your program assessments in the context of the language diversity existing in your school?

CHAPTER **6**

Working Effectively with Families, the Community, and Volunteers

Key Considerations for Language Plan

- Our language plan will outline policies and procedures for working effectively with families of young **dual language learners** (DLLs).

- Our language plan will describe expectations of family involvement in the educational process.

- Our language plan will contain recommended steps for dealing with conflict involving language and/or cultural issues.

- Our language plan will set staff expectations to improve their awareness of cultural differences and set forth goals for including all of the cultures of the school community.

Principals, supervisors, and directors of successful early childhood education programs for diverse populations credit the involvement of families, volunteers, and community members with strengthening their programs. This chapter offers helpful suggestions for working successfully with people who are not school staff or employees to create an effective and supportive educational environment for the school's children and families.

Strategies for inviting and engaging family members are presented and policies for managing and orienting these important members of the school community are discussed. Contributors also provide ideas for finding appropriate community partners and communicating effectively with the community about the advantages and challenges that come with a diverse student population.

Leadership in early childhood education goes beyond managing the day-to-day tasks of immediate employees. It extends to the importance of creating a vision and giving everyone the means to follow it. Leaders also encounter difficult situations with staff, families, and children because of language and cultural differences. Contributors offer supports and techniques to help leaders cope and lead confidently in a diverse environment. The chapter concludes with an advocacy planning tool to gather information to support advocacy efforts. After reading this chapter, readers will have the information needed to plan for the enhanced connections among families, staff, and the community that will take their program to the next level of success.

A. What do administrators need to know about paid/volunteer interpreters or using family as interpreters?

■ *Diep Nguyen*

Interpreters play an important role in helping school districts provide adequate services for **English language learners** (ELLs) and their families. Some school districts contract with professional interpreting agencies as needed, but this service tends to be costly. More often, school districts use their own teachers and resource personnel to help interpret for families.

A distinction should be made between translating services and interpreting services. In both cases, it is important that the message is translated accurately, using the language register that is most appropriate and accessible to the ELLs' families and the community.

There are four main ways a school can utilize interpreter resources:

1. When legal matters are involved, it is best to pay for professionally trained interpreters and translators. Because they are professionals, their skill levels are high and they are able to interpret using specialized educational and legal language as necessary. However, sometimes cost can be prohibitive.

2. It is a common practice for school districts working with bilingual teachers and support staff to assign interpretation duties, as needed. It is advisable to (a) select specific staff based on each person's bilingual proficiency and familiarity with educational terms; (b) provide incentive for these persons to serve as interpreters; and (c) provide training to help these personnel sharpen their translation and interpreting skills.

3. Occasionally, with low-incidence languages, schools may be unable to find professional or staff interpreters. In these cases, it is acceptable to seek out volunteer interpreters from the local community social network and family members, if dealing with noncontroversial routine meetings. When using family members or community volunteers as interpreters, it is important to clarify their role in the meeting and ask that they restrict their role to being the language mediator. Sometimes, when volunteer interpreters take on the role of advocate and advisor for the parents, the result can be misunderstanding and confusion for both the school staff and the parents.

4. Interpreters are not only language resources; they also are cultural mediators between school staff and families as they fulfill their complex role as interpreters (Angelelli, 2004). Their knowledge of the ELL communities can provide insights for administrators and teachers as we seek to communicate and collaborate better with families. School districts should routinely interview, select, and train a group of interpreters who can speak the languages of the students in the school district. Having a district-wide list of persons who are trained on a yearly basis to serve as interpreters is an effective strategy to help principals meet the needs of their local communities as the student population becomes more diverse.

B. What are best practices for enrolling and welcoming diverse families?

■ Sandee McHugh-McBride

First impressions can be lasting and can have a significant impact on the comfort level of diverse families. Effective practices for enrolling diverse families in schools must be set into place in order to receive support, participation, and cooperation from them. It is important to remember that other cultures may have different expectations of the role that families play in the education of their children. In some cultures, it is respectful of the families to leave all aspects of education up to the school staff. It may be considered rude for families to request explanations of a teacher's decisions, techniques, or methods, and equally disrespectful for teachers to make suggestions about the families' childrearing methods.

Dealing with families in a welcoming, friendly manner will make them feel comfortable about attending school events. This starts with the first faces that families encounter when entering the school building. A smiling face and a welcoming office atmosphere can make a great deal of difference. This positive atmosphere creates comfortable situations resulting in positive family responses, such as helping with classroom activities, cooperating with rules and procedures, and assisting students with homework and other assignments. In these ways families motivate their young family members and aid their overall adjustment to a new school, culture, community, and language.

Calendars, schedules, and other important documents can be made available in more than one language, which demonstrates an acceptance and value of languages in general. This expression and support of more than one language shows that the school community places a value on diversity and has a respect for various cultures. Respect for **native languages** is demonstrated through an interest in the language and culture of the families, not by requesting they stop speaking their native language at home.

C. How can we get diverse families involved in their children's education and engaged in the school community?

■ Judie Haynes

When parents or guardians bring a child into your school who does not speak English, they should be greeted by informed school secretaries or intake personnel. This may be the family's first experience with a school in the United States. Constructive communication sets the tone for future interactions between the school and families whose **dominant language** is not English.

School personnel and teachers should learn a few words in the languages of the students. This is not difficult to do when there are language resources online in hundreds of languages. If you can't find information about the language of a new student arrival, ask the parents or students to teach you a few words. One principal recorded words of greeting in various languages on her cell phone so that she could refer to them when greeting the parents of her **English language learners** (ELLs).

Many schools have translated notices and interpreters or students who speak the **majority languages** of ELLs. Efforts should be made to provide these services to families of all the languages spoken in the school. Teachers and administrators cannot build relationships with parents if there is no translated information available (Zacarian & Haynes, 2012b).

Getting parents involved in school activities can be a way to engage them in their child's education. School teachers and administrators should encourage parents to come into the school on a regular basis. Involve families in school projects that include their children. Parents can share information with their child's class about their native country. ELLs feel very proud when they see their parents working around the school or their mother comes in to talk to the class about their country. Encourage parents to volunteer to work in the school office or library, in after-school programs, and as chaperones for field trips. Schools need to encourage parents to share their concerns, ideas, questions, and expectations. Communication needs to be a two-way street, not a one-way message from the school to the parents.

One of the most pressing mandates of schools is to develop respect for the cultures in the school. This respect needs to be shared by administrators, school secretaries, custodians, cafeteria workers, instructional aides, and teaching staff. In order to cope with the challenges they face, ELLs need a good relationship with the classroom teacher and classmates (Haynes, 2007). Families pick up on insensitive or negative attitudes very quickly. The more comfortable new learners of English feel in their classrooms and in their schools, the quicker they learn. Conversely, the more anxiety students experience, the less language they will comprehend. Teachers and other school personnel need to focus on the positive. School personnel should learn about the cultures of the students in their school, and imparting this information should be part of a professional development program.

Teachers need to give ELLs lots of encouragement and praise for what they *can* do. Don't dwell on all that they can't yet do. Create frequent opportunities for ELLs' success in your school and in your classrooms.

■ Sandee McHugh-McBride

There are several ideas that schools can use to get diverse families more involved in their children's education. Sending home monthly newsletters keeping parents informed of school and community events, programs, open houses, conferences, concerts, and celebrations is helpful. Schools may include an orientation meeting at the beginning of the year, which can be held for a brief part of "Back to School" night, getting the families to attend both events. Making telephone calls or writing home notes will keep families informed of their children's progress. Diverse families are included and encouraged to attend all activities, including field trips, school plays, concerts, after-school programs, and so forth. They should not be left out because they cannot speak English fluently.

Schools can engage families in the curriculum by asking for their contributions to international festivals, storytelling, poetry readings, plays, musical concerts, artwork, as well as sharing their special skills, talents, and cultural traditions. Some activities teachers have successfully used in the classroom include inviting family members into the classroom to share a hobby, interest, or career with the class. This builds a sense of belonging in both the families and the students. For example, one father came to school to show how he made his famous empanadas. An uncle played his guitar and sang native songs as well as American songs in class. Another older sibling arrived in his military uniform and spoke about his travels. One child represented her family by demonstrating how her grandmother taught her to crochet. These types of experiences help build confidence and motivation in the students. School becomes a happy, comfortable place that they look forward to attending.

Another approach to successful family involvement includes having meetings and workshops to teach families various educational games, the value of reading stories aloud (in any language), using puppets to practice language skills, instructing computer skills, and so on. One idea is for teachers to demonstrate reading aloud to the students in the classroom, using questioning techniques that require higher-level thinking skills, such as predicting and making inferences. Families can better grasp these methods by actually watching teachers demonstrate this during a workshop. Teachers can explain the reason behind the techniques so that the families understand the purpose and value of them. Families should be given the opportunity to ask questions. As a result, they are better equipped, and thus more confident, in participating in their children's education at home and within the school community.

RECOMMENDED RESOURCE

U.S. Department of Education Office of Communications and Outreach. (2005). *Helping your child with homework*. Washington, DC: Author.

D. How do we partner with families to access their funds of knowledge?

■ Leslie Sevey

Administrators and teachers serving students and families often wonder how they can connect with them to take greater advantage of the unique assets and resources they possess.

When answering this question, it's helpful to connect to the concept of funds of knowledge. Using this concept, early childhood educators of **English language learners** (ELLs) begin with the belief that families' "accumulated bodies of knowledge and skills essential for household functioning and well-being" can be utilized by teachers to "develop curricula and teaching techniques that have roots in the experience of the students and of the community" (González, 1995, p. 3). By utilizing the funds of knowledge model, programs and schools can build on children's cultural knowledge and strengths, thus ensuring positive self-images for language-minority children and the development of meaningful and relevant curriculum (Cummins, 1994).

Teachers and schools can engage with families and create opportunities for dialogue by using a home visiting approach. If visits to the home are challenging for the teacher or concerning for the family, visits can take place in more neutral spaces, such as parks, community centers, or local eateries. Unlike a traditional model of home visiting, where the purpose is often to teach, the emphasis in this approach is on forming relationships of mutual trust whereby families are invited to "tell their stories." The stories can often begin with an invitation to answer questions such as, "Where have you been?" and "How did you get to where you are?" (González, 1995, p. 6). These stories can become opportunities for the children and families to engage in literacy experiences. One such example is the early authors program, where "children, parents, and educators author books together in both English and the **home languages** of the children. The books are based on family histories, the children's lives, and the children's interests. Family photographs and children's drawings are used to illustrate the books" (Weiss, Caspe, & Lopez, 2006).

Not only are the stories important in identifying the funds of knowledge, but the process of collecting them is also important in establishing reciprocal relationships with families. Other opportunities can be found to reflect on the meaning of the collected information. Teachers might form study groups to reflect on and analyze the potential funds that the families offer as a way to develop meaningful curriculum for ELLs. These study groups can be an important resource and support to the teachers as they work together to identify the possibilities for responsive curriculum development.

Topics of study evolving out of the funds of knowledge from the families and students provide opportunities for students to engage in curricula "with familiar contextual cues" (Gonzalez, 1995, p. 6). When families possess knowledge about topics that the students are familiar with, such as plant cultivation, carpentry, banking, law, or archeology (depending on the life experience of the parents in question), the curricula can be enhanced to engage the students in meaning-based experiences that provide opportunities for communication and critical-thinking skills. In addition to enhancing the curricula, teachers, students, and families can try on new roles in which parents and students become teachers and teachers become learners. This new dynamic allows for all participants to contribute to the process of educating young children and each member is valued for his or her contributions.

RECOMMENDED RESOURCE

Moll, L., González, N., & Amanti, C. (Eds.). (2005). *Funds of knowledge: Theorizing practice in households, communities, and classrooms.* Mahwah, NJ: Lawrence Erlbaum.

E. How do we connect with community resources to enhance the effectiveness of our program?

■ *Leslie Sevey and Nancy Cloud*

Early childhood educators are well aware of the importance of establishing strong partnerships with families to enhance their educational efforts with children. Because of this, the National Association for the Education of Young Children (NAEYC) established the Engaging Diverse Families Project to learn of exemplary practices and programs that effectively reach families from diverse cultural and linguistic communities. Of the six principles they have established for family engagement practices, two pertain to utilizing community resources to enhance the effectiveness of programs:

- *Principle 3: Effective programs and teachers engage families in ways that are truly reciprocal.* This means that programs invite families to share their unique knowledge and skills as critical assets to the life of the school. Following this principle, we would seek information about students' lives, families, and communities so that it can be integrated into curriculum and teaching practices. Bi-directionality in the flow of information is key.
- *Principle 4: Programs provide learning activities for the home and in the community.* Programs use learning activities that take place naturally in the home and community to enhance each child's learning.

But how can we learn about these natural learning activities? Learning about community resources can be done through a process called "community mapping" (Ordoñez-Jasis & Myck-Wayne, 2012). This is an inquiry-based method that unearths sociocultural assets and natural resources present in each community. Through systematic analysis using field notes; interviews; and photos or videos of educational spaces, places, or settings in the community, educators identify community-based learning opportunities. Some barriers to this analysis include the time that community mapping takes, the documentation skills (such as for taking field notes) needed, and gaining permission to film certain locations. But with a little advance planning, time, and preparation, it is certainly feasible and very worthwhile.

What kinds of learning spaces may exist in communities? When families are recent arrivals to the United States, they may interact with resettlement agencies on a regular basis. Often these centers are gathering spaces where parents and children attend activities, use their native language, take English classes, and socialize with other recent arrivals while learning about their new community and its resources. There may be community churches offering services in other languages, social clubs (e.g., Portuguese Social Club), food stores that offer staples needed to prepare traditional dishes, and restaurants that families frequent where they build social networks with owners and other patrons. Other possible spaces are dance studios in which folkloric or other culturally inspired dance styles are taught or performed, bookstores or community libraries with native language or bilingual book collections, and nature centers and community gardens where native vegetables are grown. Communities may host musical events and festivals and contain theaters, art galleries, or children's museums with responsive collections. Families may have located language classes to ensure that their children learn to read and write their **native languages**.

By discovering where families go for outings (e.g., parks, lakes, or beaches) and which recreational activities they engage in on a regular basis (e.g., soccer leagues, zoos or aquariums, Boys/Girls Clubs), we can find natural learning activities to integrate into our early childhood programming. All of these spaces have human resources in the form of volunteers or paid staff who can become our "cultural informants" and professional collaborators. Business leaders also know their communities well, and by interviewing them we can learn of ways to fully engage the community and thus enhance the early education of culturally and linguistically diverse children.

Community mapping is a promising strategy for connecting with community resources to enhance the effectiveness of your program. The results can be shared with families in the form of booklets or orientation videos to ensure that all families have the same information about community-based educational settings in their community.

RECOMMENDED RESOURCES

Hepburn, K. S. (2004). *Building culturally and linguistically competent services to support young children, their families and school readiness.* Baltimore, MD: Annie E. Casey Foundation. Available from www.aecf.org/upload/PublicationFiles/HS3622H325.pdf. See Family Involvement, pp. 64–72.

National Association for the Education of Young People (NAEYC). (2008–2010). *Engaging diverse families project.* Available from www.naeyc.org/familyengagement. This site will help you learn more about exemplary early childhood programs that are successfully engaging their communities.

F. What can/should we put on our school website to connect with and inform families who speak different languages?

■ *Karen N. Nemeth*

There are many advantages to providing a user-friendly, informative website about your school community. New families can easily learn more about your school and their responsibilities. They can also find out about opportunities to become engaged in the school community. With an effective website you will be able to provide public information in multiple languages that will inform **newcomer** families and send a clear message welcoming diverse families.

Keep in mind that immigrant families may have school experiences that are very different from what occurs in the United States. Rather than assuming that everyone who reads your website is familiar and knows what to look for, start thinking about it as something completely new. What is the most important information to put on the opening slide? School calendar? Addresses of schools and offices? Key dates and requirements? These should be visible so that new families won't have to dig to find them.

Also be sure to use very simple, direct language throughout the site. Instead of a tab for "transitions," consider listing "getting ready for kindergarten." Instead of a tab for "board offices," consider listing frequently asked questions with the office that can help with those questions. Make it easy for parents to contact someone at the district who will get right back to them—they may not have email and may be accessing the website via the local library or their smart phone. You might also post a few key links to services that families may need, so they can find them without the embarrassing task of coming to the school building and asking about them.

Some districts and schools also post literacy activities, study tips, and other learning resources for young children in a variety of languages. I know one district that invites staff members and other members of the school community to record their voices reading stories in their **home languages**. These recordings are posted on the school website so families can take advantage of these welcoming early literacy connections. Another way to welcome families and help them prepare their children to be comfortable in their new school is to post videos demonstrating emergency procedures such as fire drills.

Most programs obtain photo, video, and website release forms from families as they register. Try to respect the fact that some families who are not familiar with the school or with English may not realize what they are signing. Use caution when posting photos of children or staff, but don't be so cautious that you make it impossible for families to find what they need.

G. What should administrators consider when setting attendance policies in diverse early childhood education programs?

■ *Karen N. Nemeth*

Research has shown that poor attendance in the early years can have damaging effects on school success later on. Many administrators have been working on strategies to improve school attendance (Applied Survey Research, 2011). Unfortunately, families who come from different countries and who speak different languages may be the hardest to reach, although their children may benefit most from regular school attendance. Here are some factors to consider when planning and creating policy related to school attendance.

Keep in mind that attendance and parental responsibility are treated differently in different countries. Don't assume that the immigrant families who come to your school have an automatic understanding of your policies. They need explicit information to help them understand and acclimate to their new school culture. Administrators should do everything possible to provide information that is in simple language and is translated into every language needed.

Sometimes, perhaps quite often, poor attendance is a symptom of deeper issues with a family. Here again, families of **dual English language learners** (DLLs)/**English language learners** (ELLs) may be the hardest to reach because of the language barriers. Even though reaching out to these families may be difficult, it is of the utmost importance. Assign a social worker or employ an interpreter to talk with the family about issues at home such as depression or addiction issues, health problems that make it hard for the child to attend school or for the parent to get the child ready for school, financial problems, lack of transportation, or complications because of the parent's shifts or work responsibilities.

Children who are DLLs/ELLs may be more likely to be victims of bullying and teasing at school (Chang et al., 2007). Parents or other family members may also feel uncomfortable, embarrassed, or intimidated when they come to school. Explore these possible causes for absenteeism. Observe how your office staff, bus drivers, and even kitchen staff interact with people from different backgrounds. Provide professional development for all staff to help them interact with diverse children and families in a more welcoming way and to help them spot signs of bullying.

Encourage family engagement by offering supports, events, and resources the families really need. Establish a positive rapport so that families feel more connected to the school and staff is better able to step in when family problems arise. When offering special events or volunteer opportunities, think carefully about the needs and interests of the families so you attract more participants. Rather than expecting families to come to an evening workshop where you point out what's wrong with their parenting skills, consider offering an English as a second language class or computer training instead. The important thing is to get the families into the school building to raise their comfort level and help them feel that school is a positive and important place for the whole family.

It is also a good idea to help families build relationships with one another. This helps each family feel more welcome and more comfortable as part of the school community. It may be possible to ask more experienced bilingual parents to serve as ambassadors to help **newcomer** families understand everything that they need to know at the school.

Provide information about the importance of regular school attendance for each child's success in school and beyond—but make sure this information is truly accessible to all families. Be careful, though, not to go too far with rewards for good attendance; these often push families to send children to school with obviously contagious ailments or injuries. Provide information about the critical need for sleep—now considered to be one of the most important health and behavioral concerns in early childhood, and a factor that can certainly have an impact on attendance.

Interview families about their particular needs. Perhaps some families can't make it to the bus stop on time. Parents may not be able to send their child to school on days when they have to leave early for work or stay late. Are there options for transportation? Are before and after school care available? If the goal truly is to improve attendance, some traditional rules, policies, and services may have to be reconsidered in light of increasing linguistic diversity in the school.

H. How should we advocate for English language learners and their families to ensure they get the social services they need?

■ *Karen N. Nemeth*

Children of immigrants are more likely to live in poverty than other children. Their families may face the stress of acclimating to a new culture and language along with the added challenge of navigating a new community with inadequate income, health care, or other resources. Immigrant families may not have a clear understanding of the services that might be available to help, or they may be afraid of the consequences of asking for assistance. School personnel can help in four important ways:

1. Make sure that all staff, not just the school social worker, are well informed about the different agencies and services in the community so they can help to connect families quickly when needs arise.
2. Build partnerships with local organizations and agencies that can offer help, services, or social and cultural connections. By establishing these relationships, you can smooth the way to quick access to appropriate supports as soon as they are needed. This strategy also gives you the opportunity to provide service organizations and agencies with accurate information about the languages and needs of families that are enrolling in your program.
3. Look for a variety of formal and informal service providers in your area. Examples include the following:
   - Childcare resource and referral agencies provide childcare referrals for before/after school care, subsidies, and information on parenting in multiple languages.
   - Communities of faith may have immigrant support networks, food, or clothing drives.
   - The county welfare agency can help with housing assistance, food stamps, or welfare, often in more than one language.
   - The public library may help families learn English, apply for jobs, learn to use computers, or research other information that may help them.
   - Community colleges and universities may be able to connect families with volunteers or tutors who speak their languages.

4. You can lead a general advocacy approach that builds positive community awareness and acceptance of families from different countries and the wealth of talents and assets they can contribute to the school.

I. Who are the constituents that I need to build relationships with in the district and community?

■ *Barbara Tedesco*

As a former building principal of a bilingual magnet school, I made it a point to build relationships with all constituents—from the crossing guards to the neighbors surrounding the school, the mayor and council, fire and police departments, the town library, civic and religious groups, and local retailers. Within the school there were open lines of communication between and among central office administration, the board of education, parents/family members, teachers, support staff, and students. I consistently communicated our need and my gratitude. Our school parent–teacher organization networked with other parent groups within the school district. I also reached out to the senior citizens and invited them to participate in tutoring or recording readings of popular books onto tapes.

As an urban school, we built a relationship with a suburban school that donated books to our school library. In addition, it is important to build partnerships with local colleges and universities. We became a professional development school and trained many pre-service general education as well as bilingual and English as a second language teachers who subsequently were hired in our district.

■ *Diep Nguyen*

Who the constituents are in your school district and community depends largely on the power structure that is at work in your community and what is at stake. Perhaps the question can be best answered by examining three principles of community engagement that are necessary for any successful program serving **English language learners** (ELLs).

1. *Everyone is important and each has a unique role to play in the collaborative work of educating children.* The key to engaging and including all constituents in the education process is to take the time to explore with each person/group the way in which they can play a constructive, specific role in the process. If you take the time to negotiate this role and show appreciation for their contributions, most people are more than happy to advocate with you on behalf of the children. The process of negotiating is also an opportune time to share with each person or group the vision that you have for a project and how their unique perspectives and work contribute toward this common goal. Parents and leaders of the ELL community appreciate knowing that their engagement not only benefits their own children but also provides a unique contribution to the larger school community.

2. *Constituents move in and out of the spheres of influence, depending on what is at stake and who else is involved. It's the long-term relationship with school leaders that keeps them engaged.* Many parents, teachers, and community leaders volunteer their time to help in school matters. Some people are engaged over a long period of time; others volunteer for short-term projects. Everyone wants to be informed, whether they play a critical role or are marginally engaged. Parents of ELLs may be reluctant at the beginning to become

engaged and take on a leadership role. As a school leader, it is important that you take time to cultivate relationships with parents of ELLs, to nudge them to engage with and take on these leadership roles. With encouragement, parent leaders emerge and provide a critical link between school and community. It is also essential that you maintain relationships with key constituents in the ELL community, keep them informed, and check in with them from time to time, even if they are not playing a critical role in a particular project. In the end, it is the positive relationship that you maintain with each person that will invite them to re-engage and provide assistance when you need their participation and leadership.

3. *In every community there are formal leaders and informal leaders. Informal leaders often play an important gatekeeping role for their community.* Because it takes time to build relationships and gain access to diverse communities, school leaders often rely on the formal community leaders to represent the interests of a particular group. However, it is equally advantageous to find out who the informal community leaders are. They often can help you gain access to informal groups of parents and community members. They also can become your cultural mediators and guides as you learn how to work respectfully and collaboratively with members of their community. Seeking out informal leaders and asking them to be your cultural mediators/guides helps you become a school leader who serves young ELLs and their families in a more culturally responsive manner.

In the end, it matters less that a school leader knows all the key constituents. What is more important is that a school leader uses the principles of inclusion, collaboration, and relationship building when working with both formal and informal community leaders.

J. What can administrators and staff do to become more culturally aware and sensitive?

■ *Janet Gonzalez-Mena*

Becoming culturally aware and sensitive is important for everyone in education and isn't necessarily an entirely intellectual process. Emotional triggers may be what moves someone to begin acknowledging, understanding, and accepting cultural differences. Such triggers can cause discomfort; that's okay—it's the beginning of awareness. It's fine to use your brain and try to learn about the different cultures represented in the program where you work, but you can't become an expert on every culture you encounter. Even anthropologists can't do that; they have to focus and specialize. One thing they learn is that you can't predict behavior or attitudes just by knowing a person's culture. So, start by realizing that no one expects you to be an expert—only to be aware and sensitive. When you set sensitivity as a goal you become a learner; that is what is important.

What helped me become culturally aware and sensitive was to discover I had a culture. As a European-American (married to a man from Mexico), I thought of myself as "just regular"; it was other people who had culture. Discovering myself as a cultural being was an eye opener. I began to see I needed to start with myself before I could begin to be sensitive to and understand the diversity I encountered. I remember when I first was exploring the idea that I had a culture, someone said to me with anger, "How could you not know you are also a cultural being? It's *your* culture that dominates everything." Ouch.

It took the feminist movement to help me begin to see how the hierarchy of privilege works. I had already experienced enough male privilege and how it operates to begin to understand "white privilege," which is a useful term bringing race and culture together when looking at domination patterns. I didn't like the idea that I had privilege that many other people lack. At first I felt guilty and defensive. After all, I told myself, I didn't ask to be born into privilege, and I've done the best I can to promote equity and social justice. Yes, that was true, but then an image of myself riding a white horse in to "save" other people hit me. That was a turning point in my life. I began to see how much more effective in making change I'd be as a partner to those who lacked my area of privilege.

Anyone in a position of power will learn a great deal by creating partnerships with people who have less power and privilege. It all starts with sensitivity and awareness, no matter what your culture, race, or gender.

RECOMMENDED RESOURCES

Gonzalez-Mena, J. (2008). *Diversity in early care and education: Honoring differences* (4th ed.). Washington, DC: National Association for the Education of Young Children and New York: McGraw-Hill.

Gonzalez-Mena, J. (2013). *Fifty strategies for working and communicating with diverse families.* Upper Saddle River, NJ: Pearson.

K. What strategies help administrators and staff cope with conflict in diverse environments?

■ *Laura Ascenzi-Moreno*

All healthy environments are diverse. Therefore, administrators and staff always have to interface with differences in their work. One important way to ensure that people's differences in opinions, ways of working, and outlook enrich the environment rather than spin out of control into a conflict is to ensure that there is a shared common vision and ownership in that vision.

Even with a shared common vision, there are still conflicts, both internal to the school and external to the school community. Internal conflicts can happen between staff, between administration and staff, or between staff and parents. When internal conflict does occur, it is essential that a space is created to hear the concerns of the parties in conflict, even if the issue at the center of the conflict cannot be completely resolved. For example, at one urban school parents advocated for months to acquire assistant teachers in order to alleviate large class size with a number of **emergent bilingual** students. However, when the budget for the coming year was received, the administrator realized that there were no funds to support this endeavor. Rather than let parents discuss this matter in a forum, the principal simply relayed the information to them. This in turn created further conflict and distrust of the principal. The end result in sentiment would have been very different if the principal had allowed parents to have a voice.

Another case highlights the importance of the administrator in educating the entire community. In one suburban community, the demographics rapidly changed. This community received a very rapid influx of Ecuadorian immigrants. The principal invested in developing a dual language, bilingual program for these students. This type of programming was an excellent choice not only for educational reasons but also for political ones. A dual language, bilingual program would bring together Latino and non-Latino students. However, the non-Latino population was not ready for this change. In fact, many non-Latino parents were reluctant to place their children in these classes because of the presence of immigrant children in them. In order to combat this bias, the principal took a multipronged approach. First, for parents' night she hired translators so that the Latino parents could participate and be known in the school community. At these meetings, the strengths of the dual language, bilingual program were highlighted and demystified. These measures aided parents to get to know the new population at the school rather than view them as other.

Conflict also can be external. At one school, the school district was imposing a reading program on a dual language school. This reading program was designed for students whose **home language** was English. As such, it was a poor fit for this school. The school mobilized parents and teachers to form a coalition against the incursion of this ill-fitting curriculum. This type of mobilization reflects a strong, community-based vision. One parent at the school, looking back at the conflict, says,

> Programs come and go . . . but the school was created by parents who had ownership of the **dual language program**. They believed in the ideas and found value in the teacher-made curriculum, which they knew addressed the needs of their children and the community, rather than bringing in prescribed curriculum that had no attachment to the community. There were deep roots in what they believed in and they backed the curriculum designed at the school. (Ascenzi-Moreno & Flores, 2012)

Conflicts are bound to occur. They can serve as the foundation for a common vision and understanding among constituents, which ultimately strengthens the community.

L. How should administrators handle difficult conversations with parents who speak different languages?

■ *Janet Gonzalez-Mena*

Difficult conversations are a big problem if teachers and administrators don't speak the language of the parents. Obviously translators are vital. My first piece of advice is to avoid using the children of the parents, if at all possible. First of all, young children don't have the vocabulary to deal with the more sophisticated concepts that may come up in talks with parents. Second, translation puts children in a position above their parents, which is a reversal of relationships. Third, if the conversation is about the child, it may be uncomfortable for everybody if the child is the translator. The child is not a neutral party to the conversation, as a translator should be.

Another issue with translators is finding one who knows both languages well. I remember a story of a family with a sick child who needed surgery. The family didn't speak English, so a translator was brought in. No matter what the doctor explained, the family absolutely refused to give permission. The medical staff was in a frenzy because the surgery was so important. Luckily, they brought in a second translator, and then the parents signed the release. It turned out that the first translator didn't know the word for "surgery" and had used the word for "butcher" instead. No wonder the parents refused!

Of course, in a difficult conversation, both parties should do what they can to understand the perspective of the other. If they find themselves on opposite sides, they can use the advice of the 12th-century poet Rumi, who said, "Out beyond the fields of wrong doing and right doing there lies a field. I'll meet you there." In that field they can use the advice of Copple and Bredekamp (2009, p. 49): move from "either/or" to "both/and thinking"— instead of polarizing.

RECOMMENDED RESOURCE

Gonzalez-Mena, J. (2013). *Fifty strategies for working and communicating with diverse families.* Upper Saddle River, NJ: Pearson.

M. How can administrators foster buy-in from all staff and constituents in support of a language plan or vision?

■ *Laura Ascenzi-Moreno*

The most important step an administrator can take when developing a vision and a corresponding language plan is to open the doors to all constituents while developing them. Although opening up the process may take longer, the investment in incorporating a larger circle of community members into the vision makes it stronger and more relevant to the community.

In one case, in order to revamp the school's arts program and align it to the needs of **emergent bilingual** students, the school hosted a retreat that involved parents, arts teachers, bilingual classroom teachers, and administrators. These school players came together to envision an arts program that supported language development. This shared space allowed all parties to voice their opinions about how this could be accomplished. Furthermore, the dialog allowed for constituents to address misconceptions across the community. For example, parents initially were unaware of how the arts program was linked to academic work. Prior to the retreat, they viewed the arts as "fun" for students. After the retreat, parent leaders had a solid idea of how the arts were configured at this school to support bilingual language development. Lastly, one key component of the retreat was the collaborative development of a mission statement for how the arts program would enrich language development. These shared experiences, although labor intensive, broaden the community that is invested and owns the school's language plan or vision.

It is important to note that these experiences must be renewed across time. As time passes, community members change and the immediate power of a community coming together to forge common goals weakens. Therefore it is vital that through school activities and forums, both existing and new community members have the opportunity to engage in the acceptance or revision of common goals.

N. What do we know about the value to *all* students of growing up bilingual?

■ *Karen N. Nemeth*

A growing body of research is creating a compelling case for changing the way American schools operate. Rather than thinking of bilingual education as a special service provided to some children of immigrant families, we should begin to think of bilingualism as a goal for all children. To make this possible, learning in two languages has to happen right from the start.

An article from the *New York Times* summarized some of the key findings on topic. The title alone, "Why bilinguals are smarter," is enough to convince some people (Bhattacharjee, 2012). The writer describes cognitive advantages that would be a benefit to any child, not just children who are new to English. For example, keeping two language systems in mind seems to act like exercise for the brain, enabling bilingual children to be better at solving certain problems, at starting and stopping activities, at certain **executive function** skills, with working memory, and at learning a new language.

We know that in other countries, growing up with two languages is a matter of course. The facts don't support the American resistance to new languages. Furthermore, the National Association for Bilingual Education's mission statement captures the answer to this question:

> By using native and second languages in everyday life, we not only develop intercultural understanding, but we also show by example that we respect and can effectively cross cultural and linguistic barriers.
>
> **Bilingualism** and **biliteracy** for all is an admirable goal for every individual. We embrace this mantra and advocate learning more than two languages and cultures. We are a global society and we must be at the cutting edge in living and creating unity within diversity.

In her 2013 update of her well-known 2008 report, Linda Espinosa finds even stronger evidence for the value of helping young children grow up with two languages. She reminds us that there is no evidence that learning in two languages causes any harm or delay. In fact, support of the **home language** in the early years is likely to help the child do better in both the home language *and* English later on. Apparently, the more we support the child's ability to access and use information they have stored in either of their languages, the stronger foundation they have for future learning in both languages. These cognitive advantages are augmented by the social and emotional advantages of having support for the home language and the breadth of experience that comes from learning a new language. Espinosa (2013) recommends: "Support bilingualism for all children whenever possible; **dual language programs** are an effective approach to improving academic achievement for DLL children while also providing many benefits to native English speakers" (p. 20).

Understanding the impact of the research described in this report can substantially change the approach early childhood educators take toward working with diverse populations. These findings shift the focus from thinking of **English language learners/dual language learners** as children encumbered with a deficit to thinking of bilingualism as a goal for all children in our schools that must be pursued as early as possible. With this in mind, the guidance offered in this book can empower administrators to facilitate extraordinary change—not only in their own schools, but also in communities throughout the United States.

Resources and Questions

ADVOCACY PLANNING TOOL

	Activity	Languages	Training Provided	Policy/ Handbook
List tasks that parents can do to support the school				
List programs for parents to help them support their child's learning				
List tasks that volunteers can do				
List community resources to support your program				
List staff in your school/ district/program who need to learn more about your work with ELLs/DLLs				
Describe your program's vision for educating diverse children effectively				

QUESTIONS FOR REFLECTION

- How are your efforts to engage with parents being adapted to reach families who come from different languages and cultures?

- What plans do you have in place to train bilingual volunteers to use their language assets effectively when helping out in your school?

- What members of the staff or community seem to be creating obstacles or objections to your work with diverse young children? How can you identify opportunities to educate them about your program and turn them into allies?

Glossary

Academic fluency: The student's ease in using academic vocabulary to comfortably speak, understand, read, and write about academic topics. Compare to Conversational fluency.

Academic language proficiency: The level of proficiency required to participate and achieve in content-area instruction, generally measured by some form of assessment. In contrast to more easily attained conversational or informal fluency, academic language proficiency may take 6–8 years or more to attain, according to James Cummins (2000).

Additive bilingualism: The process by which, or context in which, a second or additional language is learned while maintaining the first language. It is sometimes contrasted with subtractive bilingualism, wherein a student loses some of the first language while learning the second language.

Bilingual education: Providing educational content in two languages. Bilingual education can take many forms, but all of these are planned educational programs that use two languages for instructional purposes. All U.S. bilingual programs aim for eventual high English-proficiency and academic-achievement levels as important goals (some bilingual programs have additional goals). The different types of bilingual education programs usually are defined by their goals and the balance of teaching time between English and the non-English language. Compare to Developmental bilingual education (DBE) program and Dual language programs.

Bilingual education teacher: A teacher who is certified as a bilingual education teacher or has a bilingual education endorsement on his or her certificate, having satisfied state requirements for language proficiency and coursework that qualify him or her to teach in a bilingual education program. This term distinguishes a teacher who has specific qualifications to teach in a specifically designated bilingual education program from a certified teacher who happens to be bilingual.

Bilingualism: The state of being able to use two or more languages. When used informally, this term may be applied to someone who easily speaks and understands two languages very well. In school settings, the term "bilingual" often has more clearly specified criteria. Knowing and using more than two languages is called multilingualism.

Biliterate/Biliteracy: The ability to read and write very well in two languages.

Cognates: Pairs of words in two etymologically related languages that have similar meanings and sound very similar, such as elephant and *elefante*. Showing young dual language learners (DLLs) the connections between cognates in their home language and English is a successful strategy to help them develop their English language skills.

Comprehensible input: Language input provided in the classroom in way that is easier for DLL students to understand. This includes the intentional choice of familiar words along with scaffolding cues for understanding new words such as visual or gestural supports.

Consultation method: An alternative to push-in or pull-out services, in which an English as a second language (ESL) teacher provides consultative support to the classroom teacher but does not provide direct services to a particular child. This method is used in some early childhood programs, particularly at the preschool level. The ESL teacher assists in assessing the child's language support needs and collaborates with the classroom teacher to plan the teaching strategies to meet the child's needs. Supports are not provided in isolated periods of direct service, which means they can be embedded in the child's school day, all day, every day, by the classroom teacher and any other specialists who might work with that child. Compare to Pull-out supports/instructions/methods and Push-in supports/instructions/methods.

Conversational fluency: The level of informal fluency in a language that is sufficient to support conversations and informal interactions, but is not quite at the level needed for full participation in academic learning—also known as playground fluency. Compare to Academic fluency.

Developmental bilingual education (DBE) program: A type of bilingual education that targets ELLs and aims for high levels of proficiency in English and in the students' home language, along with strong academic development. Students generally participate in these programs for at least five to six years, receiving content-area instruction in English and in their home language. Developmental bilingual programs are also sometimes referred to as one-way developmental bilingual programs, maintenance bilingual programs, or late-exit bilingual programs.

Developmentally appropriate practice: A term used informally to refer to educational practices that are appropriate for the developmental, cognitive, and/or language proficiency levels of the student. In early childhood education, this term has a more formalized meaning that includes a child-centered approach to learning rather than a teacher-led approach, as described in publications by the National Association for the Education of Young Children.

Dominant language: In some programs, contexts, or locations, a term that refers to the language in which the student has the greatest proficiency and fluency. In other contexts, educators may use the term to describe the majority language of an area. It is important to be clear about the meaning when this term is used. See also Primary language.

Dual language learner (DLL): Any child from birth through age 8 who has a home language other than English, regardless of what type of program he or she may be in. Whether they have been learning in two languages from birth or began life with one language and came to a new community or school where they begin to learn a new language, children in the early years are still in the process of learning about language and continue to need support in both their home language and English.

Dual language programs: Schools or classrooms that are specifically established to provide education in two languages to support bilingualism and biliteracy. One-way dual language immersion provides instruction in the two languages for children who enter the program speaking only one of the languages being taught. Two-way dual language immersion programs enroll children who speak either one or both of the languages being taught so they can all learn their own and one another's languages. The goal of this type of program is to achieve desired academic outcomes and encourage cross-cultural communicative competence.

Emergent bilingual: A term used by some states and programs to indicate young students who are becoming proficient in a second or additional language. It may be used instead of English learner.

English as a second language (ESL) program: A type of English language development program that provides specialized instruction in English to students who are identified as limited English proficient (LEP). ESL instruction is provided by teachers who have certification or endorsement in ESL and should be adapted to meet the language proficiency needs of each student. ESL programs are provided as an alternative to bilingual education programs or when a district does not have sufficient numbers of students who speak the same language or teachers with the needed languages to offer bilingual education.

English language development: The process of learning to understand and use the English language, regardless of policies, standards, or programs.

English language development programs: Services included in ELD policies that may be in the form of ESL, bilingual education, sheltered English, or other adaptations and supports.

English language development standards: Standards used by most states to address the development of English language skills. Some states may use the ELD standards created by the World-Class Instructional Design and Assessment (WIDA) organization.

English language learner (ELL)/English learner (EL): A student who speaks a non-English language and is enrolled in a U.S. school. These terms generally are interchangeable and one or the other is prevalent in different states or districts. They are often used in educational programs and policies to identify students who are determined to be "limited English proficient" and in need of ELD services. Recently, this term has been replaced by "dual language learner" for children aged 8 and under by many national organizations and local programs.

Executive functions: Adaptive aspects of brain function that allow a person to (for example) maintain focus despite distractions or to control shifts in attention. Executive functions are key to school success, and research has shown that they are often more highly developed in bilingual people.

Full English proficient (FEP): The label given by school districts to students who have met their requirements for demonstrating readiness to exit from ELD services. It does not necessarily indicate full academic fluency in the new language.

Home language: A language other than English used in the home of a young child or student. Although this is often the first language learned by the child, it can sometimes be introduced by an influential person in the child's life who speaks the language in the home. See also Native language.

Language immersion program: A program for students in preschool through later grades that is designed to immerse them in a new language. U.S. language immersion programs are run as private schools or enrichment programs to help monolingual English speakers become fluent in a new language while attaining educational goals.

Limited English proficient (LEP): The official designation of a student in need of ELD services in school. This term is falling out of favor in the education world because of the negative connotations of using the word "limited" when these students actually have the benefit of knowing more than one language.

Majority language: The language spoken by the majority of people in a described location (school, community, or state), or the official language of the location—even if fewer than half of the people in the area are fluent in that language. Compare to Minority language.

Metalinguistic awareness: The ability to recognize the components and features of language in general and of the particular languages being developed by the student. This skill is more highly developed in bilingual people.

Minority language: A language that is spoken by less than half of the people in a described location, or a language that is not the official language or most powerful language influence in a state or area. Compare to Majority language.

Native language: The first language learned by a child; also called L1. Subsequent languages are called L2, L3, and so forth, according to their position in the sequence of learning. In early childhood education, the presence of any language in the home in the early years should be considered in planning for the child's educational needs, so the term "home language" is now used more frequently than "native language." See also Home language.

Newcomer: A student who has just arrived in the United States and most likely speaks no English. Newcomer programs are offered by some schools with specific linguistic, cultural, and personal supports available to aid adjustment.

Primary language: The language that is determined to be stronger or used more frequently by the student; also called the "dominant language." In certain federal and state government documents, the term primary home language other than English (PHLOTE) is used. In some contexts, however, this term is used simply to indicate the language the child started to learn first. It is important to be clear about the meaning of this term when using it in documents or conversations. See also Dominant language.

Pull-out supports/instructions/methods: A format for ESL or ELD services in which the teacher pulls the child out of the classroom and works with one or more DLLs. In some cases, this support is conducted by providing activities that are unrelated to what is happening in the child's main classroom and cannot be observed or repeated by the general education teacher. Pull-out strategies are more effective when there is ample time and support for collaboration between the ESL and classroom teacher so they can plan activities that will be relevant to the child for that class and will feed effectively into what the child would have learned by remaining in class. Compare to Consultation method and Push-in supports/instructions/methods.

Push-in supports/instructions/methods: A format for ESL or ELD services in which the ESL teacher goes into the DLL child's regular classroom to provide services, ideally blending with and capitalizing on the curricular activities in the classroom. In this model, the child does not lose learning time leaving the classroom and returning, and the teacher can observe the types of supports provided by the ESL teacher so they can be repeated at other times. Although there are advantages to this model, it necessitates that language support services are provided in the midst of a busy classroom where the ESL and classroom teachers must find ways to collaborate. Push-in is a form of co-teaching, with widely varying levels of actual teacher-to-teacher planning and collaboration. Compare to Consultation method and Pull-out supports/instructions/methods.

Sequential language learning: The learning of a new language three or more years after the child has begun life speaking a first language (Paradis, Genesee, & Crago, 2011).

Sheltered content-area instruction: A program model that offers grade-level content to DLLs using specialized ESL instructional strategies to support content learning and English language learning at the same time.

Sheltered English immersion: A program model for DLLs that combines ESL instruction, sheltered content-area instruction, and primary language support. It may also be called structured English immersion.

Sheltered instruction observation protocol (SIOP): A research-based approach for sheltered content-area instruction that helps ELLs develop oral language proficiency while building academic English literacy skills and content-area knowledge. The SIOP Institute trademark and copyright are owned by LessonLab/Pearson Education.

Simultaneous language acquisition: The learning of two or more languages at the same time, for example, when a father and mother speak different languages to the child. The child is considered to be experiencing simultaneous language acquisition if one or more of the languages is introduced before he or she turns 3 years old, and sequential language acquisition if the second language is introduced after age 3.

Transitional bilingual education: An education program provided mostly in the student's home language for the purpose of preparing him or her for exit to general education in English as soon as possible.

Adesope, O. O., Lavin, T., Thompson, T., & Ungerleider, C. (2010). A systematic review and meta-analysis of the cognitive correlates of bilingualism. *Review of Educational Research, 80*(2), 207–245.

Adi-Japha, E., Berberich-Artzi, J., & Libnawi, A. (2010). Cognitive flexibility in drawings of bilingual children. *Child Development, 81*(5), 1356–1366.

Alanís, I. (2011). Learning from each other: Examining the use of bilingual pairs in dual language classrooms. *Dimensions of Early Childhood, 39*(1), 21–28.

Alanís, I. (2013). Where's your partner? Pairing bilingual learners in preschool and primary grade dual language classrooms. *Young Children 68*(1), 42–47.

Alanís, I., & Rodriguez, M. A. (2008). Sustaining a dual language immersion program: Features of success. *Journal of Latinos and Education, 7*(4), 305–319.

Andersson, U. (2010). The contribution of working memory capacity to foreign language comprehension in children. *Memory, 18*(4), 458–472.

Angelelli, C. (2004). *Revisiting the interpreters' role.* Philadelphia: John Benjamins.

Applied Survey Research. (2011). *Attendance in early elementary grades: Associations with student characteristics, school readiness, and third grade outcomes.* San Jose, CA: Author. Available at www.attendanceworks.org/wordpress/wp-content/uploads/2010/04/ASR-Mini-Report-Attendance-Readiness-and-Third-Grade-Outcomes-7-8-11.pdf

Ascenzi-Moreno, L., Espinosa, C., Ferholt, S., Loeb, M., Lugo-Salcedo, B., & Traugh, C. (2008). Learning through descriptive inquiry at the Cypress Hills Community School. *Language Arts, 85*(5), 392–400.

Ascenzi-Moreno, L., & Flores, N. (2012). A case study of bilingual policy and practices at the Cypress Hills Community School. In O. García, B. Octu, & Z. Zakharia (Eds.), *Bilingual community education and multilingualism* (pp. 219–231). Bristol, UK: Multilingual Matters.

Asher, J. (1996). *Learning another language through actions* (5th ed.). Los Gatos, CA: Sky Oaks.

Asher, J. J. (1969). The total physical response approach to second language learning. *Modern Language Journal, 53*(1), 3–17.

August, D., & Shanahan, T. (2006). *Developing literacy in second language learners. Report of the National Literacy Panel on Language Minority Children and Youth.* Mahwah, NJ: Lawrence Erlbaum.

Baker, J. A., Dilly, L. J., & Lacey, C. L. (2003). Creating community-oriented classrooms. In C. Howes (Ed.), *Teaching 4- to 8-year-olds* (pp. 1–24). Baltimore, MD: Paul Brookes.

Ballantyne, K. G., Sanderman, A. R., & Levy, J. (2008). *Educating English language learners: Building teacher capacity.* Washington, DC: National Clearinghouse for English Language Acquisition. Available at www.ncela.gwu.edu/practice/mainstream_teachers.htm

Barac, R., & Bialystok, E. (2011). Cognitive development of bilingual children. *Language Teaching, 44*(01), 36–54.

Barnett, W. S., Yarosz, D. J., Thomas, J., Jung, K., & Blanco, D. (2007). Two-way monolingual English immersion in preschool education: An experimental comparison. *Early Childhood Research Quarterly, 22*(3), 277–293.

Barrueco, S. (2012). Assessing young bilingual children with special needs. In S. M. Benner (Ed.), *Assessment of young children with special needs: A context-based approach* (2nd ed., pp. 237–248) New York: Routledge.

Barrueco, S., López, M. L., Ong, C. A., & Lozano, P. (2012). *Assessing Spanish-English bilingual preschoolers: A guide to best measures and approaches.* Baltimore: Paul Brookes.

Bartel-Haring, S., & Younkin, F. L. (2012). Family distance regulation and school engagement in middle-school aged children. *Family Relations Interdisciplinary Journal of Applied Family Studies, 61*, 191–206.

Beach, R., Campano, G., Edmiston, B., & Borgmann, M. (Eds.). (2010). *Literacy tools in the classroom: Teaching through critical inquiry, grades 5–12.* New York: Teachers College Press.

Bedore, L. M., Peña, E. D., Summers, C., Boerger, K., Resendiz, M., Greene, K., . . . Gillam, R. B.

(2012). The measure matters: Language dominance profiles across measures in Spanish/English bilingual children. *Bilingualism: Language and Cognition, 15,* 616–629.

Bell, D. (2010). *Scaffolding phonemic awareness in preschool aged English language learners.* (Unpublished doctoral dissertation). Florida State University, Florida.

Bhattacharjee, Y. (2012, March 25). Why bilinguals are smarter. *New York Times,*. Retrieved from www .nytimes.com/2012/03/18/opinion/sunday/the -benefits-of-bilingualism.html?_r=0

Bialystok, E. (2001). *Bilingualism in development: Language, literacy, and cognition.* Cambridge, UK: Cambridge University Press.

Bialystok, E. (2007). Acquisition of literacy in bilingual children. *Language Learning,* 45–77.

Bialystok, E. (2011). Coordination of executive functions in monolingual and bilingual children. *Journal of Experimental Child Psychology, 110*(3), 461–468.

Bialystok, E., Barac, R., Blaye, A., & Poulin-Dubois, D. (2010). Word mapping and executive functioning in young monolingual and bilingual children. *Journal of Cognition and Development, 11*(4), 485–508.

Bialystok, E., Craik, F. I. M., & Ryan, J. (2006). Executive control in a modified antisaccade task: Effects of aging and bilingualism. *Journal of Experimental Psychology: Learning, Memory, and Cognition, 32,* 1341–1354.

Bialystok, E., & Feng, X. (2009). Language proficiency and executive control in proactive interference: Evidence from monolingual and bilingual children and adults. *Brain and Language, 109*(2), 93–100.

Bialystok, E., & Viswanathan, M. (2009). Components of executive control with advantages for bilingual children in two cultures. *Cognition, 112*(3), 494–500.

Biemiller, A. (2006). Vocabulary development and instruction: A prerequisite for school learning. In D. K. Dickinson & S. B. Neuman (Eds.), *Handbook of early literacy research* (Vol. 2, pp. 41–51). New York: Guilford.

Birch, S. H., & Ladd, G. W. (1998). Children's interpersonal behaviors and the teacher–child relationship. *Developmental Psychology, 34*(5), 934.

Blumenfeld, H. K., & Marian, V. (2011). Bilingualism influences inhibitory control in auditory comprehension. *Cognition, 118*(2), 245–257.

Bobb, S. C., Wodniecka, Z., & Kroll, J. F. (2013). What bilinguals tell us about cognitive control: Overview to the special issue. *Journal of Cognitive Psychology, 25*(5), 493–496.

Bohman, T. M., Bedore, L. M., Peña, E. D., Mendez-Perez, A., & Gillam, R. B. (2010). What you hear and what you say: Language performance in Spanish-English bilinguals. *International Journal of Bilingual Education and Bilingualism, 13*(3), 325–344.

Booth, A., & Dunn, J. F. (1996). *Family-school links: How they affect educational outcomes.* Mahwah, NJ: Lawrence Erlbaum.

Bredekamp, S., Isenberg, J., & Jalongo, M. (2003). *Major trends and issues in early childhood education: Challenges, controversies, and insights.* New York: Free Press.

Brisk, M. E. (Ed.). (2008). *Language, culture, and community in teacher education.* Mahwah, NJ: Lawrence Erlbaum.

BUILD Initiative. (2012). *Top ten recommendations for state leaders implementing kindergarten entry assessments.* Available at www.elccollaborative.org/ assessment/77-kindergarten-entry-assessment.html

Burchinal, M., Field, S., Lopez, M., Howes, C., & Pianta, R. (2012). Instruction in Spanish in prekindergarten classrooms and child outcomes for English language learners. *Early Childhood Research Quarterly, 27,* 188–197.

Cabell, S. Q., Justice, L. M., Piasta, S. B., Curenton, S. M., Wiggins, A., Turnbull, K. P., & Petscher, Y. (2011). The impact of teacher responsivity education on preschoolers' language and literacy skills. *American Journal of Speech-Language Pathology, 20*(4), 315–330.

Calderón, M. E. (2011a). *Teaching reading and comprehension to English learners, K–5.* Indianapolis, IN: Solution Tree.

Calderón, M. E. (2011b). Teaching writing to EAL pupils in secondary schools. *Better: Evidence-based Education. 3*(2), 8–9.

Calderón, M. E., Hertz-Lazarowitz, R., & Slavin, R. E. (1998). Effects of bilingual cooperative integrated reading and composition on students making the transition from Spanish to English reading. *Elementary School Journal, 99*(2), 153–165.

California Department of Education. (2009). *Preschool English learners: Principles and practices to promote language, literacy, and learning—a resource guide.* Sacramento: Author.

Camilli, G., Vargas, S., Ryan, S., & Barnett, W. S. (2010). Meta-analysis of the effects of early education interventions on cognitive and social development. *Teachers College Record, 112,* 579–620.

Carini, P. & Himley, M. (2009). *Jenny's story: Taking the long view of the child, Prospect's philosophy in action.* New York: Teachers College Press.

Carlo, M., August, D., & Snow, C. (2005). Sustained vocabulary-learning strategy instruction for English-language learners. In E. H. Hiebert & M. L.

Kamil (Eds.), *Teaching and learning vocabulary* (pp. 115–136). Mahwah, NJ: Lawrence Erlbaum.

Center for Law and Social Policy (2012). *Supporting our youngest children: Early Head Start programs in 2010. March 2012, Brief No. 11*. Available at www.clasp.org/admin/site/publications/files/EHS-Trend-Analysis-Final.pdf

Chang, F., Crawford, G., Early, D., Bryant, D., Howes, C., Burchinal, M., . . . Pianta, R. (2007). Spanish speaking children's social and language development in pre-kindergarten classrooms. *Journal of Early Education and Development, 18*(2), 243–269.

Cho, R. M. (2012). Are there peer effects associated with having English language learner (ELL) classmates? Evidence from the early childhood longitudinal study kindergarten cohort (ECLS-K). *Economics of Education Review, 31*, 629–643.

Christian, D. (1994). *Two-way bilingual eductaion: Students learning through two languages*. Educational Practice Rep. No. 12 ed. Santa Cruz, CA and Washington, DC: National Center for Research on Cultural Diversity and Second Language Learning.

Chumak-Horbatsch, R. (2012). *Linguistically appropriate practice: A guide for working with young immigrant children*. North York, Canada: University of Toronto Press.

Collier, V. P., & Thomas, W. P. (2009). *Educating English learners for a transformed world*. Albuquerque, NM: Fuente Press.

Connecticut Administrators of Programs for English Language Learners. (2011). *English language learners and special education: A resource handbook*. Hartford, CT: Connecticut Department of Education.

Copple, C. & Bredekamp, S. (Eds.). (2009). *Developmentally appropriate practice in early childhood programs serving children from birth through age 8* (3rd ed.). Washington, DC: National Association for the Education of Young Children.

Council for Exceptional Children/National Association for Bilingual Education. (2002). *Determining appropriate referrals of English language learners to special education: A self-assessment guide for principals*. Arlington, VA and Washington, DC: Authors. Available at www.dcsig.org/files/DeterminingAppropriateReferralsOfEnglishLanguageLearnersToSpecialEducation.pdf

Council for Exceptional Children Division for Early Childhood. (2010). *Responsiveness to ALL children, families and professionals: Integrating cultural and linguistic diversity into policy and practice*. Available at www.dec-sped.org/uploads/docs/about_dec/position_concept_papers/Position%20Statement_Cultural%20and%20Linguistic%20Diversity_updated_sept2010.pdf

Cummins, J. (1981). The role of primary language development in promoting educational success for language minority students. In California State Department of Education (Ed.), *Schooling and language minority students: A theoretical framework* (pp. 3–49). Sacramento, CA: California State Department of Education.

Cummins, J. (1994). Knowledge, power and identity in teaching English as a second language. In F. Genesee (Ed.), *Educating second language children: The whole child, the whole curriculum, the whole community* (pp. 33–58). Cambridge, UK: Cambridge University Press.

Cummins, J. (2000). *Language, power, and pedagogy: Bilingual children in the crossfire*. Clevedon, UK: Multilingual Matters.

Cummins, J. (2001). Bilingual children's mother tongue: Why is it important for education? *progforum, 7*(19), 15–20.

Dashler, D., Palinscar, A., Biancarosa, G., & Nair, M. (2007). *Informed choices for struggling adolescent readers: A research-based guide to instructional programs and practices*. Newark, DE: International Reading Association.

Delfino, A., Johnson, J. F., & Perez, L. (2009). Winning schools for ELLs. *Educational Leadership 4*, 66–69.

Department for Education and Skills. (2006). *It is not as simple as you think: Cultural viewpoints around disability*. Annesley, UK: Department for Education and Skills Publication.

Derman-Sparks, L., & Olsen Edwards, J. (2010). *Anti-bias education for young children and ourselves*. Washington, DC: Library of Congress.

Diamond, A. (2013). Executive functions and cognitive training. *Lecture at the Harvard Faculty of Arts and Sciences, week 6, Psychology 1609*. (Unpublished document.)

Dickinson, D. K., McCabe, A., & Anastasopoulos, L. (2003). A framework for examining book reading in early childhood classrooms. In A. van Kleeck, A. A. Stahl, & E. B. Bauer (Eds.), *On reading books to children: Parents and teachers* (pp. 95–113). Mahwah, NJ: Lawrence Erlbaum.

Duran, L. K., Roseth, C. J., & Hoffman, P. (2010). An experimental study comparing English-only and transitional bilingual education on Spanish-speaking preschoolers' early literacy development. *Early Childhood Research Quarterly, 25*(2), 207–217.

Ellwein, M. C., Walsh, D. J., Eads, G. M., & Miller, A. (1991). Using readiness tests to route kindergarten students: The snarled intersection of psychometrics, policy and practice. *Educational Evaluation and Policy Analysis, 13*(2), 159–175.

Espinosa, L. (2006). Social, cultural and linguistic components of school readiness in young Latino children. In L. M. Beaulieu (Ed.), *The social development of young children from diverse backgrounds.* Baltimore, MD: National Black Child Development Institute Press.

Espinosa, L. (2010). *Getting it right for young children from diverse backgrounds. Applying research to improve practice.* Boston: Pearson.

Espinosa, L. (2012, June). *State early learning guidelines/ standards and young dual language learners.* Power point presentation at the BUILD/CCSSO, ECEA-SCASS meeting on Standards and Assessments for Young Dual Language Learners, Indianapolis, IN.

Espinosa, L. (2013). *Challenging common myths about young dual language learners: An update to the seminal 2008 report. A PreK-3rd Policy to Action Brief.* New York: Foundation for Child Development.

Farver, J. A., Xu, Y., Lonigan, C. J., & Eppe, S. (2013). Home literacy environment and Latino Head Start children's emergent literacy skills, *Developmental Psychology, 49*(4), 775–791.

Finger, I., Billig, J. D., & Scholl, A. P. (2011). Effects of bilingualism on inhibitory control in elderly Brazilian bilinguals. In C. Sanz, & R. P. Leow (Eds.), *Implicit and explicit language learning: Conditions, processes, knowledge in SLA and bilingualism* (pp. 219–229). Washington, DC: Georgetown University Press.

Fong, A. B., Bae, S., & Huang, M. (2010). *Patterns of student mobility among English language learner students in Arizona public schools.* (Issues & Answers Report, REL 2010–No. 093.) Washington, DC: U.S. Department of Education, Institute of Education Sciences, National Center for Education Evaluation and Regional Assistance, Regional Educational Laboratory West. Available at http://ies.ed.gov/ncee/edlabs

Friesen, D., & Bialystok, E. (2013). Control and representation in bilingualism: Implications for pedagogy. *Innovative Research and Practices in Second Language Acquisition and Bilingualism, 38,* 223.

Fuller, B. (2007). *Standardized childhood: The political and cultural struggle over early education.* Stanford, CA: Stanford University Press.

Garbin, G., Sanjuan, A., Forn, C., Bustamante, J. C., Rodriguez-Pujadas, A., Belloch, V., . . . Ávila, C. (2010). Bridging language and attention: Brain basis of the impact of bilingualism on cognitive control. *Neuroimage, 53*(4), 1272–1278.

García, E. E., & Frede E. A. (2010). *Young English language learners: Current research and emerging directions for practice and policy.* New York: Teachers College Press.

Garcia, E. E., Jensen, B. T., & Scribner, K. P. (2009). English language learners represent a growing proportion of U.S. students. To meet these students' needs, we must understand who they are. *Educational Leadership, 66,* 7, 8–13.

García, O. (2009). *Bilingual education in the 21st century: A global perspective.* Malden, MA: Wiley-Blackwell.

Gass, S. M., Behney, J. N., & Uzum, B. (2013). Inhibitory control, working memory and L2 interaction. In K. Drozdzial-Szelest & M. Pawlak (Eds.), *Psycholinguistic and sociolinguistic perspectives on second language learning and teaching* (pp. 91–114). Berlin: Springer.

Gass, S. M., & Mackey, A. (2013). *Stimulated recall methodology in second language research.* Mahwah, NJ: Lawrence Erlbaum.

Genesee, F. (2008, September). *Early dual language development. Zero to three.* Available from http://main.zerotothree.org/site/DocServer/29-1_Genesee.pdf

Genesee, F., Lindholm-Leary, K., Saunders, W., & Christian, D. (2006). *Educating English language learners: A synthesis of research evidence.* Cambridge, UK: Cambridge University Press.

Genesee, F., Paradis, J., & Crago, M, B. (2004). *Dual language development and disorders: A handbook on bilingualism and second language learning.* Baltimore, MD: Paul Brookes.

Gentner, D., & Namy, L. L. (2006). Analogical processes in language learning. *Current Directions in Psychological Science, 15*(6), 297–301.

Gibson, T., Peña, E., & Bedore, L. (2014). The relation between language experience and receptive-expressive semantic gaps in bilingual children. *International Journal of Bilingual Education and Bilingualism, 17*(1), 90–110.

Gold, B. T., Kim, C., Johnson, N. F., Kryscio, R. J., & Smith, C. D. (2013). Lifelong bilingualism maintains neural efficiency for cognitive control in aging. *Journal of Neuroscience, 33*(2), 387–396.

Goldenberg, C. (2013). Unlocking the research on English Learners: What we know—and don't yet know—about effective instruction. *American Educator, Summer,* 4–11.

Goldenberg, C., Hicks, J., & Lit, I. (2013). Teaching young English learners. In D. R. Reutzel (Ed.), *Handbook of research-based practice in early education* (pp. 140–160). New York: Guilford.

González, N. (1995). The funds of knowledge for teaching project. *Practicing Anthropology, 17*(3), 3–6.

Gottlieb, M. (2006). *Assessing English language learners: Bridges from language proficiency to academic achievement.* Thousand Oaks, CA: Corwin.

Gottlieb, M., & Ernst-Slavit, G. (2013). Academic language: A foundation for academic success in mathematics. In M. Gottlieb & G. Ernts-Slavit (Eds.), *Academic language in diverse classrooms: Promoting content and language learning* (pp. 1–38). Thousand Oaks, CA: Corwin.

Gottlieb, M., & Nguyen, D. (2007). *Assessment and accountability in language education programs: A guide for teachers and administrators.* Philadelphia: Caslon.

Graham, S., & Perin, D. (2007). *Writing next. Effective strategies to improve writing of adolescents in middle and high schools.* New York: Carnegie Corporation of New York.

Graves, M. F. (2006). *The vocabulary book.* New York: Teachers College Press.

Greenberg, A., Bellana, B., & Bialystok, E. (2012). Perspective-taking ability in bilingual children: Extending advantages in executive control to spatial reasoning. *Cognitive Development 28*(1), 41–50.

Gregory, E. (1996). *Making sense of a new world: Learning to read in a second language.* London: Chapman.

Gutiérrez-Clellen, V. F., & Kreiter, J. (2003). Understanding children bilingual acquisition using parent and teacher reports. *Applied Psycholinguistics, 24,* 267–288.

Gutiérrez-Clellen, V., Simon-Cereijido, G., & Sweet, M. (2012). Predictors of second language acquisition in Latino children with specific language impairment. *American Journal of Speech-Language Pathology, 21,* 64–77.

Halle, T., Hair, E., Wandner, L., McNamara, M., & Chien, N. (2012). Predictors and outcomes of early versus later English language proficiency among English language learners. *Early Childhood Research Quarterly, 27,* 1–20.

Hammer, C. S., Komaroff, E., López, L. M., Rodríguez, B., Scarpino, S. E., & Goldstein, B. (2012, June). *The role of language exposure, language usage, and parental characteristics in predicting bilingual preschoolers' language abilities.* Poster session presented at Head Start's 11th National Research Conference: Research on Young Children and Families: Effective Practices in an Age of Diversity and Change, Washington, DC.

Hammer, C. S., Lawrence, F. R., & Miccio, A. W. (2008). Exposure to English before and after entry to Head Start: Bilingual children's receptive language growth in Spanish and English. *International Journal of Bilingual Education and Bilingualism, 11*(1), 30–56.

Hardin, B. J., Roach-Scott, M., & Peisner-Feinberg, E. S. (2007). Special education referral, evaluation, and placement practices for preschool English language learners. *Journal of Research in Childhood Education,* 39–54.

Haynes, J. (2007). *Getting started with English language learners: How educators can meet the challenge.* Alexandria, VA: Association for Supervisors and Curriculum Developers.

Hemmeter, M. L., Ostrosky, M., & Fox, L. (2006). Social and emotional foundations for early learning: A conceptual model for intervention. *School Psychology Review, 35,* 583–601.

Hilchey, M. D., & Klein, R. M. (2011). Are there bilingual advantages on nonlinguistic interference tasks? Implications for the plasticity of executive control processes. *Psychonomic Bulletin & Review, 18*(4), 625–658.

Hirsh-Pasek, K., Golinkoff, R., Berk, L., & Singer, D. (2009). *A mandate for playful learning in preschool: Presenting the evidence.* New York: Oxford University Press.

Howard, E. R., Christian, D., & Genesee, F. (2003). *The development of bilingualism and biliteracy from grade 3 to 5: A summary of findings from the CAL/CREDE study of two-way immersion education* (Research Report 13). Santa Cruz, CA and Washington, DC: Center for Research on Education, Diversity & Excellence.

Howes, C., & Ritchie, S. (2002). *A matter of trust: Connecting teachers and learners in the early childhood classroom* (Vol. 84). New York: Teachers College Press.

Ibrahim, R., Shoshani, R., Prior, A., & Share, D. (2013). Bilingualism and measures of spontaneous and reactive cognitive flexibility. *Psychology, 4*(7A), 1–10.

Jacobson, P. F., & Schwartz, R. G. (2005). English past tense use with bilingual children with language impairment. *American Journal of Speech Language Pathology, 14*(4), 313–323.

Justice, L. M., McGinty, A. S., Piasta, S. B., Kaderavek, J. N., & Fan, X. (2010). Print-focused read-alouds in preschool classrooms: Intervention effectiveness and moderators of child outcomes. *Language, Speech, and Hearing Services in Schools, 41*(4), 504–520.

Kamil, M. L., & Hiebert, E. H. (Eds.). (2005). *Teaching and learning vocabulary: Bringing research to practice.* Mahwah, NJ: Lawrence Erlbaum.

Karger, J., & Hitchcock, C. (2003). *Access to the general education curriculum for students with disabilities: A brief legal interpretation.* Washington, DC: National Center on Accessing the General Curriculum. Available at www.cast.org/publications/ncac/ncac_accesslegal.html

Klingner, J. K., & Harry, B. (2006) The special education referral and decision making process for

English language learners: Child study team meetings and placement conferences. *Teachers College Record, 108*(11), 2247–2281.

Kohnert, K. J., & Bates, E. (2002). Balancing bilinguals ii: Lexical compehension and cogitive processing in children learning Spanish and English. *Journal of Speech Language & Hearing Research, 45*, 347–359.

Kohnert, K. J., Bates, E., & Hernández, A. (1999). Balancing bilinguals: Lexical-semantic production and cognitive processing in children learning Spanish and English. *Journal of Speech Language & Hearing Research, 42*(6), 1400–1413.

Kovács, Á. M., & Mehler, J. (2009). Cognitive gains in 7-month-old bilingual infants. *Proceedings of the National Academy of Sciences, 106*(16), 6556–6560.

Krashen, S. (1982). *Principles and practice in second language acquisition.* Oxford, UK: Pergamon.

Kuipers, J. R., & Thierry, G. (2013). ERP-pupil size correlations reveal how bilingualism enhances cognitive flexibility. *Cortex, 49*(10), 2853–2860.

Lindholm, K. J. (1990). Bilingual immersion education: Criteria for program development. In A. Padilla, H. Fairchild, & C. Valadez (Eds.), *Bilingual education: Issues and strategies* (pp. 91–105). Newbery Park, CA: Sage.

Lindholm, K. J., & Gavlek, K. (1994). *California DBE projects: Project-wide evaluation report, 1992–1993.* San Jose, CA: Author.

Lindholm-Leary, K. (2001). *Dual language education.* Clevedon, UK: Multilingual Matters.

Lindholm-Leary, K. (2004). The rich promise of two way immersion. *Educational Leadership*, 56–59.

Lindholm-Leary, K. (2005). *Review of research and best practices on effective features of dual language education programs.* Washington, DC: Center for Applied Linguistics. Available at www.lindholm-leary.com/resources/review_research.pdf

Lindholm-Leary, K., & Block, N. (2010). Achievement in predominantly low SES/Hispanic dual language schools. *International Journal of Bilingual Education and Bilingualism, 13*(1), 43–60.

Lindholm-Leary, K., & Borsato, G. (2001). *Impact of two-way bilingual elementary programs on students' attitudes toward school and college* (Research Report 10). Santa Cruz, CA and Washington, DC: Center for Research on Education, Diversity & Excellence.

López, L. M., & Greenfield, D. B. (2004). The cross-language transfer of phonological skills in Hispanic Head Start children. *Bilingual Research Journal, 28*(1), 1–18.

López, L. M., Ramirez, R., & Ferron, J. (2013, April). *A Contextual understanding of the development of language for dual language learners.* Paper presented at the Society for Research in Child Development Biennial Conference, Seattle, WA.

Luk, G., Anderson, J. A., Craik, F. I., Grady, C., & Bialystok, E. (2010). Distinct neural correlates for two types of inhibition in bilinguals: Response inhibition versus interference suppression. *Brain and Cognition, 74*(3), 347–357.

Magnuson, K., & Waldfogel, J. (2005). Early childhood care and education: Effects on ethnic and racial gaps in school readiness. *The Future of Children, 15*(1), 169–196.

Magruder, E. S., Hayslip, W. W., Espinosa, L. M., & Matera, C. (2013). Many languages, one teacher: Supporting language and literacy development for preschool dual language learners. *Young Children, 68*(1), 8–15.

Marietta, G. & Brookover, E. (2011). *Effectively educating preK–3rd English language learners (ELLs) in Montgomery County public schools.* New York: Foundation for Child Development. Available at http://fcd-us.org/sites/default/files/FCDCaseStdy MntgmryCtyELLS.pdf

McGroarty, M., & Calderón, M. (2005). Cooperative learning for second language learners. In P. A. Richard-Amato & M. A. Snow (Eds.), *Academic success for English language learners* (pp. 174–194). White Plains, NY: Pearson.

Moffitt, T. E., Arsenesault, L., Belsky, D., Dickson, N., Hancox, R. J., Harrington, H. L., . . . Caspi, A. (2011). A gradient of childhood self-control predicts health, wealth, and public safety. *Proceedings of the National Academy of Sciences of the United States of America, 108*(7), 2693–2698.

Morales, J., Calvo, A., & Bialystok, E. (2013). Working memory development in monolingual and bilingual children. *Journal of Experimental Child Psychology, 114*(2), 187.

Nagy, W. (2005). Why vocabulary instruction needs to be long-term and comprehensive. In E. H. Hiebert & M. L. Kamil (Eds.), *Teaching and learning vocabulary. Bringing research to practice* (pp. 27–44). Mahwah, NJ: Lawrence Erlbaum.

National Association for the Education of Young Children. (1995). NAEYC position statement: Responding to linguistic and cultural diversity. Recommendations for effective early childhood education. Available at www.naeyc.org/files/naeyc/file/positions/PSDIV98.PDF

National Association for the Education of Young Children. (2005). Screening and assessment of young English language learners. Available at www.naeyc.org/files/naeyc/file/positions/ELL_Supplement_Shorter_Version.pdf

National Association for the Education of Young Children. (2008). Developmentally appropriate practice in early childhood programs serving children from birth through age 8. Available at http://old web.naeyc.org/about/positions/dap4.asp

National Association for the Education of Young Children. (2012). NAEYC position statement: Technology and interactive media as tools in early childhood programs serving children from birth through age 8. Available at www.naeyc.org/files/naeyc/file/positions/PSTECH98.PDF

National Staff Development Council. (2001). *Definition of professional development*. http://learningforward.org/who-we-are/professional-learning-definition#.UuSosHn0D-k

Nemeth, K. (2009). *Many languages, one classroom: Teaching dual and English language learners*. Lewisville, NC: Gryphon House.

Nemeth, K., & Brillante, P. (2011). Solving the puzzle: Dual language learners with challenging behaviors. *Young Children* 66(4), 12–17.

Neuman, S. (2006). The knowledge gap: Implications for early education. In D. K. Dickinson & S. B. Neuman (Eds.), *Handbook of early literacy research* (Vol. 2, pp.29–40). London: Guilford Press.

Neuman, S. B. (1999). Books make a difference: A study of access to literacy. *Reading Research Quarterly, 34*, 286–301.

New Jersey Department of Education. (2010). Preschool program implementation guidelines. Available at www.state.nj.us/education/ece/guide/imp guidelines.pdf

New Jersey Department of Education. (2013). NJ Administrative Code 6A:15, Bilingual Education. Available at www.state.nj.us/education/code/cur rent/title6a/chap15.pdf

O'Connor, E., & McCartney, K. (2007). Examining teacher-child relationships and achievement as part of an ecological model of development. *American Educational Research Journal, 44*(2), 340–369.

Office of Head Start. (2008). *Dual language learning: What does it take?* Washington, DC: U.S. Department of Health and Human Services. Available at http://eclkc.ohs.acf.hhs.gov/hslc/tta-system/teaching/eecd/Individualization/Learning%20in%20Two%20Languages/DLANA_final_2009%5B1%5D.pdf

Office of Head Start. (2013). *Quick facts*. Available from www.acf.hhs.gov/programs/ohs/quick-fact

O'Neill, R., Horner, R., Albin, R., Sprague, J., Storey, K., & Newton, J. (1997). *Functional assessment and program development for problem behavior: A practical handbook*. Pacific Grove, CA: Brooks/Cole.

Ordoñez-Jasis, R., & Myck-Wayne, J. (2012). Community mapping in action: Uncovering resources and assets for young children and their families. *Young Exceptional Children, 15*(3), 31–45.

Pandey, A. (Ed.) (2000). Symposium on the Ebonics debate and African-American language. *World Englishes: Journal of English as an International and Intranational Language, 19*(1), 1–4.

Pandey, A. (2005, June). *Not without our children: The collaborative continuity approach to language and literacy enhancement*. Proceedings of the Hawaii International Social Sciences Conference, The East-West Center.

Pandey, A. (2010). *The child language teacher: Intergenerational language and literary enhancement*. Manasagangothri, Mysore: Central Institute of Indian Languages.

Pandey, A. (2012a). *Language building blocks: Essential linguistics for early childhood practitioners*. New York: Teachers College Press.

Pandey, A. (2012b). *Resource guide to language building blocks*. Available at www.tcpress.com/pdfs/9780807753552_supp.pdf

Pandey, A. (2012c). Issues in education: Language building blocks for climbing the learning tree. *Childhood Education, 88*(6), 388–390. Available at www.tandfonline.com/doi/abs/10.1080/00094056.2012.741485?journalCode=uced20

Pandey, A. (2013a). *Mother tongue as building blocks in education* (ACEI Radio show, syndicated on BAM Radio, Feb. 20). Available at www.acei.org/news-publications/acei-radio.html

Pandey, A. (2013b). When "second" comes first—Hindi to the eye? Sociolinguistic hybridity in professional writing. In Canagarajah, S. (Ed.), *Literacy as translingual practice: Between communities and classrooms* (pp. 215–227). New York: Routledge.

Pandey, A. (2013c). Expert: Considering students' home language could help school performance. (Radio interview, WUWM Public Radio, March 13). Available at www.wuwm.com/post/expert-considering-students-home-language-could-help-school-performance

Paradis, J. (2010). The interface between bilingual development and specific language impairment. *Applied Psycholinguistics, 31*(2), 227–252.

Paradis, J., Crago, M., Genesee, F., & Rice, M. (2003). French-English bilingual children with SLI: How do they compare with their monolingual peers? *Journal of Speech, Language, and Hearing Research, 46*(1), 113–127.

Peregoy, S. (1991). Environmental scaffolds and learner responses in a two-way Spanish immersion kindergarten. *Canadian Modern Language Review, 47*(3), 463–476.

Peregoy, S., & Boyle, O. (1990). Kindergarteners write! Emergent literacy of Mexican American children in a two-way Spanish immersion program. *Journal of the Association of Mexican American Educators, 1,* 6–18.

Peregoy, S. F., & Boyle, O. F. (2008). *Reading, writing, and learning in ESL: A resource book for teaching K–12 English learners* (5th ed.). Boston: Pearson.

Pew Hispanic Center. (2009, December). *Between two worlds: How young Latinos come of age in America.* Washington, DC: Author.

Phillips, L., & Twardosz, S. (2003). Group size and storybook reading: Two-year-old children's verbal and nonverbal participation with books. *Early Education and Development, 14*(4), 453–478.

Pianta, R. C. (1999). *Enhancing relationships between children and teachers. School psychology book series.* Washington, DC: American Psychological Association.

Pica, T. (2000). Tradition and transition in English language teaching methodology. *System, 28,* 1–18.

Pivneva, I., Palmer, C., & Titone, D. (2012). Inhibitory control and L2 proficiency modulate bilingual language production: evidence from spontaneous monologue and dialogue speech. *Frontiers in Psychology, 3,* 57.

Poulin-Dubois, D., Blaye, A., Coutya, J., & Bialystok, E. (2011). The effects of bilingualism on toddlers' executive functioning. *Journal of Experimental Child Psychology, 108*(3), 567–579.

Price, P., Tepperman, J., Iseli, M., Duong D., Black, M., Wang, S., . . . Alwan, A. (2009). Assessment of emerging reading skills in young native speakers and language learners. *Speech Communication, 51,* 968–984.

Prior, A., & MacWhinney, B. (2010). A bilingual advantage in task switching. *Bilingualism: Language and Cognition, 13*(2), 253–262.

Purnell, P. G., Ali, P., Begum, N., & Carter, N. (2007). Windows, bridges and mirrors: Building culturally responsive early childhood classrooms through the integration of literacy and the arts. *Early Childhood Education Journal, 34*(6), 419–424.

RAND Reading Study Group. (2002). *Reading for understanding: Toward an R & D program in reading comprehension.* Santa Monica, CA: RAND.

Reese, L., & Goldenberg, C. (2008). Parental involvement and the academic achievements of Hispanic students: Community literacy resources and home literacy practices among immigrant Latino families. *Marriage & Family Review, 43,* 109–139.

Reeves, J. (2006). Secondary teacher attitudes toward including English-language learners in mainstream classrooms, *Journal of Educational Research 99*(3), 131–142.

Restrepo, M. A., Castilla, A. P., Schwanenflugel, P. J., Neuharth-Pritchett, S., Hamilton, C. E., & Arboleda, A. (2010). Effects of a supplemental Spanish oral language program on sentence length, complexity, and grammaticality in Spanish-speaking children attending English-only preschools. *Language, Speech, and Hearing Services in Schools, 41*(1), 3–13.

Restrepo, M. A., Morgan, G. P., & Thompson, M. S. (2013). The efficacy of a vocabulary intervention for dual-language learners with language impairment. *Journal of Speech, Language, and Hearing Research, 56,* 748–765.

Reyes, A. (2006). Reculturing principals as leaders for cultural and linguistic diversity. In K. Tellez & H. C. Waxman, (Eds.), *Preparing quality educators for English language learners. Research, policies, and practices* (pp.145–165). Mahwah, NJ: Lawrence Erlbaum.

Roben, C., Cole, P., & Armstrong, L. M. (2012). Longitudinal relations among language skills, anger expression, and regulatory strategies in early childhood. *Child Development, 84*(3), 891–905.

Roberts, T. A. (2009). *No limits to literacy for preschool English learners.* Thousand Oaks, CA: Corwin.

Roberts, T. A. (in press). Not so silent after all: Examination and analysis of the silent stage in childhood second language acquisition. *Early Childhood Research Quarterly.*

Robinson, P., Mackey, A., Gass, S. M., & Schmidt, R. (2012). Attention and awareness in second language acquisition. In S. M. Gass & A. Mackey (Eds.), *The Routledge handbook of second language acquisition* (pp. 247–267). New York: Routledge.

Rodríguez, J. L., Díaz, R. M., Duran, D., & Espinosa, L. (1995). The impact of bilingual preschool education on the language development of Spanish-speaking children. *Early Childhood Research Quarterly, 10,* 475–490.

Rothbart, M. K., Ellis, L. K., Rueda, M. R., & Posner, M. I. (2003). Developing mechanisms of temperamental effortful control. *Journal of Personality, 71*(6), 1113–1143.

Rothbart, M. K., & Rueda, M. R. (2005). The development of effortful control. In U. Mayr, E. Awh, & S. Keele (Eds.), *Developing individuality in the human brain: A tribute to Michael I. Posner* (pp. 167–188). Washington, DC: American Psychological Association.

Rumberger, R. W., & Larson, K. A. (1998). Student mobility and the increased risk of high school dropout. *American Journal of Education, 107,* 1–35.

Russakoff, D. (2011). *Pre-K–3rd: Raising the educational performance of English language learners, Policy to action brief number 6.* New York: Foundation for Child Development.

Samson, J., & Collins, B. (2012). *Preparing all teachers to meet the needs of English language learners: Applying research to policy and practice for teacher effectiveness.* Washington, DC: Center for American Progress.

Santos, R. M., Fowler, S. A., Corso, R. M., & Bruns, D. (2000). Acceptance, acknowledgement, and adaptability: Selecting culturally and linguistically appropriate early childhood materials. *Teaching Exceptional Children. 32*(3), 14–22.

Sanz, C. (2012). *Multilingualism and metalinguistic awareness. The encyclopedia of applied linguistics.* New York: Wiley.

Sareen, H., Visencio, D., Russ, S., & Halfon, N. (2005). *The role of state early childhood comprehensive systems in promoting cultural competence and effective cross-cultural communication.* National Center for Infant and Early Childhood Health Policy at UCLA.

Saunders, W. M., Foorman, B. R., & Carlson, C. D. (2006). Is a separate block of time for oral English language development in programs for English learners needed? *Elementary School Journal, 107,* 181–197.

Saunders, W., Goldenberg, C., & Marcelletti, D. (2013). English language development: Guidelines for instruction. *American Educator,* 13–39.

Schecter, S. R., & Cummins, J. (Eds.). (2003). *Multilingual education in practice: Using language as a resource.* Portsmouth, NH: Heinemann.

Scott-Little, C., Kagan, S. L., & Stebbins Frelow, V. (2005). *Inside the content: The breadth and depth of early learning standards.* Greensboro, NC: Regional Educational Laboratory at SERVE.

Scott-Little, C., Lesko, J., Martella, J., & Milburn, P. (2007). Early learning standards: Results from a national survey to document trends in state-level policies and practices. *Early Childhood Research & Practice, 9*(1).

Sénéchal, M., & LeFevre, J. (2002). Parental involvement in the development of children's reading skill: A 5-year longitudinal study. *Child Development, 73,* 445–460.

Senesac, K. B. V. (2002). Two-way bilingual immersion: A portrait of quality schooling. *Bilingual Research Journal, 26*(1), 85–101.

Serving Preschool Children through Title I Part A of the ESEA. (2012). Available at www2.ed.gov/policy/elsec/guid/preschoolguidance2012.pdf

Shor, I., & Pari, C. (1999). *Education is politics: Critical teaching across differences, K–12: A tribute to the life and work of Paulo Freire.* Portsmouth, NH: Boynton Cook.

Simon-Cereijido, G., & Gutiérrez-Clellen, V. F. (2014). Bilingual education for all: Latino dual language learners with language disabilities. Special issue of the *International Journal of Bilingual Education and Bilingualism, 17*(2), 35–54.

Sleeter, C., & Grant, A. (1999). *Making choices for multicultural education: Five approaches to race, class and gender* (2nd ed.). Upper Saddle River, NJ: Prentice Hall.

Society for Neuroscience. (2008, September). The bilingual brain. Brain briefings. Washington, DC: Author.

Soltero, S. W. (2004). *Dual language: Teaching and learning in two languages.* Boston: Allyn and Bacon.

Soltero, S. W. (2011). *Schoolwide approaches to educating ELLs: Creating linguistically and culturally responsive K–12 schools.* Portsmouth, NH: Heinemann.

Stipek, D., Ryan, R., & Alarcón, R. (2001). Bridging research and practice to develop a two-way bilingual program. *Early Childhood Research Quarterly, 16*(1), 133–149.

Strain, P. S., & Joseph, G. E. (2006). You've got to have friends: Promoting friendships for Preschool children. *Young Exceptional Children Monograph Series, 8,* 57–66.

Sunderman, G., & Fancher, E. (2013). Lexical access in bilinguals and second language learners. *Innovative Research and Practices in Second Language Acquisition and Bilingualism, 38,* 267.

Tabors, P. (2008). *One child, two languages: A guide for early childhood educators of children learning English as a second language* (2nd ed.). Baltimore, MD: Paul Brookes.

Tazi, Z. (2011). *The effects of bilingual instruction on the English emergent literacy skills of Spanish-speaking preschool children.* (Doctoral Dissertation). City University of New York, ProQuest, UMI Dissertations Publishing, 2011. 3456939.

TESOL (2010). Position Paper on Language and Literacy Development for Young English Language Learners. Available at hwww.tesol.org/docs/pdf/371.pdf?sfvrsn=2

Thomas, W., & Collier, V. (2002). *A national study of school effectiveness for language minority students' long-term academic achievement.* Santa Cruz, CA and Washington, DC: Center for Research on Education, Diversity & Excellence.

Thomas, W. P., & Collier, V. P. (2003). The multiple benefits of dual language. *Educational Leadership, 61*(2), 61–64.

U.S. Department of Education. (2002). No Child Left Behind (NCLB) Act of 2001, Public Law 107-110. Available at http://www2.ed.gov/policy/elsec/leg/esea02/index.html

U.S. Department of Education.(2013). Elementary and Secondary Education Act Part A. Available at http://www2.ed.gov/policy/elsec/leg/esea02/pg40.html

U.S. Department of Education. (2013). Individuals with Disabilities Education Act. Available at http://idea.ed.gov/explore/view/p/,root,regs,300,D,300%252E306

U.S. Department of Education. (2013). Title IX General Provision 9101 [25]. Available at http://www2.ed.gov/policy/elsec/leg/esea02/pg107.html

Valdes, G., & Figueroa, R. (1994). *Bilingualism and testing: A special case of bias.* Norwood, NJ: Ablex.

Walker, A., Shafer, J., & Liams, M. (2004). Not in my classroom: Teacher attitudes towards English language learners in the mainstream classroom. *NABE Journal of Research and Practices, 2,* 130–160.

Weiss, H., Caspe, M., & Lopez, E. (2006). *Family involvement in early childhood education.* (Family Involvement Makes a Difference: Evidence that Family Involvement Promotes School Success for Every Child of Every Age No. 1). Cambridge, MA: Harvard Family Research Project. Available at www.hfrp.org/publications-resources/browse-our-publications/family-involvement-in-early-childhood-education

Whitebook, M., Bellm, D., Lee, Y., & Sakai, L. (2005). *Time to revamp and expand: Early childhood teachers' preparation programs in California's institutions of higher education. Executive Summary.* Berkeley, CA: Center for the Study of Childcare Employment.

Wilcox, M. J., Gray, S. I., Guimond, A. B., & Lafferty, A. E. (2011). Efficacy of the TELL language and literacy curriculum for preschoolers with developmental speech and/or language impairment. *Early Childhood Research Quarterly, 26,* 278–294.

Winsler, A., Díaz, R. M., Espinosa, L., & Rodríguez, J. L. (1999) When learning a second language does not mean losing the first: Bilingual language development in low-income, Spanish-speaking children attending bilingual preschool. *Child Development, 70*(2), 349–362.

Wodniecka, Z., Craik, F. I., Luo, L., & Bialystok, E. (2010). Does bilingualism help memory? Competing effects of verbal ability and executive control. *International Journal of Bilingual Education and Bilingualism, 13*(5), 575–595.

Wong Fillmore, L., & Snow, C. (2000). *What teachers need to know about language.* (Special Report).

ERIC Clearing House of Language and Linguistics. (ERIC Document Reproduction Service No. ED-99-CO-0008).

World-Class Instructional Design and Assessment. (2013 Draft). *Early language development standards.* Madison, WI: Board of Regents of the University of Wisconsin System on behalf of the WIDA Consortium.

Yang, S., Yang, H., & Lust, B. (2011). Early childhood bilingualism leads to advances in executive attention: Dissociating culture and language. *Bilingualism: Language and Cognition, 14*(3), 412–422.

Zacarian, D. (2011). *Transforming schools for English learners: A comprehensive framework for school leaders.* Thousand Oaks, CA: Corwin.

Zacarian, D. (2013a). *Mastering academic language: A comprehensive framework for supporting student achievement.* Thousand Oaks, CA: Corwin.

Zacarian, D. (2013b). *Serving English learners: Laws, policies and regulations.* Available at www.colorincolorado.org/pdfs/policy/ELL-Policy-Guide.pdf

Zacarian, D., Finlayson, B., Lisseck, K., & Ward Lolacono, N. (2010). Early education and care policies and guidelines for children whose home languages are in addition to or other than English. Boston: Massachusetts Department of Early Education and Care. Available at www.mass.gov/edu/docs/eec/laws-regulations-and-policies/20101203-dual-lang-edu-policies.pdf

Zacarian, D., & Haynes, J. (2012a). *Teaching English learners across the content areas.* Alexandria, VA: Association for Supervisors and Curriculum Developers.

Zacarian, D., & Haynes, J. (2012b). *The essential guide for educating beginning English learners.* Thousand Oaks, CA: Corwin.

Zacarian, D., & Silverstone, M. (in press). *The real core: Creating community around a classroom.* Thousand Oaks, CA: Corwin.

Zehler, A. M., Fleischman, H. L., Hopstock, P. J., Pendzick, M. L., & Stephenson, T. G. (2003). *Descriptive study of services to LEP students and LEP students with disabilities: Findings on special education LEP students.* Washington, DC: U.S. Department of Education, Office of English Language Acquisition, Language Enhancement, and Academic Achievement for Limited English Proficient Students (OELA). Available at www.ncela.gwu.edu/files/rcd/BE021199/special_ed4.pdf

Index

Note: Page numbers followed by f or t indicate figures or tables, respectively.

Language development, 56–77
culture and, 69–70
and executive function skills, 74–76
factors influencing, 61–64, 62f
and fluency in sequentially learned second language, 60–61
graphic of, 76t
home language learning and maintenance in, 64–67
home literacy practice in, 73–74
knowledge of, 29
with language disabilities, 102–105
oral, 67–69
process of, 58–60
reading and writing in, 70–73
Language development needs of preK vs. K–3 students, 13–14
Language development standards, 49–50, 49f, 50t
Language disabilities, ELLs with, 102–105
Language-facilitative trigger, 63
Language immersion programs, 9, 22, 29, 80, 89–90
Language learning. *See also* Language development
autonomous, 64
culture in, 69–70
home language, 64–67
vs. language acquisition, 63
reading and writing in, 70–73
of sequential second language, 60–61
Language learning needs of preK vs. K–3 students, 13–14
Language minority children, 7
Language objective and assessment method, 122
Language proficiency
assessment of, 40–42
language development standards and, 49–50, 49f, 50t
Language proficiency tests, 40–42
Language-rich environment, 98
Language use in dual language program, 85
Large group activities in special education plan, 103
Latinate languages, 66
Leadership, 2–35
developmentally appropriate practice in, 16–17
formal and informal, 144
interviewing and hiring of staff by, 17–18
knowledge about young dual language learners by, 5–6
and knowledge needed by general education teachers, 28–30
and knowledge needed by staff before starting work, 18–20
nationally accepted terms for young children who speak different languages in, 7–8

Leadership (*Cont.*)
preK children vs. K–3 children in, 9–10
preK children vs. K–3 childrens' language learning and development needs in, 13–14
preK children vs. K–3 curricula models in, 11–13
professional development and ongoing support by, 20, 25–28
resources and organizations for, 23–25
roles of various practitioners in, 20–23
self-assessment checklist for, 34
skills and dispositions needed by teachers in, 15–16
supervision of staff in multilingual classroom by, 33–34
support of effective collaboration and planning among staff by, 30–33
terms used by states and practitioners for young children who speak different languages in, 8–9
Learning spaces in communities, 139
Limited English proficiency (LEP), 7, 109
screening tool or assessment for, 40
Linguistically privileged child, 69
Linguistics, knowledge of, 29
LinkedIn groups, 25
Literacy
opportunities for, 70
in primary language vs. English, 82
Literacy acquisition
continued first language development and, 72
in dual language learners, 6
foundations for, 70–73
home language learning in support of, 64–67, 148
oral language development and, 67–69
oral participation and, 70–71
Literacy instruction, time allotment for, 71
Literacy practices at home, 38–39, 73–74
Long-term commitment to dual language program, 84–85
"Looping," 94
Low-incidence languages
effective services for, 48
interpreters for, 134
Lunchtime, 14

M
Maintenance model, 91
Manipulatives in special education plan, 103
Materials
age- and stage-appropriate, 97–98
in classrooms, 94–96
Measure of developing English language (MODEL) assessment, 45
Memorized chunks, 59
Mentoring, 26